Kant's Theory of Action

Kant's Theory of Action

Richard McCarty

OXFORD
UNIVERSITY PRESS

OXFORD
UNIVERSITY PRESS

Great Clarendon Street, Oxford OX2 6DP

Oxford University Press is a department of the University of Oxford.
It furthers the University's objective of excellence in research, scholarship,
and education by publishing worldwide in

Oxford New York

Auckland Cape Town Dar es Salaam Hong Kong Karachi
Kuala Lumpur Madrid Melbourne Mexico City Nairobi
New Delhi Shanghai Taipei Toronto

With offices in

Argentina Austria Brazil Chile Czech Republic France Greece
Guatemala Hungary Italy Japan Poland Portugal Singapore
South Korea Switzerland Thailand Turkey Ukraine Vietnam

Oxford is a registered trade mark of Oxford University Press
in the UK and in certain other countries

Published in the United States
by Oxford University Press Inc., New York

© Richard McCarty 2009

The moral rights of the author have been asserted
Database right Oxford University Press (maker)

First published 2009

British Library Cataloguing in Publication Data
Data available

Library of Congress Cataloging in Publication Data
Data available

Typeset by Laserwords Private Limited, Chennai, India
Printed in Great Britain
on acid-free paper by
the MPG Books Group, Bodmin and King's Lynn

ISBN 978-0-19-956772-0

10 9 8 7 6 5 4 3 2 1

Contents

To my father and my son,
Donald Wilson McCarty and Max Victor McCarty

Acknowledgements

A large part of the research in the history of psychology essential for this project was made possible by a Fellowship for College Teachers and Independent Scholars, generously awarded by the National Endowment for the Humanities for the academic year 1994–95. I am grateful for that support, and especially for the virtuous patience of the Endowment, which enabled me to take time rethinking, rewriting, and vastly improving the manuscript throughout the next decade. I am grateful, too, for the helpful comments of three anonymous readers, and for the editorial direction of Peter Momtchiloff. Of immeasurable benefit to me also has been the skeptical, empiricist spirit of my wife and thinking partner, Elizabeth Radcliffe. She helps me see the sensible world, at least, through Humean eyes.

Introduction

Immanuel Kant's moral theory presupposes a theory of action that has not been well understood. As a consequence, his moral theory has not been well understood, at least in parts. So this book develops an interpretation of Kant's theory of action in order to help us better understand his moral theory.

His theory of action bears only a faint resemblance to what philosophers now, over two hundred years later, call "action theory." It is at once more comprehensive than recent work in the philosophy of action, and more limited. Kant's interest in human action overlaps with his broader, metaphysical theories of freedom and causation, which are topics that today's action theorists generally wish to avoid. At the same time, his views on desire and human motivation are constrained by an eighteenth-century "empirical psychology" that most today would see as too restricting. So by contemporary standards, Kant's theory of action will seem overblown in some respects, and in a bad sense, metaphysical; while in other respects it will seem underdeveloped psychologically, archaic, and idiosyncratic. Accordingly, the following chapters are not offered in order to stake out any distinctly Kantian territory on the map of contemporary action theory. They are offered instead for the benefit of students of Kant's moral theory, at all levels, and for students of his wider philosophy.

In general, philosophers are interested in human action because actions are subject to evaluation: they can be praised and criticized. But this interest leads to two, apparently antithetical types of investigations. *Metaphysical investigations* of action focus on freedom and responsibility, while *psychological investigations* focus on causation and motivation. Everyone sees judgments of praise and blame as inappropriate when a person was forced to act, when he had no freedom of choice, and could not have done otherwise. The metaphysical investigation of human action therefore aims at establishing the conditions for an action's being freely chosen. But everyone also assumes that people's characters are exhibited in their actions; that what a person is like, psychologically, explains what she does. Without this assumption our assessments of people as good or bad, virtuous or vicious, seem pointless.

The psychological investigation of human action therefore focuses on the explanatory link between character and action. But it naturally appears antithetical to the metaphysical investigation. Its purpose, after all, is to explain the psychological conditions determining action—conditions in virtue of which, given the circumstances, a person could not have done otherwise.

In explaining Kant's theory of action, this book will show how he combined, in a single theory, the apparently antithetical theses of metaphysical freedom and psychological determinism. But the way that combination will be presented here is controversial. Kant's philosophy is widely recognized as an attempt at reconciling human freedom with the causal determinism of nature. Yet recent interpreters have tended to exclude from that determinism the determinism of psychological states giving rise to action. That is, nowadays it is common to assume that Kant rejected psychological determinism: the thesis that human actions invariably result from contests of desires, motives or natural inclinations, so that whatever we choose to do is always causally determined by the strongest psychological force. It is thought that this brand of determinism cannot be reconciled with Kant's metaphysics of action: with his theory of free choice. But the chapters that follow show how psychological determinism *is* compatible with Kant's metaphysics of action. In doing so they show also how psychological determinism can be compatible with Kantian moral theory. They even show how Kantian moral theory can benefit from embracing psychological determinism in the theory of action it presupposes.

It needs to be acknowledged here, however, that some recent interpreters of Kant's moral theory actually agree that his philosophy allows us to say that our free actions can be explained by the psychological forces of desire. They say that this is true at least *from a certain standpoint*. For they see his theory of action as presenting two, alternate perspectives we can adopt in considering human conduct. They say that in viewing an action as freely chosen we take one perspective on it, while in viewing it as psychologically determined we adopt the other perspective. "Perspectivist" interpretations therefore appear to allow us to combine metaphysical freedom and psychological determinism in one theory of action. But I think grave philosophical difficulties arise for any perspectivist synthesis. Foremost among them is a problem posed by this simple question: How is the same, self-identical action to be identified independently of the two perspectives we can take on it? Such identification ought to be possible. For we ought to be able to say, *of the same action*, that it was freely chosen, and that it is causally determined by the psychological states of the agent. But how can we say this unless we have some way of regarding the action independently of the two standpoints of freedom and psychological determinism? And if some part of Kant's philosophy would even allow us to think of an action independently of both freedom and determinism, would it be consistent with other views he held?

It will be an objective of this book to show how perspectivist or so-called "two-standpoints" interpretations of Kant's wider philosophy lead to insurmountable difficulties in this theory of action. As an alternative, I defend here what is usually called a "two-worlds" interpretation. I show how Kant combined freedom and psychological determinism through his assumption that we act in two worlds, *literally*. In one world, which is timeless ("noumenal"), we may be supposed to act freely, independent of any prior, psychological condition that could cause our acting one way rather than another. In the other world, which is this temporal ("phenomenal") world, our actions are supposed always to be causally determined by prior psychological states. Our actions in the temporal world are assumed to be "appearances" of what we do in the timeless world; and that is how the same action can be both psychologically determined, and metaphysically free.

A central thesis here is that Kant's theory of action requires assuming that our actions are explained by psychological forces. The main argument for this thesis is that making that assumption is the only way to solve what I shall present here as "the problem of justification and explanation." If that problem cannot be solved, that is, if we cannot show how what justifies action can explain it, then, I think, justification turns out to be irrelevant. For there seems to be no point in our saying, "This is what I ought to do," if the thought or reason behind such a statement does not have any power to explain our doing what we recognize we ought to do. My contention here will be that, in Kant's view, the thoughts or reasons that justify statements of that type, and so that justify actions, can explain them through deterministic psychological forces; and only in that way can the relevance of practical, moral justification be preserved.

Kant is usually supposed to have accepted a version of what is nowadays known as "moral internalism." This is the doctrine that someone's making a moral judgment like the above would require her also having a motive to act in accordance with that judgment. He is thought to have believed this because he also believed that 'ought' implies 'can,' that recognizing that we *ought* to do something, morally, implies our having a motive by which we *can* do it. In his unique terminology this motive is the "moral incentive," and it is identified in his moral theory as "respect for the moral law." The problem of justification and explanation may therefore seem to be solved quite easily by Kant's having embraced the internalist doctrine behind 'ought' implies 'can.' For by this doctrine, someone who recognizes that she ought to do something is guaranteed a motive of respect for law to explain her doing it. Hence, the "ought" that justifies her action seems capable of explaining it; so, problem solved.

Not exactly, I think. For I think the doctrine of internalism merely sets us on the way toward a solution to the problem. It can guarantee only that we *have* a motive for doing whatever we recognize we ought to do. But it does not go so far as to show how the guaranteed motive can explain the action that ought to be done. To see why, just consider the fact that when we recognize that there is something we ought to do, we typically also have another motive for doing something else. The doctrine of internalism is not presumed to guarantee that in recognizing a justification for an action we have a motive for doing it, *and no motive for doing anything else.* Internalism guarantees only that in recognizing that we ought to do something we have a certain motive, among our other motives.

But in order to solve the problem of justification and explanation it must be shown how our having the motive for acting on a recognized justification can explain our acting on it despite our also having other motives, for acting otherwise. In other words, solving the problem requires identifying the "mechanism," or "procedure," that explains how, when there are multiple motives for acting, one of those motives prevails. Suppose it were like this—suppose that just as moral internalism says, whenever we recognize a moral justification for an action we are guaranteed to have an explaining motive for it, among the other motives we have at the time. Suppose also that which of those motives we end up acting on is always left to sheer chance. If things were like this, then even if we were to act on the motive implied by the recognized moral justification, that justification could not explain our action. Nothing could explain it, in fact; because chance defies explanation.

Here some will be quick to offer that, for a rational agent, what would explain action on a recognized justification is an act of free choice. That is, a rational agent who acts on the motive guaranteed by a recognized justification would do so by her own free choice. Or, if she acts otherwise, on a different motive, then she would do *that* by her own free choice. Either way, it will be said, a free choice between available motives always explains what a rational agent does. In the following chapters, however, I argue not only that this was not Kant's view, but also that it is false. In Kant's theory of action, I argue, what explains someone's acting on a recognized justification is the preponderant psychological force of the motive provided by that justification.

But this conclusion will likely be thought to entail that we have no free will. For it implies that we are basically passive with respect to the compelling psychological forces of our desires or motives. It implies that we do not freely decide which of our available motives to act on. My response to this point will be to agree that the solution does imply this, and to say that this implication is nevertheless consistent with Kant's theory of action. For I do not think Kant believed we have the freedom to choose, from the survey of our available desires or motives, which ones will move us to action. As I explain his theory of action in the following chapters, it will become clear why he thought instead that our freedom is *otherworldly*. Starting with Chapter 4, we begin to see why he thought that by a free choice in another world we become what we are like in this world, and what we are like in this world—our "empirical character"—is what explains our actions on the justifications we recognize.

To some this solution to the problem will seem rather extreme, however. They might even offer that if *that* is what is required to solve the problem of justification and explanation, then it seems more reasonable to live with the problem. But I do not agree that this is an extreme solution. It is a metaphysical solution, to a problem that is also metaphysical. So the apparent extremity of the solution matches the extremity of the problem. The metaphysical problem arises from a characteristic insight of Kant's, which is that nothing in the natural, empirical world can account for the categorical *ought* of morality. This insight implies that not all of the justifications for our actions, not all of the reasons why we ought to act one way or another, can be natural justifications. And because that is so, not all of the explanations of our actions can be natural explanations. So one way to present the metaphysical problem is by asking this: Assuming there are non-natural justifications for actions, how can there be non-natural explanations of actions as events in the natural, temporal world, the world where every event is fully determined by a natural cause?

It seems to me that there is only one plausible answer to this question. There is only one plausible way the prospect of non-natural, metaphysical action-explanations can be coordinated with the thoroughgoing determinism of the natural world. We must presuppose a metaphysical explanation for the natural world itself: for the whole series of its causes and effects. We must assume that the natural series of events, which includes our actions, advances through time in one way rather than another, because it is the appearance of one non-natural, metaphysical reality rather than another. We must suppose that the natural world has the contents, events and causal laws it has, because of the contents, whatever they may be, of the metaphysical reality "behind" it—a metaphysical reality for which we may be partially responsible. Only this assumption, I think, makes it possible for what justifies our actions, non-naturally, to explain them.

The preceding is a very abstract, cosmological representation of the solution to the problem. And it can be expected to provoke a number of critical reactions. One that will be dismissed rather easily in due course is the objection that Kant's own theory of knowledge does not allow us to talk sensibly about any metaphysical reality "behind" the empirical world, much less to describe it as being one way rather than another. A number of other objections are more clever than this, however, and they will be harder to dismiss in later chapters.

But here it may be worth saying something about a certain sheepishness or embarrassment that admirers of Kant might feel, or might be expected to feel, over this solution to the metaphysical problem. Since so many of our contemporaries are given over almost completely to naturalistic ideals, we seem to set ourselves up for ridicule if we would seriously entertain the "wild metaphysics" of other worlds, and of otherworldly explanations of what happens in this world. Yet here we can quickly, and, I think, effectively, forestall any such reproaches stemming from the champions of philosophical naturalism. We need only direct them to contemporary physics, the home office of naturalistic explanation. Multiple-worlds hypotheses, and "higher dimensions," are commonplace there. Increasingly at this level contemporary science has begun to resemble science fiction. Even conservative physicists now modeling the inflation of the cosmos only milliseconds after the "singularity" of its onset—the so-called "big bang"—are convinced that everything in the natural universe, including space-time, has developed from an antecedent reality. For all we can know, that reality would be another world existing somehow apart from the known space-time reality of this world. And physicists unashamedly admit to being incapable of describing that reality in naturalistic terms, incapable even of imagining it. They understand that naturalistic methods of explanation are exhausted, in principle, when we come to nature's edge: when we run out of distances to measure, because we are literally out of space, and when the temporal sequence from cause to effect is unintelligible, because we are literally out of time.

So long as it is assumed that our actions can be justified independently of naturalistic concepts, and so long as we assume that what justifies action must be capable of explaining it, we must agree that the explanation of our actions cannot be completely natural. If it therefore turns out that the possibility of non-naturalistic justification of action would imply a world of free agents acting independently of the conditions of the natural world—and we shall see in later chapters why it might—then we should be entitled to think that actions in this world can depend upon actions in that world. These are explanatory principles that no conscientious naturalist should be able to see any grounds to dismiss, and that admirers of Kant's practical philosophy need offer no apology for entertaining.

The first three chapters of this book focus on psychology. Chapter 1 clarifies some of the more unique aspects of Kant's theory of action, which are familiar to any student of his moral theory—what it means to act on a "maxim," for instance. Chapter 2 develops his psychology of "incentives," which are the motive forces that explain our actions. In Chapter 3 we consider and reject the best reasons for assuming that, in Kant's theory, human actions are supposed to be explained by the so-called "power of free choice" (*freie Willkür, arbitrium liberum*).

The next couple of chapters turn to metaphysics. Chapter 4 presents the two-worlds cosmology that accounts for our freedom of action. It explains how we act in two worlds, and how what we do in the other world would be related to what we do in this world. Chapter 5 then considers and rejects the best reasons for interpreting Kant's theory of action as a theory just about two standpoints we can take on actions, instead of a theory about two words.

The last two chapters explore problems in moral psychology. Chapter 6 is about Kant's theory of moral motivation by the feeling of respect for the moral law. It also offers a solution to a persisting problem for Kantian ethics, a problem about "moral worth." Sometimes our actions are motivated not by respect for law, but by admirable inclinations like benevolence, gratitude, and sympathy. A central argument of Chapter 6 is that even if such actions must be denied genuine moral worth, because they are not motivated by respect for "duty," there is no reason to deny that they are virtuous. This solution requires distinguishing between "moral worth" and "virtue" as terms of appraisal. And it becomes plausible, as we shall see, once we recognize the explanatory power of psychological forces. The seventh and final chapter focuses on Kant's views on "radical evil" and "good will." Since we are not perfectly rational, or perfectly good, Kant saw no alternative but to say that human beings are evil by nature. He did not take this to imply that no one has a good will, however. As will be suggested near the end of Chapter 7, it seems that Kant assumed we all have a good will. For to have a good will is apparently nothing other than to be predisposed to feel respect for, and so to be motivated by, purely moral considerations. That is why we all, as rational agents, can be thought to have incomparable moral worth, or dignity.

A concluding section will present a brief sketch of some of Kant's views on the rational basis for moral hope. Though we are all evil, we have grounds to hope for the restoration of our originally good nature, provided we are committed to personal moral progress. We also have grounds to hope for happiness in proportion to our virtue. These hopes can be expected to be fulfilled in another world, however; though it is hard to say what that hoped-for world would be like.

My hopes for this book are considerably more modest, of course. I hope that through my research in Kant's theory of action our understanding and appreciation of his still intriguing moral theory can be enhanced. I began work on this project a number of years ago, prompted mainly by the nagging problem in Kant's moral theory that I believe I have solved here, in Chapter 6. It is sometimes called the "Schiller problem," and it stems from a popular reading of Kant's initial arguments in his *Groundwork of the Metaphysics of Morals*. In order to act virtuously, Kant seems to say there, we must act with single-minded resolve to do our moral duty. The sterner the resolve the greater the virtue, apparently. Yet Friedrich Schiller's witty comment on this idea was that if that were so, then it would be better actually to hate our friends. For then our friendly actions toward them would be all the more virtuous.

At the time I began thinking about this problem the prevailing view was that its solution would lie in a clearer understanding of the complexities of Kant's theory of action. His conception of how rational agents act on "maxims" was thought to allow for the possibility of multiple levels of human motivation, and "overdetermination." It was thought to allow for our resolving to act dutifully on one level, or according to one maxim, while choosing to act on admirable inclinations like friendship or sympathy, on another level, or according to another maxim. The resulting action would therefore be both "morally worthy," as an expression of a commitment to duty, and morally admirable, as an expression of a friendly or sympathetic character.

Through research in the history of German psychology prior to Kant, principally in the metaphysics and ethics of Christian Wolff, I discovered how acting on maxims had been understood in Kant's day. I learned also about rationalist conceptions of "desire" and "volition," which helped in understanding Kant's theory of action. But I began to make what I see as substantial progress in this project only after studying his lectures in what he called "empirical psychology." There I found that Kant can be correctly understood as having embraced a variation on what is today recognized as a "Humean," or "belief-desire" model of action. Maxims can be understood as playing the same functional role in action that desires play in the Humean model. Maxims are not identical with Humean desires, however. They are principles, and can be stated in propositional form. But in the rationalist tradition in which Kant matured as a philosopher, this was true also of all desires and volitional states. A desire, in this tradition, was considered to be a thought (representation) that something is good. And that is what a maxim is. In order to act on a maxim, just as in order to act on a desire in the Humean model, one also needs a belief that some action "falls under" the maxim, or can satisfy the desire. Then whether one will in fact act that way always depends upon the psychological force of the maxim, or as Humeans would say, upon the strength of the desire. The psychological force of a maxim is, in Kant's terminology, the "incentive" it incorporates.

That, incidentally, is why he referred to respect for the moral law as the "moral incentive." The relative strength of an incentive constitutes the potential of its maxim to cause action, considering what else the agent may be motivated to do instead. And that is why Kant recognized that we have a moral obligation to make progress in strengthening our respect for the moral law. In other words, the psychological strengths of incentives to action *matter*. On this point, at least, the Humean and Kantian theories of motivation are in complete agreement.

How, then, does this interpretation of Kant's theory of action lead to a solution to the Schiller problem? It prompts us to abandon the now orthodox interpretation of Kant's view of freedom of choice. That popular interpretation says that in freely choosing to act we select an incentive to make into a principle for our action, and then we choose to act on it. But I think this is a misunderstanding of Kant's theory of action. And once it is seen that the causal forces of incentives are responsible for what we choose to do, a new light is shed on the evaluation of human action. The friendly person is not someone who freely chooses friendliness as the motive for what she does. She is rather someone in whom friendship is a strong incentive, stronger than patriotism, perhaps, or the profit motive, even self-love. And when the incentive of friendship causes her to do something for her friend, her action is virtuous. It would not have what Kant called "moral worth," however. For actions merit *this* special appraisal only when they are motivated by the incentive of respect for the moral law.

An illuminating insight here is this. In Kant's view, when it comes to caring for our friends, we are not expected to decide between doing so from the motive of duty or from the motive of friendship. That doesn't make sense; because human action doesn't work that way. In Kantian moral theory, accordingly, we are not expected to decide, whenever possible, in favor of acting on the motive of duty—as if it were our duty to decide to do our duty from duty; as if our moral vocation were to accumulate as much "moral worth" as we can. We do not choose to act by choosing from among our motives. Rather, the relative strengths of our motives determine how we choose. So I might well visit my friend in the hospital, because of the strength of my motive of duty. But if I do, this tells us something about my character; something not very admirable, I think—and this news will not be very comforting to my friend. I could defend myself, perhaps, by observing that my action from the motive of duty would at least have "moral worth." But even so, it is consistent with Kantian ethics that I ought to be a better friend—that my motive of friendship should be stronger. It ought to be strong enough to accomplish what I cannot accomplish by acting from the motive of duty: cheering up my friend.

To this type of solution to the Schiller problem it would ordinarily be objected that it must resolve all our free choices into events causally determined by psychological forces. But my response will be that this need not be so for *all* our free choices. If we have our characters in this world by an act of our own free choice, an act taking place in the other, noumenal world, then that choice would not be determined by any psychological causes. And if this is so, then what we are caused to do here and now, through the relative strengths of our desires, can be seen as resulting from our own free, otherworldly choice. Suppose that we have each freely chosen the characters we now portray in this grand theater of the empirical world. And suppose, accordingly, that on this cosmic stage we now act always "in character," as dictated by some metaphysical script. So long as we are each free in the choice by which our characters in this world are determined, we are just as free in being here and now caused to act in character, through the psychological forces of our desires.

The preceding are some of the main themes in the chapters to follow, and they run contrary to prevailing views about Kant's practical philosophy. For this reason the development of these themes will require presenting arguments critical of widely held, alternative interpretations. These critical arguments will sometimes be textually based. But other times they will be conceptual. They will show, that is, that some common ways of interpreting Kant's thoughts on how human beings act are philosophically unsound, and so, if we can, we should avoid interpreting him in these ways. Where possible in the following chapters I have isolated criticisms of others' interpretations in footnotes. Sometimes this was not possible, however; especially when the extended development of an argument required identifying competing interpretations by the persons at their sources, or when it was most convenient to do so. In all cases I have endeavored to present the views of others with whom I disagree as clearly, succinctly, and as charitably as possible.

As I have indicated above, my aim in what follows is to enhance understanding of the theory of action implicit in Kant's moral theory. This should result in enhanced understanding and appreciation of Kantian ethics. And I am sure that many whose views are discussed in the following chapters, even if they cannot agree with my arguments here, share my enthusiasm for this project.

1

Acting on Maxims

"Maxims" are central to Kant's moral theory. So also are "imperatives." Both concepts are borrowed from the structure of practical reasoning, by which, in Kant's theory of action, our actions are supposed to be justified. For similar purposes other theories of action employ concepts like desires and intentions, means and ends, and reasons for action. A principal aim of this chapter is to show how the maxims and imperatives of Kant's theory of action relate to these more familiar concepts employed by other theories.

Another aim of this chapter will be to set the agenda for the book. This occurs toward the end, where a question will be raised about the relation between practical reasoning and action. Very broadly, the question will be: Is practical reasoning supposed merely to *justify* action, or can it also *explain* it? More narrowly, the question is: Are the conclusions of practical reasoning just advice or recommendations about how we ought to act? Or can practical reasoning actually issue in actions, as conclusions following from its premises? I think Kant's view was that practical reasoning both justifies and explains action. It seems to me that most writers on Kant's practical philosophy are convinced of this also. But I do not find among them a satisfactory explanation of how practical reasoning can do both. So near the end of the chapter I'll pose a problem related to practical reason's ability both to justify and to explain action. The solution I'll offer for this problem will be a central contribution of this book. And in order to develop and clarify this solution it will be necessary to set out the basic principles of Kant's theory of human motivation, which is the objective of the next chapter.

Here we begin with a brief statement about what Kant thought action is, and proceed from there to explain his concept of a *maxim*. Next follows a section on the role of maxims in practical reasoning. After that, maxims will be connected with some more familiar concepts in action theory: concepts like desire, intention, and will. An explanation of the role of *imperatives* in practical reasoning will then follow. This will pave the way, near the end, for exploring the problem posed by our leading question: the question about whether practical reasoning merely justifies action, or also explains it.

1.1 Action

Kant understood action as making a difference in the world. His reason for thinking of action so broadly will become clearer in a later chapter. Here it will suffice to point out that his most general term referring to action is *Handlung,* which encompasses everything done by human beings, as well as by every other causal agent in the world.[1] In a lecture he once defined "action" broadly as "the determination of the power of a substance as a cause of a certain accident."[2] We may think of the human mind as a substance, and of an intentional bodily movement as a type of accident. If we do, then the mind's causally determining this movement, through its own power, would fall under Kant's broader definition of action. But so also would a billiard ball's rolling, or a cup of water's freezing.

Kant's technical term for the type of action of primary interest to moralists and action theorists is "deed" (Latin: *actus, factum;* German: *That*). He defined this term as follows: "An action is called a *deed* insofar as it comes under obligatory laws and hence insofar as the subject, in doing it, is considered in terms of the freedom of his choice. By such an action the agent is regarded as the *author* of its effect, and this, together with the action itself, can be *imputed* to him. ..."[3] Several sections of this chapter immediately following present explanations of other technical terms Kant

---

[1] The concept of "causality leads to the concept of action, this to the concept of force, and thereby to the concept of substance"; Immanuel Kant, *Critique of Pure Reason,* trans. and ed. Paul Guyer and Allen W. Wood (Cambridge: Cambridge University Press, 1998), A204/B249. "For according to the principle of causality actions are always the primary ground of all change of appearances. ..." (A205/B250).

[2] Immanuel Kant, *Lectures on Metaphysics,* trans. and ed. Karl Ameriks and Steve Naragon (Cambridge: Cambridge University Press, 1997), 329/28:565.

[3] Immanuel Kant, *The Metaphysics of Morals,* trans. Mary Gregor (Cambridge: Cambridge University Press, 1991), 50/6:223.

used to explain his concept of action, in the sense of a "deed." We begin
with the term, "maxim."

1.2 Maxims

Most of what is known about Kant's theory of action comes from his
moral theory, which, as a theory of action-evaluation, contains an implicit
theory of action. The moral theory's primary evaluative principle, the
"categorical imperative," indicates that actions can be evaluated as morally
right or wrong based on their maxims. Kant defined a maxim as a
"subjective principle of volition," or "of acting."[4] But these are not
especially helpful definitions; and a number of disputes over how to
interpret his moral theory revolve around the correct understanding of his
concept of a maxim.

We are fortunate that Kant provided several examples of maxims in
illustrating how to apply the categorical imperative. A very simple example
is "to let no insult pass unavenged" (*Practical Reason,* 17/5:19). Some
more complicated examples are "to shorten my life when its longer
duration threatens more troubles than it promises agreeableness," and,
"when I believe myself to be in need of money I shall borrow money
and promise to repay it, even though I know that this will never happen"
(*Groundwork,* 32/4:422).

Our interest in maxims here, and throughout the chapters to follow, will
focus on how they function in practical reasoning. From the assumption in
Kant's moral theory that actions can be evaluated by their maxims we can
infer his assumption that every action has a maxim. Most commentators
are convinced that human actions can be distinguished from other causes
in the world by their relations to maxims. Maxims seem to be essential for
human actions; and for this reason I shall assume throughout this book that
something has gone wrong if we arrive at a point where we must admit

---

[4] See Immanuel Kant, *Groundwork of the Metaphysics of Morals,* trans. and ed. Mary Gregor (Cambridge: Cambridge University Press, 1997), 14n./4:401n., 31n./4:420n. See also Immanuel Kant, *Critique of Practical Reason,* trans. and ed. Mary Gregor (Cambridge: Cambridge University Press, 1997), 17–18/5:19–20; and *Metaphysics of Morals,* 51/6:225.

that a human action is not related to, or is not in the normal way based on, a maxim. I think most commentators will agree, also, that in Kant's theory of action maxims are presumed to "rationalize" actions. For any action having occurred, its maxim is supposed to give the reason for it, in some sense.

As "subjective" principles, maxims are to be distinguished in Kant's theory of action from "objective" principles, which are called "laws" or "imperatives." A law or imperative will indicate a course of action that ought, rationally to be done. Kant described the difference between maxims and laws, or imperatives, as follows:

> The former [a maxim] contains the practical rule determined by reason conformably with the conditions of the subject (often his ignorance or also his inclinations), and is therefore the principle in accordance with which the subject *acts;* but the law is the objective principle valid for every rational being, and the principle in accordance with which *he ought to act,* i.e., an imperative.   (*Groundwork,* 31n. 4:421n.)

This suggests that Kant assumed that *how* we act depends always upon what seems reasonable to us, given our knowledge, or lack of it, and our subjective prompts to actions. The latter would include desires or inclinations, but might not be limited to these. The maxim principles upon which we act reflect this kind of qualified reasonableness, which we can here call "subjective reasonableness."[5] But how we rationally *ought* to act, independently of our ignorance or our inclinations, is expressed by laws and imperatives. These may be called principles of "objective reasonableness." Imperatives will be discussed more fully below, in Section 1.9. Before they can be explained properly it is necessary to understand several more points about acting on maxims, and especially the structure of maxim-based practical reasoning.

1.3 The Practical Syllogism

If maxims provide *reasons* for actions, then a structure of rational argument seems like an appropriate model for relating maxims to actions. It seems that our actions should be representable as following somehow from our

---

[5] See Kant's distinction between "objectively" and "subjectively practical reason" at *Practical Reason,* 125/5:151.

maxims, in the way that conclusions follow from premises.[6] Notes from one of Kant's lectures show that he explained to his students that a maxim is the major premise of a practical syllogism.[7] Maxims were defined this way also in their textbook.[8] And among Kant's contemporary readers it was common to think about action and practical reasoning in terms of the practical syllogism. This is because of the influential theories of Christian Wolff, one of the most well known and prolific writers of the German Enlightenment. Wolff's simplistic model for the reasoning structure of the practical syllogism was as follows: 1) X is good; 2) Doing Y will achieve X; 3) Therefore, doing Y is good.[9] Statement 1) in this model, the major premise, is what Wolff called the maxim.

[6] As I see it, there is necessarily a maxim behind every rational, voluntary action; and usually more than one. I think this is implied by the assumption in Kant's ethical theory that every action is either obligatory, wrong, or morally permissible. If the categorical imperative's formula of universal law is really the complete ("supreme") moral principle Kant said it is, then it must be able to determine whether any action is obligatory, wrong, or permissible. Since it is supposed to be able to do this by testing the maxim of any action, it follows that every action that can be judged either obligatory, wrong or permissible, is based on a maxim. This conclusion, which seems to be confirmed by Kant's statement quoted in the following note, is contrary to the conclusion reached by several others. These interpreters view maxims as guiding principles that agents consult only in moral deliberation, as if the great majority of our actions are not based on maxims. See Rüdiger Bubner, "Another Look at Maxims," in Predrag Cicovacki, ed., *Kant's Legacy: Essays in Honor of Lewis White Beck* (Rochester, NY: University of Rochester Press, 2001), 245–59 at 251; Michael Albrecht, "Kants Maximenethik und ihre Begründung," *Kant-Studien* 85 (1994): 129–46 at 132; and Patricia Kitcher, "What is a Maxim?" *Philosophical Topics* 31 (Spring and Fall 2003): 215–43 at 235–6.

[7] "[Action is voluntary] insofar as it comes about according to maxims (maxims ... [are] principles practically subjective ... because they would be the major premise ... in practical syllogisms)" (*Lectures on Metaphysics*, 380/28:678).

[8] The ethics text Kant used throughout his teaching career referred to a maxim as the "*maioribus propositionibus sylligismorum practicorum.*" See Alexander Gottlieb Baumgarten, *Ethica Philosophica* (1751), §§246, 449; repr. in Immanuel Kant, *Kant's gesammelte Schriften,* vol. 27 pt. 2. no. 1, (Berlin: Walter de Gruyter, 1923), 800, 857.

[9] Christian Wolff, *Vernünfftige Gedancken von der Menschen Thun und Lassen, zu Beförderung Ihrer Glückseeligkeit* [*Deutsche Ethik*] (Frankfurt, 1733; facsimile, Hildesheim: Georg Olms, 1976), §§190, 400. Wolff schematized an enthymemic practical syllogism as follows: "*This thing or circumstance is of such and such character. Therefore, it is good (or evil).* The premise to be found would be this: *A thing or circumstance of such and such character is good (or evil).* And hereby is the maxim revealed, according to which the person judges whether something may be good or evil" (§193). Moses Mendelssohn, who agreed with Wolff and on many points, wrote that:

In every legitimate action that a human being undertakes, he silently makes the following rational inference: Whenever the property A is encountered, my duty requires me to do B. The present case has the property A; therefore, and so on. The major premise of this rational inference is a maxim, a general rule of life, which we adopted at some earlier time and which must naturally come to mind on the occasion of the present case.

Moses Mendelssohn, *Philosophical Writings*, trans. and ed. Daniel O. Dahlstrom (Cambridge: Cambridge University Press, 1997), 295.

Kant was frequently critical of Wolff's philosophical views, especially in his lectures. But there seems to be no record of his ever having criticized Wolff's conception of maxims and of their role in the practical syllogism. Nor did Kant ever offer any alternative explanation of what maxims are, nor of how they function in practical reasoning. He relied on the concept of a maxim to make crucial points in his moral theory. Yet in his presentations of that theory his explanations of maxims are cryptic, at best. It therefore seems most likely that Kant assumed maxims were already well enough understood by his audience, through their acquaintance with Wolff's practical philosophy.[10]

Wolff was a mind–body dualist, and he relied on Leibniz's doctrine of pre-established harmony to explain how ideas or representations in the mind coordinate with bodily movements. He explained the soul as a "power of representation" (*Vorstellungskraft, vis representationis*). But he did not mean that the soul is a mental substance *with* a power of representation. He meant that the soul is, literally, a power of representation.[11] He thought that in order to act we must first represent what we will do, in a special way. We must represent our action in a manner appropriate for God's having related our representation of it to our body's movement, when he created the world. Whenever we act, we must represent our doing something as "good" (or our omitting doing it as "bad"). This is the form of the concluding thought in the Wolffian practical syllogism: "Doing *Y* is good." And because of its unique relation to bodily movement Wolff called this thought a "moving reason" (*Bewegungs-Grund*) or a motive (*motivum*).[12] But he did not suppose that moving thoughts like this simply happen in the mind. Rather, he thought that for rational minds like ours, they would fol-low from representations of objects or conditions as "good" to bring about, which are major premises of practical reasoning, that is, maxims. They would also presuppose causal judgments, as minor premises, about how to act in order to bring about those objects or conditions represented as good.[13]

---

[10] Cf. Patricia Kitcher, "Kant's Argument for the Categorical Imperative," *Noûs* 38 (2004): 555–84 at 559–60; and "What is a Maxim?" 221–5.

[11] Christian Wolff, *Vernünfftige Gedancken von Gott, der Welt und der Seele des Menschen, Auch Allen Dingen Überhaupt* [*Deutsche Metaphysik*], (Halle, 1751; facsimile, Hildesheim: Georg Olms, 1983), §§742–53.

[12] See the Glossary (*Das erste Register*) of Wolff's *Deutsche Metaphysik*, where he equates *Bewegungs-Grund* and *Motivum*, 673.

[13] Cf. Wolff's *Deutsche Ethik*, §190.

But to today's students of Kant's moral theory it might initially seem that he must have disagreed with Wolff's conception of maxims. None of the examples of maxims we read in his writings on moral theory seems to fit the Wolffian format, after all. Yet it is relatively easy to adapt Kant's examples of maxims to play the role of major premises in the practical syllogism.[14]

A Wolffian maxim always represents something *as good* (or *as bad*). So the maxim's formal predicate need not be included in its statement if we understand beforehand that we are being given an example of a maxim. When Kant wrote "to let no insult pass unavenged" as a simple example of someone's maxim, he could have expected his readers to understand this as an expression of the person's thinking of this policy as good. Kant's examples of maxims taking the form of conditional statements can be adapted similarly. The person contemplating acting on the principle "when I believe myself to be in need of money [, to] borrow money and promise to repay it, even though I know that this will never happen," can be imagined to think that acting on this complex, conditional policy would be good.

Although Wolff's schema for the practical syllogism contains just a few simple statements, it can be easily extended to a practical sorites, or a polysyllogism. In this way, the reasoning behind our actions can include hierarchies of action-policies. In one of Kant's more complicated examples of how to evaluate a maxim by the categorical imperative he considered a man contemplating suicide. "His maxim . . . is: from self-love I make it my principle to shorten my life when its longer duration threatens more troubles than it promises agreeableness" (*Groundwork,* 32/4:422). This seems to be a maxim for maxim-making. Its complexity suggests a chain of reasoning from a very general maxim, through intermediate maxims of lesser generality, to a motivating conclusion. Something like the following:

1. My happiness (i.e., self-love) is good. (*Maxim I*)
2. By experiencing more agreeableness than troubles I satisfy my self-love. (*Judgment*)

---

[14] Cf. Beck's schema for the Kantian practical syllogism: "To avenge a wrong is always my purpose—Maxim or principle. To tell this lie would avenge a wrong—Rule. Therefore, I purpose to tell this lie—Decision"; Lewis White Beck, *A Commentary on Kant's Critique of Practical Reason* (Chicago: University of Chicago Press, 1960), 81.

3. Therefore, [from self-love, I make it my principle that] acting in order to experience more agreeableness than troubles is good. (*Maxim II*)

4. By shortening my life when its longer duration threatens more troubles than agreeableness I will experience more agreeableness than troubles. (*Judgment*)

5. Therefore, [from self-love, I make it my principle that] shortening my life when its longer duration threatens more troubles than agreeableness is good. (*Maxim III*)

6. My life's longer duration now threatens more troubles than agreeableness. (*Judgment*)

7. Therefore, shortening my life now is good. (*Maxim IV*)

8. By jumping off this bridge now I will shorten my life. (*Judgment*)

9. Therefore, jumping off this bridge now is good. (Wolffian *Motive*)

We can see here, in statement 5, how Kant's complicated example of the suicide maxim can be integrated into a practical sorites. It is helpful to point out here also that Kant distinguished two kinds of maxim: there are "maxims of action," and "maxims of ends."[15] The first maxim in the above example would be a maxim of ends, since it is a simple statement that something, happiness, is good to bring about. The rest are maxims of action that express the goodness of ways of acting, or of policies of action. They are all derived by inferences of practical reasoning from the leading maxim, in descending degrees of generality. And the final conclusion of this reasoning, called a motive by Wolff, represents a particular action as something good to do, here and now. From this mental representation the relevant movement of the body could be expected to follow because of the way God has ordered the matter of the world, at least according to Wolff.

Kant did not follow Leibniz and Wolff in thinking of minds and bodies as related through pre-established harmony, however. So he did not think it would be up to God to connect the thoughts that conclude our practical

---

[15] The distinction between maxims of action and maxims of ends is implicit at *Metaphysics of Morals*, 198/6:395; cf. also 193/6:389. Some commentators have found at least three kinds of maxim in Kant's ethical writings. Atwell found that Kant recognizes "incentival," "actional", and "dispositional" maxims. See John E. Atwell, *Ends and Principles in Kant's Moral Thought* (Dordrecht: Martinus Nihoff, 1986), ch. 3. Potter offers a comparable interpretation, distinguishing three "elements" of maxims: "our moral character as moral agents (our moral goodness or evil), the end or goal of our actions, and the kind of action itself." See Nelson Potter, "Maxims in Kant's Moral Philosophy," *Philosophia* 23 (July 1994): 59–90 at 69.

reasoning with our bodies' movements. His own explanation of how we get from maxims in the mind to behavior in the external world is not something we can pursue here. It will suffice for now to say that Kant recognized certain kinds of mental representations as themselves capable of causing intentional bodily movements.[16]

The practical sorites, with its leading maxim and descending hierarchy of sub-maxims, may seem like a contrived device for representing practical reasoning. But it is relatively easy to translate the whole business into the somewhat more familiar structure of final and intermediate ends. We need only think of the action named in the syllogism's conclusion as a means to be taken to achieve an immediate end. This end, in turn, can be seen as a means to achieving a more final end, and so on, until we reach the ultimate end. So in the suicide example, the agent jumps off the bridge as a means of shortening his life, but this action ultimately serves the end of happiness or self-love, ironically. The practical sorites is a way of expressing sequences of means to ends in the rationalist tradition of practical reasoning, where mental states like desires are seen as thoughts or representations in the mind (the "power of representation"). Ends are represented as things that are good to bring about, and contemplated actions are represented as means to achieving those ends.

1.4 Intentions

The generality of maxims has been a point of controversy among recent commentators on Kant's moral theory. This controversy has some bearing on how the concept of an intention can be supposed to apply in his theory of action. For reasons we need not pursue here, some have found it best to think of maxims as only the most general personal policies, or "life rules." They have recommended that actions be thought of as following not directly from maxims, but always through agents' particular, context-informed *intentions*.[17] Their idea is that maxims would be too general to be of much use in the context of action. So the principles upon which

[16] See *Lectures on Metaphysics*, 259/29:891, 261/29:894, 376/28:675.

[17] See, for example, Onora O'Neill, *Constructions of Reason, Explorations in Kant's Practical Philosophy* (Cambridge: Cambridge University Press, 1989), 84, 129. See also Kitcher, "What is a Maxim?" 219–21.

we typically act, they say, are intentions. These are always less general than maxims, and as such they are adaptable to the particulars of our circumstances. Hence, according to this view, the connection between a maxim and an action is always mediated by an intention. I agree with this view, at least on the point that the intentions upon which we act are not maxims. But I do not agree that maxims are only the most general policies of a person. From the preceding example of several maxims hierarchically ordered in a practical sorites it should be clear that maxims are capable of exhibiting various degrees of generality. In this I agree with what seems to be the majority of Kant's recent interpreters.[18]

Kant used words besides "maxim" to suggest intentions in acting: words like *Absicht, Vorsatz,* and *Gesinnung.*[19] In many contexts, however, it seems that "maxim" and English "intention" can be used synonymously. The important exception is when agents' intentions are to perform particular actions, at particular times and places. For maxims, as principles, cannot refer to actions as particulars.

In the simplest form of a practical syllogism the agent's intention in performing the action will be reflected in the minor premise. Typically, that will be where a particular action is represented as capable of causing the object or condition the maxim represents as good. So if the maxim is "Exercising is good," and the minor premise is "Walking in the neighborhood now is an effective way to exercise," then the agent moved to action by these premises intends: "to walk in the neighborhood now as an effective way to (in order to) exercise." Some might insist that the intention here should refer to the action only, or be expressed as just "to walk in the neighborhood now." The end at which the action aims should not be represented in its intention, it may be said. But it seems common for English speakers to think of intentions in acting as capable of referring to both means and ends. It seems meaningful to ask someone "What is your intention?" even when knowing what she is doing, or how she is acting. So here the "intention" asked about can be expected to refer not only to the known action, but also to the queried end.

---

[18] See, for example, Henry E. Allison, *Kant's Theory of Freedom* (Cambridge: Cambridge University Press, 1990), 91–4.

[19] With the possible exception of *Gesinnung,* which he sometimes uses synonymously with "maxim," Kant's terms suggesting English "intention" do not seem theoretically significant (see below, 7.2). *Gesinnung* is often translated "disposition," but Kant uses it sometimes to refer to maxims (e.g., *Practical Reason,* 49/5:56, 73/5:86), and sometimes to refer to particular motives for actions (e.g., 125/5:552).

It therefore seems correct to say that intentions, at least when they are intentions to perform particular actions, can include references ends. For that reason intentions seem to be represented in the minor premises of practical syllogisms.

Intentions seem capable of referring to actions apart from their ends, however. And if we also allow that they can be general, then we are well on the way to seeing how maxims can be approximately the same as general intentions. In other words, "maxim" and "intention" can sometimes apply to the same mental representation. For example, I may form the general intention to exercise, or to exercise more, without specifying in my intention why I would exercise, or the particular way I would exercise. I might think that "My becoming more physically fit is good," and then judge that "By exercising I would become more physically fit." So I would conclude that "Exercising is good." The reasoning here takes the form of a practical syllogism starting with a maxim, and concluding with a less general maxim, *via* a minor premise about the effect of exercising. When I derive the maxim that exercising is good, there seems to be no reason why it cannot be said that I have derived a general intention to exercise.[20] So the controversy over whether we act upon maxims or intentions does not pose a well-formulated problem. Intentions are mental states of various degrees of generality, and so they can be maxims, even if some intentions are too particular to be maxims.

1.5 Desires

Kant used "desire" in both a narrow and a broad sense. The narrow sense of the term refers to desires based in sense-experience. Habitual desires in this sense are called "inclinations," and Kant most frequently used this term when referring to sense-based desires. The broad sense of "desire" is somewhat less common in his writing, and it can refer to any motivational state. It is desire, as is sometimes said, "in the philosophers' sense."[21]

---

[20] Of course forming or adopting a general intention doesn't necessarily mean that one will act on it. General intentions include New Year's resolutions, as well as all those other good but ineffective intentions that pave the road to hell.

[21] Frierson explains this sense of desire relatively well in writing that "when desire is taken in this sense, there are no actions that are not preceded by and caused by desires, and no desires that do

Kant's two words for "desire" in German are *Begierde* and *Begehr*. He was not completely consistent in the way he used them, but the former usually suggests sense-based desire. The latter most often refers to desire in general, and it is typically used in contexts where intellect-based motivational states are included in the discussion. For reasons we need not explore here, Kant was on the cutting edge of German philosophical psychology in defending a "three-faculty psychology." This means that unlike most of his predecessors he saw the human mind as capable of three basic types of operation: cognition, feeling, and desire. Since his name for the mind's practical or motivational faculty was the "faculty of desire" (*Begehrungsvermögen*), any "determination" or "state" of this faculty can be referred to as a desire (*Begehr*). It can therefore be correct to classify as a desire, in this broad sense, even what Kant called "respect for the moral law," the special attitude effective in moral motivation (see Ch. 6).

The rationalist tradition in which Kant was educated, whose figureheads in Germany were Leibniz and Wolff, explained the human mind as a power capable of representing the world either cognitively or appetitively. In this tradition, cognitive mental states would represent their objects by implicitly applying concepts like "true," or "real," while appetitive states would represent their objects with the concept of "good."[22] In more contemporary jargon, and speaking very loosely, the idea is that in cognition we would represent things as they are — our representations are expected to adapt themselves to the world — while in desiring we would represent things that ought to be — the world would be expected to adapt

not lead to actions (at least in the absence of external impediments)"; Patrick R. Frierson, "Kant's Empirical Account of Human Action," *Philosophers' Imprint* 5 (December 2005): 1–34 at 9. But I do not agree with the parenthetical qualification that the impediments that would explain a desire's not leading to action are only "external," i.e., non-psychological. I will show later why this qualification makes the strength of one's desire indistinguishable from the strength of one's body (3.7). It seems to me also that Kant makes passing references to someone's having a desire or inclination that is frustrated by, and so does not lead to action because of, an "internal" impediment that is another, conflicting desire: in many cases, a moral desire. Moreover, a passage from the second *Critique* seems to indicate that what I believe Frierson would call a moral desire "fails to express its effect in actions only because subjective (pathological) causes hinder it" (68/5:79). Partly for these reasons I also disagree with Frierson's interpretive claim that "In contrast to customary English usage, Kantian desires mark an end to deliberation, not factors taken into account in deliberation" (10).

[22] "The soul has two faculties, the cognitive and the appetitive. We are certain of this by experience. ... It is also clear that each of these faculties can function faultily. The cognitive faculty can stray from the truth and the appetitive faculty from goodness. ..." Christian Wolff, *Preliminary Discourse on Philosophy in General*, trans. R. J. Blackwell (Indianapolis, IN: Bobbs-Merrill, 1963), 35.

to our representations. Here desire is not assumed to be a psychological state distinct from the thought or representation of something's goodness: as if we think of something as good and then we desire it on that account (or vice-versa). Rather, in this tradition, to desire just is to think of or represent something as good. Another way to put the point is to say that desires have objects in exactly the way thoughts have objects, because desires are thoughts. They are thoughts of the goodness of their objects.

Kant was steeped in this tradition of philosophizing about desire, and he never criticized it. That is, he never objected to the idea that desires represent their objects as good, while aversions represent them as bad (cf. *Practical Reason*, 50/5:58). His definition of the mental faculty of desire suggests that desires are representations: "The *faculty of desire* is a being's *faculty to be by means of its representations the cause of the reality of the objects of these representations.*"[23] This definition does not say that the representations of desire are representations of things as "good," however. But in the second *Critique* Kant endorsed an old scholastic doctrine that we never desire anything not represented as good, and we are never averse to anything not represented as bad: "*nihil appetimus, nisi sub ratione boni; nihil aversamur, nisi sub ratione mali*" (51/5:59). Although he criticized this doctrine, he objected to it only insofar as it might restrict the idea of good (*boni*) to well-being or happiness. His view was that there is an important distinction to be made between representing something as good in the sense of well-being (*das Wohl*), and thinking of something as morally good (*das Gute*).[24]

It is worth pointing out here, before leaving the concept of "desire," that maxims are correctly seen as desires in Kant's theory of action. A representation of something as good is a desire, and, as we have seen, a maxim is a representation of something as good. Hence, to have a maxim is to desire something, at least in the broad sense of desire.

---

[23] *Practical Reason*, 8n./5:8n.; see also *Metaphysics of Morals*, 40/6:211, and *Lectures on Metaphysics*, 261/29:893–4).

[24] Kant pointed to another ambiguity in the scholastic formula. It is not clear, he wrote, whether it is to mean that in desiring something we have a basis for judging it good, or whether we first judge an object good and, as a consequence, desire it. He wrote, "[I]t may mean: we represent to ourselves something as good when and *because we desire* (will) it, or also: we desire something *because we* [*first*] *represent it to ourselves as good. . . .*" (52n./5:59n.). Subsequent remarks show that Kant prefers the first reading of the formula: that desiring (willing) determines good (see 55–6/5:64).

1.6 Will

For Kant and his contemporaries the will (*Wille*) is the most important mental faculty involved in human action. Its role is comparable to the role of the understanding, in cognition. Kant explained that for human beings "[practical] reason is required for the derivation of actions from laws," or from principles. He then characterized the will as our "capacity to act *in accordance with the representation* of laws." Hence, as he said, "the will is nothing other than practical reason."[25] We can take this to mean that whenever action follows from the premises of the practical syllogism, it does so through an operation of practical reasoning. This process is otherwise known as volition or willing. But deriving actions from principles is not the only operation Kant attributed to the will.

In the three-faculty psychology mentioned in the preceding section, the will is a division or sub-faculty of the more general faculty of desire. The will is called the "higher" faculty of desire because it is an intellectual faculty, rather than a "lower," sense-based faculty. The same type of hierarchical division is observed in the cognitive faculty as well. There, understanding is higher and the senses and sense-based imagination are lower. To Kant's way of thinking, the characteristic function of a higher faculty is to legislate a priori rules or concepts for the operations of its host faculty.[26] The understanding is higher cognition because it legislates the twelve categories for cognition of the world. In a similar way the will is higher desire, because it legislates a priori rules for actions. "Legislating" here means imposing governing concepts or norms, and these are a priori because they are not sense-based. In the cognitive faculty, an example of an a priori rule legislated by the understanding is "Every event has a cause."

[25] *Groundwork*, 24/4:412. Here I pass over the many instances where Kant seems to use the word "will" (*Wille*) in a broad sense referring to the faculty of desire; and I pass over his apparent confusion, in some earlier writing, between *Wille* and *Willkür*.

[26] Deleuze approaches this feature of Kant's system somewhat awkwardly, I think, with a distinction between "the first sense of the word 'faculty'" and "the second sense of the word 'faculty'." The latter refers to the active, "higher" faculties (understanding, reason, and judgment) that are legislative in the former; that is, in the three fundamental powers of cognition, desire, and feeling. He also substitutes the faculty of imagination for judgment as the higher, legislative faculty in the feeling of pleasure and displeasure. See Gilles Deleuze, *Kant's Critical Philosophy: The Doctrine of the Faculties,* trans. Hough Tomlinson and Barbara Habberjam (Minneapolis, MN: University of Minnesota Press, 1984), 3–10.

In the faculty of desire, the will legislates moral rules, like the universal-law formula of the categorical imperative.

In Kant's view, then, the will has two important functions. As practical reason the will runs the procedure of the practical syllogism. It derives actions from laws or principles. Our actions follow from maxims, that is, through acts of our practical reasoning, our will. But the will understood as what Kant sometimes called *pure* practical reason legislates a priori, imposing moral rules for action. An act of will in this sense, as an act of *pure* will, is the act of imposing a rule. Call it an act of self-legislation (*autonomy*).

One further point should now be made about the will. In human beings, the will is not perfectly rational. This means that in its first function of deriving actions from principles, it does not necessarily adhere to the a priori rules for action that it imposes on the faculty of desire, in its second, *pure* function. But it is at least possible to imagine beings that do have perfectly rational wills, and they would be morally perfect. These would be angels perhaps, or God.

1.7 Choice and Wish

In *The Metaphysics of Morals* Kant introduced a technical distinction between choice (*arbitrium, Willkür*) and wish (*Wunsch*). This distinction deserves more attention than it usually receives, I think. He wrote that the faculty of desire is the faculty "for *doing or refraining from doing as one pleases.* Insofar as it is joined with one's consciousness of the capacity to bring about its object by one's action it is called the *capacity for choice;* if it is not joined with this consciousness its act is called a *wish*" (42/6:213).

To understand these ideas it helps to think of choices and wishes as alternative types of determination of the faculty of desire, or as alternative types of desire. Choices and wishes are distinguished by whether or not the subject has some "consciousness" or belief that she can act in a way that will bring about the existence of a desired object: an object that her maxim represents as good. Without such a belief accompanying it, her desire is a mere wish; otherwise, it is called a choice. It must seem strange to English readers to see a "choice" classified as a type of desire, something comparable to a wish. English readers naturally think of a choice as something more like a decision than like a desire. But a desire-state is often what Kant referred to when using his term "*Willkür*," the term now usually translated "choice," "faculty of choice," or "power of choice."[27]

In his metaphysics lectures from around 1792, five years prior to publication of *The Metaphysics of Morals*, we find the following distinction among the classes of desire-state: "empty desires are called wishes (yearnings). The subject can himself be conscious of this emptiness. ...Effective desire is not yet efficient, one calls it [*arbitrium, Willkür*] as long as the opposite of my desire is also in my control."[28] In notes from lectures a few years later, just before Kant would have been writing *The Metaphysics of Morals*, we find: "There are namely two kinds of desire: *a practical desire*, i.e., the representation of the possibility of making [its object] actual ... and *a less practical desire*, which one calls wish, a desire connected with the consciousness that it does not stand in our control to be able actually to produce the object" (483/29:1013). In the same place we also find: "Now the desire with respect to such objects of which we are conscious of having adequate powers for producing, is an *act of* [*arbitrium, Willkür*], *and the faculty that corresponds to this desire is* [*arbitrium, Willkür*]. ..." (483/29:1014). These statements show that Kant used his terms *arbitrium* and *Willkür* at least sometimes to refer to a kind of desire, and other times to a faculty for having that kind of desire.

Let us now recall that a maxim can be classified as a type of desire, since it is a representation of something as good (1.5). In the practical syllogism, practical reasoning generates an action from a maxim only when the latter is connected with a minor premise. The minor premise would indicate how to act in order to bring about the object considered good in the maxim. By Kant's definitions, therefore, a maxim connected with such a premise would be a *choice* (*Willkür*), an "effective" desire, even if "not yet efficient." Otherwise, the maxim would be a *wish*. To think of something as good, without having any idea how to bring it about, is to wish for it.

---

[27] See *Lectures on Metaphysics*, 349/28:589 for Kant's comment on the etymology of "*Willkür*." The "faculty of choice" would be the capacity of desiring something with awareness of how to act in order to bring it about. Kant does not mention a "faculty of wish," however. That would be because the very point of desiring, as seen through his definition of the faculty of desire, is to cause the existence of a represented object. A wish, accordingly, is a failing desire; and one does not classify psychological possibilities of failure as faculties. The faculty of memory, for example, is not paired or contrasted with the faculty of forgetting.

[28] *Lectures on Metaphysics*, 378/28:677; cf. also 69/28:254.

Kant needed the distinction between choice and wish in order to respond to a criticism of his definition of "desire." In the second *Critique* he had defined the faculty of desire as "a being's *faculty to be by means of its representations the cause of the reality of the objects of these representations*" (8n./5:10n.). But apparently more than one critic had objected to his defining desire in terms of causality, since it seemed to imply that all desires would be causes. That would not be correct, the critics pointed out, since sometimes we desire things when we know full well that we can do nothing to cause their existence. So in the third *Critique* Kant repeated the critics' complaint, and responded. As the critics point out, he wrote:

mere *wishes* are also desires, but yet everyone would concede that he could not produce their objects by their means alone [by merely wishing].—This, however proves nothing more than that there are also desires in a human being as a result of which he stands in contradiction with himself, in that he works toward the production of the object by means of his representation *alone,* from which he can however expect no success. . . .[29]

The internal contradiction referred to here lies in representing something as good to bring about, at the same time one is convinced that it is impossible to act to bring it about. By the former, as Kant sees it, that is, by wishing, a person "works toward the production of the object by means of his representation *alone,* from which he can however expect no success, because he is aware that" his powers are inadequate to produce the object.[30]

1.8 Faculty of Choice

Our ability to desire things we believe we can bring about, that is, our ability to have "effective desires," is our "faculty of choice" (*Vermögen*

[29] Immanuel Kant, *Critique of the Power of Judgment,* ed. Paul Guyer, trans. Paul Guyer and Eric Matthews (Cambridge: Cambridge University Press, 2000), 65n./5:177n.; see also 32–3n./20:230–1n. In an appendix to Kant's "Doctrine of Right" published in 1798, he replied similarly to criticism presented by Friedrich Bouterwek; see *Metaphysics of Morals,* 163/6:356–7.

[30] This capacity we have to strive for an object without knowledge of how to attain it is a good design in nature, Kant explained: "Nature has . . . combined the determination of our power with the representation for the object even prior to knowledge of our capacity [to produce the object], which is often first brought forth precisely by this striving, which initially seemed to the mind itself to be an empty wish" (*Judgment,* 32–3n./20:230–1n.).

der Willkür, arbitrium). This faculty would be the opposite, in a sense, of our "faculty of wish," or of our ability to have "ineffective desires."[31] English-language translators and interpreters have often referred to the former faculty as the "*power* of choice." But this is a technical mistake, and it is worth understanding why.[32]

In the psychological tradition most familiar to Kant, a "power of choice" would be a nonsensical expression. This is because "choice" in his system is, along with "wish," subordinated to the faculty of desire; and the term "power" (*Kraft*) would never be applied to a subordinate faculty.[33] A faculty could be subordinate to a power; and a faculty could be subordinate to another, more general faculty. But a power would not be subordinate to a faculty. Christian Wolff, who developed the psychological vocabulary Kant used, had insisted quite vehemently on the importance of the distinction between *powers* and *faculties*. To his way of thinking, the soul is a power, and cognition and appetition are its most basic faculties.[34] Understanding and sensation are then sub-faculties of the soul, on the cognitive side, while will and sense-based desire are sub-faculties on the appetitive side. Ontologically, the *power* of the Wolffian soul is an actual force or effort exercised in its acts of representing. The soul's *faculties* of

---

[31] But see above, n. 27.

[32] The tendency to construe Kant's terms "*Willkür*" and "*arbitrium*" as referring to a "power of choice" may stem from some comments found in H. J. Paton, *The Categorical Imperative, A Study of Kant's Moral Philosophy* (Chicago: University of Chicago Press, 1948), 213–14. Ralph Meerbote has also recommended translating Kant's "*Willkür*" as "power of choice" in "*Wille* and *Willkür* in Kant's Theory of Action," in Moltke S. Gram, ed., *Interpreting Kant* (Iowa City, IA: University of Iowa Press, 1982), 69–84, esp. 81. These translations of "*Willkür*" and "*arbitrium*" unfortunately suggest a special "power" for free agency or choice, which is an idea that can be found in English-language moral psychology as far back as Samuel Clarke, *The Works of Samuel Clarke*, vol. II (London: J. and P. Knapton, 1738, repr.: New York: Garland Publishing Company, 1978), 566. But this is not what Kant had in mind by his use of these terms.

[33] We may note that "will" (*Wille*) is also subordinate to the faculty of desire, at least systematically. For will is the higher faculty of desire.

[34] It is unfortunate that Wolff's psychology has been misleadingly described as a "one-faculty theory." See Lewis White Beck, *Early German Philosophy; Kant and his Predecessors* (Cambridge, MA: Belknap Press, 1969), 269, 271, 287–8, and esp. 497; and John Zammito, *The Genesis of Kant's Critique of Judgment* (Chicago: University of Chicago Press, 1992), 18. Wolff wrote: "We find in experience that the soul is constantly active but its thoughts are not always of the same kind. Sometimes it has sensations, sometimes imaginings, sometimes distinct concepts, sometimes rational inferences, sometimes desires, sometimes volitions, and so forth. . . . Thus we see that much is possible in the soul . . . and considering the variations which can be brought about, we may distinguish as many different faculties [*Facultates, Vermögen*] as types of variations." Christian Wolff, *Vernünfftige Gedancken von Gott, der Welt und der Seele des Menschen, Auch Allen Dingen Überhaupt, Anderer Theil* (Frankfurt, 1740; facsimile, Hildesheim: Georg Olms, 1983), §265. This is Part II of the *Deutsche Metaphysik*, in which Wolff published an extensive commentary (*Anmerkungen*) on his earlier work and replied to criticisms.

cognition and appetition are just the various possibilities or uses of this essential power.[35]

Kant did not agree with Wolff in thinking that powers and faculties differ in just this way. Yet he indicated in his lectures, nevertheless, that he regarded them as subtly different; and he conceded that their difference is difficult to understand.[36] He agreed with Wolff that powers—forces—are the most basic explanations of activities or effects in the world. But he believed that human insight into the world's most basic powers, including the power of the soul, is limited. So he did not think that we are in any position to know that the single, most basic power of the soul is the power of representation, as Wolff had assumed. His view was that in our investigative work in the sciences we have arrived at what appears to us to be the world's most basic powers. But for all we know, the effects of these supposed powers may derive from a smaller set of still more fundamental powers. So what we now designate as a "power" must represent the limit of our understanding of an effect's explanation.[37]

Regarding the human mind, therefore, Kant's view was that in order to explain the full range of mental phenomena we must posit three basic faculties of the mind. These, as indicated above, are cognition, feeling, and desire. We cannot see how these three could be reduced to one, as a single, most basic mental power. Yet reason compels us to think that the plurality of the mind's powers must spring from some single root.[38] So due to the limits of our understanding we are entitled to refer to them as the three *powers* of the mind. But insofar as we project ahead to our possibly understanding the more basic, unitary power from which they would be derived, we should see them as the three basic *faculties* of the mind—as three different types of exercise of the single power of the soul.

---

[35] See Christian Wolff, *Deutsche Metaphysik,* §117.

[36] "Power is a faculty insofar as it suffices for the actuality of an accident. The difference between power and faculty is difficult to determine. Faculty, insofar as it is determined with respect to an effect, is power, and insofar as it is undetermined, becomes faculty. Power contains the ground of the actuality of the action, faculty the ground of the possibility of the action" (*Lectures on Metaphysics,* 182/29:823–4, see also 329/28:565).

[37] "We begin by naming causes with the same name as the powers—but this is mere naming, not explanation. One calls this naming a hidden [or occult] quality, e.g., the bell rings because the metal has a ringing effect" (*Lectures on Metaphysics,* 373/28:671).

[38] See *Pure Reason,* A648–51/B676–9. Reason compels us to posit a "single radical, i.e., absolutely fundamental, power" to which "comparatively fundamental powers" can be reduced. See also J. Gray Cox, "The Single Power Thesis in Kant's Theory of the Faculties," *Man and World* 16 (1983): 315–33.

For these reasons it actually makes little difference to Kant whether cognition, desire and feeling are called the three "powers" of the mind, or its fundamental "faculties." Although their names do include the term "faculty" (*Vermögen*), at least in the case of cognition and desire, he still sometimes referred to them as "powers." In regard to "choice" (*Willkür*), however, since this would be a sub-faculty of desire, Kant could scarcely have conceived of a "power of choice." Here the difference between "power" and "faculty" is clear, and important. And Kant never used the word "power" (*Kraft*) in referring to choice. So what, then, is meant by his phrases "*Vermögen der Willkür*" and "*arbitrium*," which are often misleadingly translated as "power of choice"? To depart momentarily from technical jargon, these signify what English speakers refer to as "will" in phrases like, "freedom of the will," or "Fire at will!" They signify the mental faculty of "will" whose operations result in our doing as we please.

Above we reviewed Kant's understanding of "will" in the technical sense as the higher, legislative faculty of desire. That is the sense of "will" used to refer to objective practical reason imposing moral principles.[39] His terms *Willkür* and *arbitrium* refer to the subjective side of the appetitive faculty.[40] They refer, technically, to our cluster of psychological abilities dedicated to desiring, forming beliefs about how to act in light of our desires, and then acting.[41]

Those who believe in free will think we exercise our freedom in exercising this cluster of abilities. But even those who doubt that we have free will agree that we routinely exercise the cluster of abilities referred to by Kant's terms *Willkür* and *arbitrium*. Their view is that our desires are the effects of prior causes not under our control, and the same goes for our beliefs. They therefore say that our actions resulting from our exercising

---

[39] Kant did not attribute freedom to the will in the objective sense of legislating practical reason. He claimed: "Laws proceed from the will, *maxims* from choice. In man the latter is a capacity for free choice; the will, which is directed to nothing beyond the law itself, cannot be called either free or unfree, since it is not directed to actions but immediately to giving laws for the maxims of actions (and is, therefore, practical reason itself)" (*Metaphysics of Morals*, 52/6:226).

[40] Christian Wolff had used the term in roughly the same way, even before Kant was born. "*In so weit nun de Seele den Grund ihrer Handlungen in sich hat, in so weit eignet man ihr einen Willkühr zu, und nennet daher willkührliches Thun und Lassen, wovon der Grund in der Seelen zu finden*" (*Deutsche Metaphysik*, §518).

[41] Recall that "wish" would refer to this same complex of abilities when the belief in how to act is absent, or when acting to satisfy a desire is believed impossible.

these abilities are, likewise, determined by prior causes over which we have no control. So from this it should be clear that the question of whether we have free will cannot be decided by determining whether or not we can exercise what Kant referred to as *Willkür* and *arbitrium*. These terms were used by his contemporaries, and by Kant himself, in referring even to animals, who were of course denied any freedom of the will.[42] So this means that as far as Kant is concerned, any conception of human freedom has to be developed independently of the concepts of *Willkür* or *arbitrium*. The explanation or characterization of human freedom has to be, in other words, an explanation or characterization of human *Willkür* or *arbitrium* as free.

1.9 Imperatives

The will's objective legislation presents actions as good (or bad) to do. For agents with perfectly rational wills, as indicated above, thoughts or representations of the laws legislated by the will would be sufficient for their doing the actions they present as good. But in our case, the will expresses its legislation in the form of principles called "imperatives." Imperatives "say that to do or omit something would be good, but they say it to a will that does not always do something just because it is represented to it that it would be good to do that thing" (*Groundwork*, 24–5/4:413).

As is well known, Kant distinguished two types of imperative: hypothetical and categorical. Only the categorical imperative is a principle of the will's objective or a priori legislation. The legislation of a hypothetical imperative always depends on some prior sense-experience. In general, hypothetical imperatives say that it would be good to do some action, or that we ought to do it, because it would be an effective means of producing something we desire as a result of sense-experience. Our desire here can be understood as a maxim representing an object of experience as good (1.5). So a hypothetical imperative may be understood as conveying the logical force of the premises of a practical syllogism.[43] When in a maxim I

---

[42] See Wolff's *Deutsche Metaphysik*, §890. See also Kant's *Metaphysics of Morals*, 42/6:213; and see below, 3.10.

[43] Here I have explained hypothetical imperatives as derived from maxims. This seems to me the most natural way to represent Kant's idea that by a hypothetical imperative we ought to do something

represent some object of experience as good to bring about, and in a minor premise I recognize how I can act in order to bring it about, practical reasoning addresses me with a (hypothetical) imperative stating that I ought to act that way.[44]

With categorical imperatives, by contrast, the logical force of the will's directive does not depend on my having thought of some object of experience as good, in one of my maxims. A categorical imperative does not tell me how I ought to act in order to bring about something I desire. Rather—and this is a crucial point of Kant's moral theory—a categorical imperative says that I ought to do something (or not), because of some intrinsic or "formal" feature of that way of acting (cf. *Practical Reason*, 19–26/5:21–8, *Groundwork*, 36/4:427–8).

A central assumption of Kantian ethics is that it is always possible for us to act as we are commanded to act by categorical imperatives. So the Kantian conception of acting on maxims needs to accommodate this guaranteed possibility. It is easy to do this by making a further assumption about rational agents. We need only assume that agents subject to categorical imperatives necessarily have a special maxim for this purpose. This would be a maxim to the effect that *obeying the moral law is good*, or that *doing one's moral duty is good*. Actions would not follow from maxims like this through

because it would be (causally) effective in bringing about something we think of as good. But as Allison sees it, imperatives are not derived from maxims, because they are rules for the evaluation or selection of maxims. "Imperatives, whether hypothetical or categorical. . . . are second-order principles, which dictate the appropriate first-order principles (maxims). . . ." (*Kant's Theory of Freedom*, 87). I agree that hypothetical and categorical imperatives can "dictate" the adoption of maxims. But I think hypothetical imperatives, at least, can do this only because of higher maxims from which they are derived. In the above example of practical reasoning about suicide from self-love, the adoption of each of the various lower-level maxims would be dictated by a hypothetical imperative based on the maxim and causal judgment immediately above it. But I also think that hypothetical imperatives, and categorical as well, can dictate action as the final conclusion of a practical syllogism. So I do not think that imperatives are only second-order practical principles dictating the adoption of maxims, following Allison.

[44] In *The Metaphysics of Morals* Kant presented the three civil authorities of a state as corresponding to the three propositions in a practical syllogism. The sovereign represents the *law* in the major premise, the executive authority represents the *command* of the minor premise, as subsumed under the law, and the judicial authority represents the syllogism's concluding judgment, or *verdict* (see 125/6:313). Here the minor premise contains a command to behave in accordance with the major premise. It does not contain a statement that doing some action would cause some effect, or would constitute some condition. Yet the minor premise can still be so represented. Suppose the major premise is the maxim that "Paying your taxes is good," and the minor premise is that "Sending $100 to the treasury will pay your taxes." The practicality of the syllogism makes it appropriate to read the minor premise as the imperative to send $100 to the treasury. The syllogism's conclusion would evidently then be the decision to obey that imperative.

minor-premise causal judgments, however. They would follow through judgments of subsumption: judgments presenting actions as instantiating the concept of obedience to the moral law, or the concept of doing one's moral duty.[45] Only with the presupposition of a special moral maxim can we understand how recognition of a categorical imperative's command can be expected to make a difference in human conduct.

1.10 Reasons for Action

Imperatives are usually thought to provide reasons for action. But so also are maxims. Since the roles these types of propositions play in practical reasoning are different, as we have seen, they apparently provide different types of reason for action. A broad distinction in types of reason for action has been attributed to the Scottish sentimentalist, Francis Hutcheson. "Justifying" or "normative reasons" are said to indicate why an action ought to be done, while "explaining" or "motivating reasons" show why an action is done, or could be done. Imperatives and maxims in Kant's theory of action seem to correspond roughly to this distinction. An imperative is a reason why I ought to do something, and a maxim is a reason why I did, would do, or could have done something.

Yet someone could plausibly *explain* why she did something by saying that it ought, morally, to have been done. So here it seems that a justifying reason might explain an action. And someone else might *justify* his action to himself, or to others, on the basis of his having a certain desire or maxim that the action would satisfy. So here, apparently, an explaining reason justifies. An additional complication arises from the fact that imperatives and maxims are propositions of practical reasoning. Imperatives are derived from maxims by reasoning, as has been shown. But they are not derived directly. In the case of a hypothetical imperative, its supporting premises include both a maxim (desire) and a judgment to the effect some action, or course of action, will be effective in producing a desired object. So supposing that someone acts as directed by a hypothetical imperative, her

---

[45] The categorical imperative that one ought not act on maxims that cannot become universal laws would follow from the maxim that obeying the moral law is good, and the judgment that avoiding acting on maxims that cannot become universal laws is a way to obey the moral law.

"reason" for acting could plausibly be the imperative, or the relevant maxim, or even the intervening causal judgment. Someone's reason for sprinkling salt on the ice-covered sidewalk, for example, could be the causal judgment (or fact) that *Salt melts ice*. Moreover, since maxims can receive rational support from still higher maxims, and more general causal judgments, any of these, in the right context, could plausibly be offered as "the reason" for someone's action.[46] Something similar could also be said for actions commanded by categorical imperatives. For the possibility of acting on a categorical imperative presupposes a special, moral maxim, as well as a judgment of subsumption: a judgment that an action has the characteristics that make it morally required.[47] So in view of all this latitude in what could count as a reason, the concept of a reason for action is, to say the least, hard to pin down.

Kant seldom wrote about reasons for action, so described. In his vocabulary, "practical laws" and "imperatives" refer to justifying reasons. The former are usually called "objective practical principles." For explaining reasons, Kant preferred terms like "maxims" and "incentive," a term to be clarified in the following chapter. A maxim is called a "subjective practical principle," while an incentive is called a "subjective determining ground" (*Bestimmungsgrund*). Kant also recognized the possibility of a law's serving as a maxim (*Pure Reason*, A812/B840), or as an incentive (*Practical Reason*, 62/5:72), and so of a justifying reason's serving as an explaining reason. But this should not commit him to holding that actions are explained only by justifying reasons.

Take a simple case of someone's acting as a means of satisfying one of her sense-based desires. Her maxim might be that *Eating something refreshing would be good;* and she might judge that *Eating the orange in the fruit bowl would be refreshing*. In order for her to act on this maxim and judgment it will not be necessary for her to draw a justifying hypothetical imperative as a conclusion. She need not say to herself, or think, "So, since I desire to eat something refreshing, and this orange would be refreshing, *I ought to eat this orange*." Her intention to eat the orange, and her action, can follow

---

[46] Above, in Section 3, an extended practical syllogism was offered to illustrate the practical reasoning of someone intent upon suicide. Any of the nine statements listed there might plausibly be offered as reasons for the action, it seems to me.

[47] On this point see the extended discussion of "reasons" for action in Kantian moral motivation in Philip Stratton-Lake, *Kant, Duty and Moral Worth* (London: Routledge, 2000), 12–77.

simply from her maxim and her judgment. No justifying reason need be involved in the explanation of her action.

Nevertheless, a rational agent has the capacity for this. Rational agents can be conscious of the reasoning process by which they act. They can also be self-critical of the maxims that explain their actions. They can judge that a maxim on which they are contemplating acting is, for one reason or another, one they ought to act on, or one they ought not act on. They can think to themselves about ways they are contemplating acting: "I ought not to act on such maxims." And thoughts like this presumably can influence how they act.

Finally, rational agents seem also to have the capacity to rank competing practical propositions as providing relatively better and worse reasons for action. They seem capable of recognizing more general maxims, or more final ends, as providing better justifications for action. They apparently can recognize unconditional justifications (categorical imperatives) as providing better reasons for action than conditional or hypothetical justifications. And these types of justifying thoughts, also, can conceivably influence action.

All of this shows, I think, that the concept of a reason for action is fluid and imprecise, and that we need not attempt to identify the exact form of reasons for action in Kant's theory of action. What will be important instead is that we understand the difference between justifying reasons and explaining reasons for action, and that we have some rough idea of how Kant's conceptions of imperatives and maxims relate to these.

1.11 Justification and Explanation

Sections 1 through 8 of this chapter showed how practical reasoning with maxims can *explain* action. Kant's theory has it that rational agents' actions are derived from their maxims, by their wills, using the reasoning structure of the practical syllogism. So to explain an action in this theory it seems sufficient to cite the maxim and minor premise from which it follows as a conclusion. For example: *He is out walking* (action); *because he thinks exercise is good* (maxim) *and because he thinks walking is a way to exercise* (minor premise). Alternatively, *He's walking in order to exercise*.

Section 9, by contrast, showed how practical reasoning with maxims can *justify* action. As Kant explained imperatives, at least valid hypothetical imperatives, they follow from maxims and causal judgments. To justify an action with a hypothetical imperative we would cite a maxim of the agent, and identify an action, in a minor premise, as a means of bringing about what is indicated in the maxim as good. For example: *You ought to sharpen your knife* (imperative); *because its cutting better would be good* (maxim) *and because sharpening your knife will make it cut better* (minor premise). Alternatively, *Because (If) you want your knife to cut better, (then) sharpen it.*

The task for the present section is to pose a problem related to the question broached at the beginning of this chapter: the question about justification and explanation. Practical reasoning seems suitable for both justifying and explaining action. The different examples we have just seen make this apparent. But there is an important complication now to be considered. It is related to the concept of an "imperative." If we were perfectly rational agents, there would be no problem in understanding how practical reasoning can both justify and explain our actions. For perfectly rational agents, the principles that justify actions suffice to explain them. We can think of perfectly rational agents as those who would desire all and only what they recognize as good through pure practical reason. So their desires would be, in effect, causal laws that explain their perfectly rational conduct.

But as we saw above, Kant assumed that the justifications for human actions are expressed in the form of imperatives. This is because, for us, what justifies action evidently does not explain it. Justification is one thing, and explanation is something else; and for us, the conditions for the one are importantly different from the conditions for the other. We can always act as we recognize we are justified in acting. But when we do, something besides the justification we recognize must explain our action. Otherwise, there could be no accounting for the counterfactual possibility of our having failed to act that way. As it happened, let us suppose, we did act in the way we recognized we ought to act. But we still could have acted otherwise, even while recognizing the way we ought to act. Thus, our recognition of the way we ought to act cannot, by itself, explain our action. Something must be added to our recognition of the way we ought to act—something presumed to be present in the factual case, and absent in the counterfactual case. This follows, again, from the presumption that justifications are expressed in the form of imperatives. So

Kant's doctrine that practical reason's justifications of human actions are imperatival seems to imply that what justifies action, for us, is not capable of explaining it.

Yet what justifies action *should be* capable of explaining it; otherwise, justification is irrelevant. People see animals as incapable of acting rationally, or on the basis of acknowledged rational justification. That is why they also see rational justification of animals' actions as pointless, irrelevant. They do not deny that animals sometimes take the most effective means to their ends, as if they were moved to action by a rational justification. What they deny is that talk of reasons and justifications even applies in the case of animal agency. They deny this precisely because they are convinced that animal actions are not explainable by practical reasoning. Any justifying imperatives that practical reason might pretend to issue for animal agents would be pointless.

David Hume, in the history of moral philosophy, applied a similar idea in arguing against rationalist moral theories. "Thus upon the whole," he wrote, " 'tis impossible, that the [justificatory] distinction betwixt moral good and evil, can be made by reason; since that distinction has an [explanatory] influence upon our actions, of which reason alone is incapable."[48] Hume's assumption here is that what justifies action must be capable of explaining it. His argument is that since reason has no explanatory influence on moral action, neither can it issue moral justifications. He made the point more generally also, even for non-moral action:

[I]f reason has no original [explanatory] influence, 'tis impossible it can withstand any principle which has such efficacy, or ever keep the mind in suspense a moment. Thus it appears, that the [justificatory] principle, which opposes our passion, cannot be the same with reason. ... Reason is, and ought always to be the slave of the passions, and can never pretend to any other office than to serve and obey them. (2.3.3.4)

Consequently, Hume continued, " 'Tis not contrary to reason to prefer the destruction of the whole world to the scratching of my finger. ... 'Tis as little contrary to reason to prefer even my own acknowledg'd lesser good to my greater, and have a more ardent affection for the former than the latter" (2.3.3.6).

---

[48] David Hume, *A Treatise of Human Nature*, ed. David Fate Norton and Mary J. Norton (New York: Oxford University Press, 2000), 3.1.1.16; see also 3.1.1.6.

Kant's theory of action seems to say, contrary to Hume, that practical reasoning *does* justify action. It does so through applications of the practical syllogism issuing in imperatives. So the problem before us is to show how, according to Kant, practical reasoning would also be capable of explaining action. We must show how practical reasoning can have an explaining influence on action through the maxims of the practical syllogism, if we are to see its imperatives, whether hypothetical or categorical, as relevant to human conduct. In the remainder of this book I shall refer to this as the problem of justification and explanation.[49]

Offering and defending a satisfactory solution to the problem of justification and explanation will be the main objective of the chapters immediately following. The solution to be offered will be that: practical reasoning from maxims *justifies* actions through logical force, but *explains* actions through psychological force. The next chapter begins by clarifying this solution, showing more concretely how it addresses the problem of justification and explanation.

We began this chapter by showing how Kant defined "action," and how "maxims" serve as subjective principles of action. They do this by functioning as major premises of a structure of practical reasoning, a structure known historically as the practical syllogism. The relation between desires and maxims, as we saw, is that maxims are desires, or at least a type of desires. Like his rationalist predecessors Kant considered a desire to be a representation of something as "good." And this is just how maxims represent objects (ends), and policies of actions. Our particular intentions in action can then be understood as reflecting minor premises of the practical syllogism. Someone intending "to do X in order to bring about Y," represents X as good to do because he judges that "X would bring about Y" (minor premise), and thinks "Y is good" (maxim). We saw in this chapter also how practical reasoning with maxims can justify action.

---

[49] Some may ask, Isn't this just the problem of skepticism about practical reason—the problem posed by the so-called "internalism requirement," that reason must be presumed capable of motivating action if moral requirements are to be derived from reason? My answer is that it is not (see Introduction). The universal availability of the moral incentive of respect seems to many to satisfy the internalism requirement. But this is not enough to solve what I am calling the problem of justification and explanation. It is not enough if we cannot see how reason can "activate" this available motive or make it explain action. What justifies action can explain action only provided it can somehow engage the mechanism that explains action. We presume that practical reason's justifications do this for perfectly rational agents. We need to see how they can do this for us.

It does this by deriving imperative conclusions from maxims: conclusion like, "You ought to X," from premises like "Y would be good to bring about" (maxim); and doing X would bring about Y (minor premise). The problem posed at the end of this chapter is to show how these two functions of practical reasoning, the explaining function and the justifying function, are coordinated, so that practical reasoning can explain the actions it can justify. This is the problem of justification and explanation. If this problem cannot be solved, then practical reason's justifications of action are irrelevant.

2

Incentives

We are not perfectly rational agents. So there is a problem in understanding how practical reasoning can both justify and explain our actions. The previous chapter proposed a solution to this problem. It is that practical reasoning justifies actions through logical force, and explains actions through psychological force. Our first objective in this chapter will be to clarify the meaning of this solution.

This chapter's title refers to Kant's concept of an "incentive," which will figure prominently in the account of how practical reason's maxims explain action. For clarification of the explanatory power of incentives we draw some crucial points from Kant's psychology lectures. We shall see here how Kant's concept of an incentive has two "dimensions," and four different types of referent. We shall see also how incentives relate to maxims: specifically, what it means for them to be "incorporated" into maxims. The relation between incentives and pleasures and displeasures, interests and practical reason will be explained here also. The central point to be established is that Kant assumed that maxims incorporate incentives as action-explaining psychological forces. That is how maxims with logical, justifying force, are capable of explaining action. The action-explaining forces of incentives are thought to derive from feelings of pleasure and displeasure, which is a doctrine I'll refer to here as Kant's "motivational hedonism."

2.1 Logical and Psychological Force

The logical force through which practical reasoning from maxims justifies action needs little explanation. A maxim is the major premise in a practical syllogism. Its function in this role is to justify or lend rational support to an intentional action. In order to do so it must be paired with a minor premise, which will typically indicate that an action would cause the object or condition that is represented in the maxim as good. When this pairing occurs, the rational agent will be led, logically, to the thought that it would be good to do that action.

For imperfectly rational agents like us, however, arriving at the thought of its being good to do something doesn't necessarily result in our doing it. Nor does it necessarily result in our intending to do it. We think of many things as good to do but we do not do them, because there is something else we prefer to do. That is why thoughts that something is good to do can take the form of imperatives commanding us to do it. The force of these commands is logical. It is the force of premises justifying a conclusion; *but it is not the kind of force that can explain action.*

The force that explains action, for us, is the psychological force of a maxim. In reasoning from a maxim and an appropriate minor premise we may be led to the conclusion that a particular action is good to do. In that case, our doing it will follow only provided that maxim's psychological force is sufficient for our doing it. The action-explaining psychological force of a maxim is what is commonly referred to as motive force. It is comparable to what people ordinarily think of as the force of desire, or desire strength.[1]

But it may now be asked: How can a force different from justifying, rational compulsion, different from the force of premises supporting a conclusion, be involved in practical reasoning? It may seem that in accepting the idea that psychological force explains action we will be abandoning one of our leading assumptions: that practical reasoning has explanatory power. To address this concern it need only be recalled here that maxims are *general* principles, which means that particular actions cannot follow from maxims except through practical reasoning. No matter how much psychological force a maxim may harbor, it cannot explain an action without a minor-premise judgment about the action. Only such a judgment can set up the agent's inference from a maxim to the conclusion that a particular action would be good to do. Motivating forces harbored in maxims, in representations of objects or conditions as good, are transmitted to the

---

[1] Worth recalling here is a fact observed in the previous chapter (1.5), that a maxim can be understood as a type of desire.

particular actions we do in no other way than through inferences of practical reasoning.

2.2 Incorporating Incentives

Kant usually referred to the psychological force of a maxim using the term, "incentive." But in order to understand his theory of action it is important to recognize that he used this term equivocally. One of the clearest cases of this equivocation comes from a discussion of moral psychology. There, he referred to both the objective moral law, and the subjective feeling of respect for the law, as the one and only "moral incentive."[2] In referring to each of these as *the* moral incentive, he either contradicted himself within the space of six pages—which is unlikely—or he assumed that his readers would understand his equivocal use of "incentive."

In light of this type of equivocation it seems correct to distinguish between subjective and objective "dimensions" of Kant's concept of an incentive.[3] In its subjective dimension, an incentive can be seen as a psychologically compelling motive force. But in its objective dimension, an incentive is what we can call the "target" of an incentive, in the subjective dimension. If the moral law is an incentive objectively considered, then respect for that law is a subjective incentive that "targets" the law. To understand this better it might help to compare an example from

[2] Kant wrote that in morally worthy action "the incentive of the human will (and the will of every created rational being) can never be anything other than the moral law" (*Practical Reason*, 62/5:72). But he later claimed that "Respect for the moral law is...the sole and also the undoubted moral incentive, and this feeling is also directed to no object except on this basis" (67/5:78). The title of the chapter in which these statements occur is: "On the Incentives of Pure Practical Reason." Its use of the plural suggests that there would be more than one moral incentive; and that is what Kant seems to demonstrate by identifying what will presently be called objective and subjective dimensions of the same moral incentive.

[3] This distinction seems implicit in Kant's claim that "the [moral] incentive of the human will (...) can never be anything other than the moral law; and thus the objective determining ground must always and quite alone be also the subjectively sufficient determining ground of action if this is not merely to fulfill the *letter* of the law without containing its *spirit*" (*Practical Reason*, 62/5:72). He seems to be invoking a similar distinction here, in a lecture illustration: "[W]hen freedom is given to me to choose one of two wholly equal ducats, then the objective incentives for the two sides would be of equal strength. I would thus reflect a moment as to which I should take until finally a subjective incentive, greed or impatience from delaying so long, would so stimulate me that I would take as best the first that caught my eye, or out of comfort, I would take that which was closest to me" (*Lectures on Metaphysics*, 268/29:902).

non-moral motivation. Money may be one of the most familiar objects serving as an incentive. But money's effectiveness as an incentive depends upon conditions within the subject to be motivated. For different people, objectively equal amounts of money may not be equally strong incentives. Whether a sum of money is an incentive at all, in fact, will depend upon subjective conditions like need. Money will not serve objectively as an incentive unless it can incite an agent, subjectively, to action. An amount of money could therefore be an objective incentive for someone's action; and his need for that money would be his subjective incentive "targeting" it.[4]

When we refer to incentives as the psychological, action-explaining forces of maxims, we have in mind their subjective dimensions. To understand how incentives can play this role in practical reasoning we must first understand their relation to maxims serving as major premises. Specifically, we must understand what it means for the psychological force of a subjective incentive to be "incorporated" into a maxim.

In an often-quoted passage from his *Religion within the Boundaries of Mere Reason,* Kant wrote something to the effect that a human being acting by free choice "cannot be determined to action through any incentive *except insofar as [he] has incorporated it into his maxim.*"[5] Many have seen this claim as crucial for understanding Kant's theory of action, and especially his theory of freedom. Most see it as telling us that subjectively forceful incentives, like natural desires or inclinations, cannot causally determine the choices and actions of a free agent, through their psychological forces. The passage

---

[4] Korsgaard seems to acknowledge what I am calling the objective dimension of incentives in explaining the difference between a person moved by duty to a beneficent act and a person moved to the same action by sympathy. She writes that "for both of these characters *the very fact that someone is in need is an incentive* and to that extent is a reason to help." See Christine M. Korsgaard, *The Sources of Normativity,* ed. Onora O'Neill (Cambridge: Cambridge University Press, 1996), 244, emphasis added. The *very fact* of someone's need is of course not a subjective, psychological state of the beneficent agent. It is an objective state of affairs that can be of interest to different agents in different ways. Shortly before this statement, however, Korsgaard used "incentive" in what appears to be a subjective, psychological sense: "An agent is confronted with an incentive—a desire or other impulse that presents a certain action as worth doing. . . ." (242–3, see also 240–1). She seems to emphasize the subjective dimensions of incentives elsewhere also when she writes that "An incentive is something that makes an action interesting to you, that makes it a live option. Desires and inclinations are incentives; so also is respect for the moral law"; Christine M. Korsgaard, *Creating the Kingdom of Ends* (Cambridge: Cambridge University Press, 1996), 165.

[5] Immanuel Kant, *Religion within the Boundaries of Mere Reason and Other Writings,* trans. and ed. Allen W. Wood and George di Giovanni (Cambridge: Cambridge University Press, 1998), 49/6:23–4.

says that in order for a free agent to act on an incentive he must first choose to "incorporate" it into his maxim. That way, it is supposed, he is not caused to act by the psychological force of the incentive. He acts instead by his own free choice. As some see it, this passage indicates that the process of deliberation in a rational agent typically concludes with a decision selecting an available incentive to be incorporated into a maxim. The psychological force of an incentive we are tempted to incorporate into our maxim might be very strong, they allow; but we need not give way to its strength. It is constitutive of our freedom, they say, that we can resist our strongest incentives. Their idea is that we can always choose to incorporate alternative and comparatively weaker incentives into our maxims instead. So the fact that an incentive bears the strong, psychological force of a desire need not affect our deliberations as free agents. The choice of which of our incentives we shall act upon, by incorporating them into maxims, is always up to us. In the next chapter (3.4) we shall return to discuss this passage from *Religion,* drawing some important clues to its meaning from its context. For now, our interest lies in the idea of a maxim's "incorporating" an incentive.

It has been difficult to understand what Kant meant by this expression. The difficulty is that a maxim is a principle of practical reasoning, with logical properties like generality and consistency. But an incentive seems to be something quite different. The lesson about freedom of choice usually drawn from the passage just quoted from *Religion* implies that incentives exhibit psychological properties like strength, or motive force. But these do not seem appropriate for "incorporation" into a principle. How can something with propositional content, something more or less general, and logically consistent or inconsistent, *incorporate* something psychologically forceful, something stronger or weaker?

The answer to this question depends on the distinction between objective and subjective dimensions of incentives. A maxim is a principle of action stating that something is good. It can be said to incorporate an incentive, in the objective dimension of that concept, simply by its referring to something, some object, as good. This means that for a rational agent to incorporate an incentive into a maxim, or to "have" a maxim, or to "adopt" one, need be nothing other than for her to think of an object as good to bring about. From here it should be relatively easy to see how objective incentives incorporated into maxims can, in their subjective dimensions, serve as the action-explaining forces of the maxims that incorporate them. It will be recalled that a maxim can be understood as a desire for something represented as good. A subjective incentive, consequently, can be understood as the psychological, motivational force of such a desire.

2.3 Moral Weakness

Kant wrote something revealing about the action-explaining forces of incorporated incentives fewer than ten pages beyond the passage cited above, in which he mentioned the incorporation of incentives into maxims. In illustrating his conception of weakness of will, which he called "human frailty," he quoted the famous lament of St. Paul, from Romans 7.

The frailty (*fragilitas*) of human nature is expressed even in the complaint of an Apostle: "What I would, that I do not!" i.e. I incorporate the good (the law) into the maxim of my power of choice, but this good, which is an irresistible incentive objectively (*in thesis*), is subjectively (*in hypothesis*) the weaker (in comparison with inclination) whenever the maxim is to be followed.[6]

In his take here on what the Apostle meant, Kant offered an explanation roughly in terms of the distinction made just above, between the objective and subjective dimensions of an incorporated incentive. In its objective dimension, the incentive of the moral law was incorporated into the Apostle's maxim. But then his obedience to the law would depend upon the action-explaining force of its subjective incentive. The Apostle's practical reasoning may have gone as follows. His maxim may have been, "Obeying the law is good." Then, upon identifying a particular action as one that would obey the law, he would have concluded that that action is good. So the action would have become justified by practical

---

[6] *Religion*, 53/6:29. In the words of St. Paul,

For the good that I would I do not: but the evil which I would not, that I do. Now if I do that I would not, it is no more I that do it, but sin that dwelleth in me. I find then a law, that, when I would do good, evil is present with me. For I delight in the law of God after the inward man: But I see another law in my members, warring against the law of my mind, and bringing me into captivity to the law of sin which is in my members. O wretched man that I am! who shall deliver me from the body of this death? (*Romans* 7:19–24)

reasoning from the maxim, and it would be commanded by a categorical imperative. But what happens next, according to Kant's analysis, is that the incorporated incentive turns out to be "weaker," in its subjective dimension, than an inclination. To complete Kant's analysis we must say, technically, that the force of the moral incentive turns out to be weaker than that of an incentive of inclination having already been incorporated into another of the Apostle's maxims.[7] So as Kant represents Christianity's most famous example of weakness of will, it comes down to a contest between two incorporated incentives, in their subjective dimensions. The inclinational incentive wins the contest because of its preponderant psychological force.[8] It is stronger in comparison with the incentive of the law, according to Kant's analysis; and that is what explains the Apostle's lamented action.

This example seems to confirm that Kant accepted the most controversial part of what was presented at the outset of this chapter, as the solution to the problem of justification and explanation: that practical reasoning

[7] As Wood sees it, this inference may not be correct. He writes: "Cases of weakness of will ... often involve an exercise of volitional agency in which someone fails to act according to a maxim, but not necessarily by adopting a contrary maxim." Allen W. Wood, *Kant's Ethical Thought* (Cambridge: Cambridge University Press, 1999), 52. But in this statement it seems that Wood is relying on a faulty but somewhat common understanding of how we act on maxims. It is the view of acting on a maxim that sees the maxim itself as a prescription we can choose whether to follow or not. Our maxim might command us to act on it, and we might choose not to heed its command (weakness of will); but that need not be the same as our choosing to act on an opposite maxim. (I take it that Wood sees the maxim referred to in the statement, upon which the agent fails to act owing to weakness, as a maxim adopted by the agent.) The problem with this relatively common view lies in how acting on a maxim is to be understood in relation to "free choice." Is making a free choice choosing *to adopt* a maxim, or is it choosing *to act* on a maxim one has adopted, or can it be either? For reasons related to a thesis that Wood endorses (in the same place) about how we act on desires or other incentives, it seem best to agree that freely choosing is nothing more than adopting a maxim (see my argument for this at 3.5). Consequently, choosing whether to act on one's adopted maxim would not be possible. For this reason also, maxims should not be thought to function in agency as prescriptions we may choose whether to follow, or not, in the way that Wood's statement above suggests. If the statement is taken instead to refer to *adopting* a maxim rather than to acting on one's adopted maxim, then the same difficulty is merely pushed back a step. All that changes with this twist on the example is that what was earlier considered to be just an "action" is now thought of as the act of adopting a maxim. Suppose the agent sees that she ought to adopt a maxim, but through weakness of will fails to do so, and her failure to do so is not describable as an action on a contrary maxim. If she ought to adopt a certain maxim, then this "ought" is a conclusion of practical reasoning from a "higher" maxim: either a maxim related to her happiness, in which case the "ought" is a hypothetical imperative, or a maxim of duty, in which case the "ought" is a categorical imperative. In either case she faces a prescribing maxim in the same way as before: a prescribing maxim she would choose to follow, or not, by adopting another maxim, or not.

[8] Here I leave it undetermined whether these incentives compete for the prize of being incorporated into a maxim, or whether each, as already incorporated, competes for getting itself acted on.

from a maxim can explain action, can explain what was done, through psychological force.[9]

2.4 Causes of Desire

Kant seems to have defined his concept of an incentive in the following passage from the *Groundwork:* "The subjective ground of desire is an *incentive;* the objective ground of volition is a *motive;* hence the distinction between subjective ends, which rest on incentives, and objective ends, which depend on motives, which hold for every rational being" (36/4:427). In the second *Critique,* however, he offered a different definition: "by *incentive* (*elater animi*) is understood the subjective determining ground of the will of a being whose reason does not by its nature necessarily conform with the objective law" (62/5:72).

It is sometimes observed that Kant must have abandoned or modified his first definition of incentives, as presented in the *Groundwork,* because he doesn't seem to follow it in the second *Critique.*[10] In the second *Critique* he referred to the objective moral law as an "incentive." But the *Groundwork* statement seems to imply that the objective moral law could serve only as a "motive," since motives are said there to "hold for every rational being." But for reasons that will emerge below, and which are somewhat technical, it seems best to say that Kant's statement in the *Groundwork* was actually not

[9] Some interpreters, Allison, for example, see the example of the Apostle's failing to act morally through weakness as illustrating a case of self-deception. But it has not been adequately explained what deception, what mis-believed proposition, is supposed to be illustrated by the case. An attempted explanation of Allison's has it that the Apostle is deceiving himself into thinking that he is not responsible for his moral transgression, owing to moral weakness (*Kant's Theory of Freedom,* 159). But this reading is entirely contrary to the spirit of Romans 7. As Kant presumably knew, St. Paul there calls himself "wretched" in a fit of self-reproach. He is not there attempting to exonerate himself on account of his weakness. If the idea is that the Apostle is supposed to have deceived himself into thinking that the course of action on the inclination was actually good, and better than obeying the moral law, then the example doesn't seem to present a case of weakness of will. Kant's analysis of the example in terms of the weakness of the moral incentive in comparison with inclination is not, in that case, very apt. For more on this point see my "Moral Weakness as Self-Deception," in Hoke Robinson, ed., *Proceedings of the Eighth International Kant Congress* (Milwaukee, WI: Marquette University Press, 1995), 587–93. For further criticism of Allison's account of weakness of will in Kant's theory of action see also Robert N. Johnson, "Weakness Incorporated," *History of Philosophy Quarterly* 15 (1998): 349–67.

[10] See, for example, Gregor's note on her translation, *Practical Reason,* 32n.

an attempt to define the concept of an incentive. His principal aim there would have been instead to distinguish sources of human motivation that are *subjective* and variable among different agents, from those that would be *objective* and invariable. It was to distinguish the ends that interest only *some* rational agents, from the ends that must interest *all* rational agents, insofar as they are rational. He used the concept of "incentive" in drawing this distinction, but, as will be seen momentarily, he did not use it precisely.

The *Groundwork* statement distinguishes between an incentive (*Triebfeder*) and a motive (*Bewegunsgrund*) as, respectively, a subjective ground of desire and an objective ground of volition. Here the parallel distinction between *desire* and *volition* follows the traditional distinction between the lower and higher faculties of desire: between sense-based and intellect-based desire (1.6). But the *Groundwork* statement need not mean that incentives would be effective only in the sense-based motivation of human beings, and not also in *volition*. For Kant would acknowledge an important role for incentives in the explanation of action on higher, intellectual desires. He did not think of incentives as necessarily sense-based, as the *Groundwork* statement may seem to imply.[11]

The point of that statement's distinction between incentive and motive was that intellectual desires are not *grounded* upon, or do not depend upon, incentives that are only subjectively valid. The point seems to be that in order for us to desire an object of sense, as a "subjective end," a subjective condition known as an incentive would be required to explain our desire. But this is not what is required in order for us to desire something intellectually, as an "objective end." What is required for this is a "motive," something that would be a source of motivation for all rational beings.

Consider now the following definition of incentives found in Kant's lecture notes:

That which is the cause of the desires is the impelling cause [*causa impulsive*] or incentive of the soul. Now, if they arose from sensibility then they are called

---

[11] Nor is it the case that Kant changed his view of incentives between the *Groundwork* and the second *Critique*. It is evident from his psychology lectures well before publication of the *Groundwork* that he saw incentives as effective in intellect-based desire and motivation: "If the [higher] cognition of the understanding has a power to move the subject to the action *merely because* the action *in itself* is good, then this motive power is an incentive which we may also call *moral feeling*" (*c*.1770, *Lectures on Metaphysics*, 72/28:257–8).

stimuli and their effect is desire aroused by stimuli or sensible desires. But if they originate from the understanding, then they are called motives [*motiva*], their effect [is called] desire aroused by motives or intellectual desires.[12]

It is clear from this statement, and other lecture notes like it, that Kant saw incentives as consisting of two classes. Incentives are either "stimuli" or "motives": causes, respectively, of either sense-based or intellect-based desires. So in the *Groundwork* statement Kant seems to have meant that the ground of a subjective, sense-based desire is a *stimulus-incentive,* while the ground of an objective, intellect-based desire is a *motive-incentive.* The Latin term "*motivum*" was commonly used synonymously with the German, "*Bewegungsgrund*" (1.3), the term Kant used in the *Groundwork* statement in contrast with "*Triebfeder.*"

The distinction between objective and subjective dimensions of incentives, established above (2.2), can be crossed with the distinction between stimuli and motives, yielding four different things that can be referred to as incentives. We can see how Kant's term "incentive" can refer to:

(*i*) an object of sense-based desire (objective stimulus), which in the *Groundwork* was called a subjective end; and

(*ii*) a psychological state (subjective stimulus) that "targets" that object, and explains the subject's having developed the desire for it.[13]

For example, I may desire to drink a glass of wine because I have tasted it and have liked it. Here the wine I tasted, as well as my liking its taste, can each be called a "stimulus" for my desiring the wine; each can therefore be called an "incentive." They are incentives in senses *i* and *ii*, respectively. But "incentive" can refer also to:

(*iii*) an intellectual object (objective motive) that is the cause or ground of an intellectual desire, and which in the *Groundwork* was called an objective end; and

(*iv*) a psychological state (subjective motive) "targeting" the object of intellectual desire.

---

[12] *Lectures on Metaphysics,* 262/29:895.

[13] The idea here is that we can develop desires for objects of experience. But we do not desire every object of experience, nor do we all desire the same objects of experience. Something therefore has to explain why some objects of experience are desired, and others are not: it has to be something subjective, otherwise everyone would desire the same objects of experience. This is the subjective dimension of Kant's concept of a stimulus-incentive.

Each of these can be referred to as a motive, as well as an incentive. The moral law and respect for the law are examples of motive-incentives, in senses *iii* and *iv* respectively.

2.5 Causes of Choice

There is a widespread assumption that the actions of human beings possessing what Kant called "free choice" (*freie Willkür, arbitrium liberum*; see 1.8) cannot be causally explained by psychological forces of incentives. The difference between a "free choice" and what Kant called an "animal choice" (*thierische Willkür, arbitrium brutum*) is very often supposed to be the difference between a chooser whose choices are free, and one whose choices are causally determined by the psychological forces of incentives. It is an assumption that has seemed to be well supported by the statement quoted above, from Kant's *Religion*. Yet it is contradicted by comments that are found in Kant's lecture notes. He told his metaphysics students that "Incentives of the soul [*elateres animi*]—incentives of the mind are called impelling causes [*causae impulsivae*] of the power of choice [*arbitrium, Willkür*]."[14] In his ethics lectures we also find the same idea: "The determining ground of choice (*causa determinans arbitrium*) is *causa impulsiva* to the action, the motivating cause. N.B. every *causa impulsiva* or trigger of the mind to action is called, *in genre, elater animi*, whether it be *motivum* or *stimulus*."[15]

These comments, especially the latter, leave little doubt about Kant's view of the causal role of subjective incentives. Whether they be intellectual (*motiva*) or sense-based (*stimuli*), incentives would be the explaining causes of effective desires, or of the desires that explain human actions (1.7). In places,

---

[14] *Lectures on Metaphysics*, 379/28:677, cf. also 484/29:1014–15. The translator of these lectures routinely substitutes "power of choice" for Kant's "*Willkür*" and "*arbitrium*," but this is inadvisable (1.8). As indicated above, sometimes "*Willkür*" and "*arbitrium*" refer to particular acts, states or "determinations" of a faculty. In the passage quoted here it is not obvious whether the faculty itself is indicated by these terms, or whether a state or determination of the faculty is indicated. That is, it is not obvious whether Kant means that incentives cause us to choose to act one way rather than another, or that incentives are causes of "effective desires" between which we might freely choose. The quotation to follow suggests somewhat more clearly that incentives causally determine how we choose to act.

[15] Immanuel Kant, *Lectures on Ethics*, ed. Peter Heath and J. B. Schneewind, trans. Peter Heath (Cambridge: Cambridge University Press, 1997), 262/27:493.

Kant may seem to have denied that incentive forces can causally determine free human choices. But as we shall see in the next chapter (3.2, 3.10), it is best to interpret his comments in those places differently.

2.6 Practical Pleasure

With incentives now identified as grounds or causes of desires we can relate them to feelings of pleasure. This is because Kant also claimed that feelings of pleasure cause desires: "That pleasure which is necessarily connected with desire (for an object whose representation affects feeling this way) can be called *practical pleasure*, whether it is the cause or the effect of the desire." He subsequently elaborated this point, in part, as follows: "As for practical pleasure, that determination of the capacity for desire which is caused and therefore necessarily *preceded* by such pleasure is called *desire* in the narrow sense; habitual desire in this sense is called *inclination.* . . ." (*Metaphysics of Morals*, 41/6:212).

These two statements, seen in light of the definitions of incentives from Kant's lectures, establish that feelings of pleasure which cause desires can be identified as "stimuli." This is the standard etiology for sense-based desire and inclination. But for intellectual desire the etiology is different. As quoted above, he wrote that practical pleasure is the pleasure that is "necessarily connected with desire . . . whether it is the cause *or the effect* of the desire" (emphasis added). He then claimed: "But if a pleasure can only follow upon an antecedent determination of the capacity for desire [, as its effect,] it is an intellectual pleasure. . . ." (ibid.). So if a stimulus-incentive is, subjectively, a desire-causing feeling of pleasure that arises from sense-experience, then a motive-incentive is, subjectively, a feeling of pleasure arising from something intellectual. It arises when an object like the moral law incites an intellectual desire. This can be seen from a later, more illuminating statement from *The Metaphysics of Morals*, where Kant compared empirical and intellectual incentives. "Moral feeling," he wrote there, "is the susceptibility to feel pleasure or displeasure merely from being aware that our actions are consistent with or contrary to the law of duty." Then he continued:

Every determination of choice [*Willkür*] proceeds from the representation of a possible action *to* the deed through the feeling of pleasure or displeasure, taking an interest in the action or its effect. The state of feeling [*äthetische Zustand*] here (the way the inner sense is affected) is either *sensibly dependent* [*pathologisches*] or *moral*. The former is that feeling which precedes the representation of the law; the latter, that which can only follow upon it.   (201/6:399)

In both types of determination of choice, the "pathological" as well as the moral, the subjective incentive that is a practical pleasure (either a stimulus or a motive) could convey psychological force sufficient to explain the agent's action.[16] For in both cases, when we move from the thought of an action to its performance ("*to* the deed") the transition, Kant wrote, goes *through the feeling of pleasure*. The difference between the practical pleasures involved in each case is a matter of their origins. It is a matter of whether they are pleasures arising from objects of sense-experience, or from an intellectual "representation of the law."

2.7 Interest

The passage just quoted from *The Metaphysics of Morals* also mentions "taking an interest." This is significant for understanding the action-explaining role of practical pleasure. A doctrine central to Kant's moral theory is that reason is *practical*. This means that reason, on its own, without the assistance of the pleasures of sense-experience, can provide psychological force sufficient to explain action it justifies. The *Groundwork* connects the practicality of reason with the concept of "interest" in this way: "An interest," Kant

---

[16] On this point compare something Kant said in a lecture about desire in general.

The faculty for producing objects by means of one's representations is the faculty of desire. The faculty of desire rests on the principle: I desire nothing but what pleases, and avoid nothing but what displeases. But representations cannot be the cause of an object where we have no pleasure or displeasure in it. This [i.e., pleasure] is therefore the subjective condition by which alone a representation can become the cause of an object. . . . (Besides the things which are moved by outer causes, there are living things which are moved by inner ones. A being is living if its power of representation can be the ground of the actuality of its objects. Life is thus the causality of a representation with respect to the actuality of its objects. Now this causality of representations with respect to the subject is the feeling of pleasure or displeasure. But with respect to the object [it is] the faculty of desire.)   (*Lectures on Metaphysics*, 261/29:893–4)

wrote, "is that by which reason becomes practical, i.e., becomes a cause determining the will" (63n./4:60n.). There are two types of interest, he explained: pure (immediate, direct), and empirical (mediate, indirect).[17] In the case of reason's pure interest, an action would be of interest because of something about its form or nature: because of "the universal validity of the maxim of the action," he said there. Reason's empirical interest in actions depends on their being seen as causes of something beyond themselves: as effective in bringing about objects or conditions previously experienced with pleasure.

Later, in the second *Critique*, Kant presented the relations among maxims, incentives, and interests as follows: "From the concept of an incentive arises that of an *interest*, which can never be attributed to any being unless it has reason and which signifies an *incentive* of the will insofar as it is *represented by reason*." This claim identifies interests as a type of incentives.[18] Then he explained that "On the concept of an interest is based that of a *maxim*" (68/5:79). By this he seems to have meant that actions motivated by interests presuppose maxims, and we can see how this follows. For an action motivated by an empirical interest it would be necessary for the agent to represent or think of as good some object of experience that the action would be expected to bring about. This thought would be a maxim of the agent. For action motivated by pure interest, on the other hand, it would be necessary for the agent to represent as good some feature of the action itself. This may be its conforming to duty or to a categorical imperative; and the thought of such actions as good to do would be a maxim.

Kant's concept of interest does not take us very far beyond what we already know about his concepts of maxims and incentives, however. To go farther, we must draw the connection that he himself drew between interest and pleasure. In the third *Critique* he explained the concept of interest in terms of pleasure or "satisfaction" (*Wohlgefallen*).[19] He wrote that "to will something and *to have satisfaction* in its existence, i.e., *to take an interest* in it, are identical" (94/5:209, emphasis added; cf. also 90/5:204). A central

---

[17] These are called "practical" and "pathological" interests at 25n./4:413n.

[18] Non-rational agents act on incentives also, but their incentives are not interests.

[19] Cf. also *Practical Reason*, 68/5:80.

distinction in his theory of aesthetic judgment presented there is between two types of pleasure: *interested* and *disinterested*. From this distinction it follows that interest would be a type of pleasure. In *The Metaphysics of Morals* Kant again related the concepts of interest and pleasure when he wrote that "a connection of pleasure with the capacity for desire that the understanding judges to hold as a general rule (though only for the subject) is called an *interest*" (41/6:212). Here the earlier distinction between pure and empirical interest is cast in terms of the "interest of reason," also called "moral interest," and the "interest of inclination."

So from these statements, and from the significance that Kant attached to the concept of interest, it seems to follow that reason can be practical, or can be a cause determining the will, only because of pleasure.[20]

2.8 Summary Review

After this conclusion, and before proceeding with what may be the most controversial thesis of this chapter, it will help to review our progress thus far. To solve the problem of justification and explanation it has been proposed that practical reasoning from maxims is capable of explaining action through psychological forces. If my maxim is that "Money is good," it incorporates the psychological force of my affection for money, my greed in the extreme case. This maxim would be capable of motivating me to act only if I recognize an action as one by which I can acquire money. Once I arrive at that recognition, an inference of practical reasoning would channel the psychological force of the incentive incorporated into the maxim to that action. That is, from the premises that, *Money is good*, and that, *This is an action by which I can acquire money*, I would draw the motivating conclusion that, *This action is good to do*.

To understand the incorporation of action-explaining psychological forces into maxims it was necessary to distinguish between objective and subjective dimensions of "incentives." In their subjective dimensions,

---

[20] Here it is illuminating to compare Kant's claim in the first *Critique* that "All practical concepts pertain to objects of satisfaction or dissatisfaction, i.e., of pleasure or displeasure, and thus, at least indirectly, to objects of our feeling" (A801n./B829n.).

incentives can be identified with practical pleasures. These may arise either from sensibility, in which case they are called "stimuli," or from the intellect, in which case they are called "motives." And the relation of incentives in their subjective dimension to desires is importantly different in each case. In the former, feelings of pleasure cause desires; in the latter, feelings would be the desires' effects. The following table illustrates these distinctions:

Table 2.1.

	Incentives		Desires
Stimuli:	i) **Object of Experience** ↓ ii) **Sense-Based Pleasure** *(cause of desire)*	→	***Sense-Based Desire*** **for Object of Experience**
Motives:	iii) **Objective Moral Law** iv) **Intellectual Pleasure** *(effect of desire)*	→ ↙	***Intellectual Desire*** **to Obey the Moral Law**

In the top row of the table, from a stimulus object of experience, which is an incentive in the objective dimension, a downward arrow represents that object as causing a sense-based pleasure. A horizontal arrow then represents this practical pleasure as causing a desire for the object. So this pleasure functions as an incentive in the subjective dimension. Both the object and the sense-based pleasure it causes are called "stimuli." These were referred to above as "incentives" in senses *i* and *ii*, respectively.

In the bottom row, from a representation of the objective moral law, as a motive (cf., *Groundwork*, 36/4:427), a horizontal arrow indicates its causing an intellectual desire to obey. This thought is therefore an incentive in the objective dimension. Its effect, as represented by the downward, back-facing arrow, is an intellectual pleasure, an incentive in the subjective dimension. Both the objective law and the intellectual pleasure it indirectly causes are called "motives." These were referred to above as incentives in senses *iii* and *iv*, respectively.

The relation of incentives to maxims and interests is shown now in the following table.

Table 2.2.

	Maxims	*Interests*
Inclinational:	"[Object of experience] is good." *(Sense-Based Desire)*	Interest of Inclination in an action judged to bring about [Object of experience]
Moral:	"Obeying the moral law is good." *(Intellectual Desire)*	Moral interest in an action judged as obeying the moral law

The sense-based and intellectual desires in the right column of the preceding table are now entered here in the left column, under *"Maxims."* Maxims, like all desires, are representations of their objects "as good" (1.5). They are either inclinational maxims, or moral maxims. The pleasures of experience that cause sense-based desires are stimulus-incentives incorporated by inclinational maxims. Feelings of intellectual pleasure called motive-incentives are incorporated by moral maxims. These are effects of the thought of, or of "determination by" the moral law. Once an action is identified as falling under either an inclinational maxim or a moral maxim, the subjective incentive that is incorporated into that maxim becomes an "interest" in the action. Interests in actions are either empirical interests of inclination, which Kant called "pathological," or they are intellectual, moral interests of reason, which he called "pure." These are the two entries in the right column of Table 2:2, under *"Interests."* In the first case, the target of these interests is the desired object of experience the action is judged capable of bringing about. Having an interest in such an action is "liking" or taking pleasure in the existence of the object it can bring about. So the interest here is mediate, or indirect. It is an interest in the action due to its capacity to bring about a pleasant object of desire. In the second case, interests target "formal" features of actions themselves, such as the universality of an action's maxim. Here, an intellectual or moral interest in an action would be pleasure taken in the action itself, due to its conformity to the moral law—or displeasure taken in the omission of the action, due to its being required by the moral law. The interest here is immediately or directly in the action; it does not depend on pleasure associated with an object whose existence it can bring about.

2.9 Motivational Hedonism

According to an old line of interpretation, Kant was a psychological hedonist about "heteronomous" motivation.[21] Here I'll discuss this now generally repudiated interpretation as a way of introducing a hedonism I believe Kant would endorse, and which I shall call "motivational hedonism." I'll be offering the label "motivational hedonism" as a species of psychological hedonism; so when I explain this doctrine, and show why I think Kant held it, I'll be showing also why I think he was a kind of psychological hedonist.

Let us say provisionally, and somewhat vaguely, that psychological hedonism is the doctrine that all action depends on feelings of pleasure. A number of passages from the second *Critique* can be, and often have been, offered as evidence for Kant's having been a psychological hedonist. In one of these passages he wrote about any principle of action for bringing about an object of sense-based desire that "the determining ground of choice is then the representation of an object and that relation of the representation to the subject by which the faculty of desire is determined to realize the object. Such a relation to the subject, however, is called *pleasure* in the reality of an object" (19/5:21). This abstruse statement seems to say that one cannot be motivated to act in order to bring about an object of sense-experience without representing that object's reality, or its existence, with pleasure.

A few paragraphs later Kant wrote about such pleasure that "It is ... practical only insofar as the feeling of agreeableness that the subject expects from the reality of an object determines the faculty of desire"

[21] The nineteenth-century source of this line of interpretation seems to be T. H. Greene. See Terrence Irwin, "Morality and Personality: Kant and Greene," in Allen W. Wood, ed., *Self and Nature in Kant's Philosophy* (Ithaca, NY: Cornell University Press, 1984), 31–56. More recent writers who interpret Kant similarly are Philippa Foot, *Virtues and Vices* (Berkeley, CA: University of California Press, 1978), 158–9, and Bernard Williams, *Ethics and the Limits of Philosophy* (Cambridge, MA: Harvard University Press, 1985), 64.

(20/5:22). After a few more paragraphs he added that when representations of empirical objects determine the will, it makes no difference whether they are intellectual or sensory representations: "the feeling of pleasure by which alone they properly constitute the determining ground of the will (the agreeableness, the gratification expected from the object, which impels the activity to produce it) is nevertheless of one and the same kind...." (20–1/5:23).

These statements are about motivation arising through sense-experience, for actions in which the agent's intention (1.4) is to bring about some sensible object or condition. They make it clear that Kant recognized feelings of pleasure as essential not only for *generating* some desires, but also for *impelling* action in order to satisfy them. That is, he would have seen feelings of practical pleasure as both the causes of desires, and as the determinants of the compelling psychological forces of these desires. The more pleasant or agreeable the object, the stronger the resultant desire for it. In terms of *incentives*, the point would be that the magnitude of the pleasure that causes a sense-based desire constitutes the strength of the incentive. In terms of *maxims*, it would be that the magnitude of the subjective incentive (pleasure) incorporated into the maxim is the basis for the degree of its action-explaining, psychological force.

The old line, hedonistic interpretation that is supported by Kant's statements quoted above has fallen out of favor today, and with good reason.[22] For unsolvable problems emerge for any theory of motivation that is only *partly* hedonistic, which is how this line of interpretation presented Kant's theory.[23] Not surprisingly, therefore, those who offered this hedonistic interpretation were also mainly critical of Kant. They supposed that his view of rational, moral motivation, through respect for the moral law, would not depend on any feelings of pleasure. For this seems to be the very point he was driving at in the relevant passages from the second *Critique*. His comments there about pleasure-based, non-moral

[22] For discussion of this interpretation see Thomas E. Hill, Jr., "Kant's Argument for the Rationality of Moral Conduct," in *Dignity and Practical Reason in Kant's Moral Theory* (Ithaca, NY: Cornell University Press, 1992), 105. See also Andrews Reath, "Hedonism, Heteronomy and Kant's Principle of Happiness," *Pacific Philosophical Quarterly* 70 (1989): 42–72.

[23] It must sound strange to refer to a theory of motivation as only "partly" hedonistic, since hedonism is a global qualification. Hedonism is the view that *all* of our actions, or desires, are pleasure based. This point, in a subtle way, anticipates the criticism that those who interpreted Kant's theory of motivation as partly hedonistic would offer.

motivation draw a sharp contrast with his view of moral motivation. So interpreters regarding Kant's view of non-moral motivation as hedonistic raised questions about this contrast. They asked, How can we expect action motivated by reason alone from an agent who would otherwise be motivated always by feelings of pleasure? It seemed to some that such a dualistic theory of human motivation, partly rationalistic and partially hedonistic, presupposes an unacceptably bifurcated, "schizophrenic" view of the self.

Here we need not pursue this line of interpretation and criticism any further. Most of Kant's interpreters today are convinced that he should be interpreted as holding a more unified theory of motivation. Most therefore reject the idea that he saw non-moral action as hedonistically motivated. Their thinking is that since Kant denied that *moral* motivation is hedonistic, and since he should be interpreted as having held a unified theory of human motivation, he should therefore be interpreted as having also denied that non-moral motivation is hedonistic. Hence, the conclusion of most recent interpreters on this point is that despite what his statements in the second *Critique* may suggest, Kant was not a psychological hedonist.[24]

If psychological hedonism is the doctrine that all human motivation can be traced to a desire for pleasure (or an aversion to pain), then hardly any one has attributed this doctrine to Kant. For he very clearly intended to deny that we are moved, in moral motivation, by any desire for pleasure. Yet I think his view was that feelings of practical pleasure are nevertheless essential for human motivation, in every case; and that there are ways for practical pleasures to function in all human motivation that do not commit us to the doctrine that we are always moved to action by desires for pleasure.

By *psychological* hedonism, broadly construed, I understand any theory saying that human motivation and action depend upon feelings of pleasure

---

[24] See Allison, for example: *Kant's Theory of Freedom*, 35, 102–3. Kerstein, on the other hand, is one of only a few commentators who argue that Kant was a psychological hedonist; see Samuel J. Kerstein, "Kant's (Not So Radical?) Hedonism," in Volker Gerhardt, Rolf-Peter Horstmann, and Ralph Schumacher, eds., *Kant und die Berliner Aufklärung, Akten des IX. Internationalen Kant-Kongress*, Bd. III (Berlin: Walter de Gruyter, 2001), 247–55. Herman, also, has seen reasons to give the prospect of Kant's being a hedonist a second look. See Barbara Herman, "Rethinking Kant's Hedonism," in *Moral Literacy* (Cambridge, MA: Harvard University Press, 2007), 176–202. The issue for Kerstein and Herman is whether Kant can be plausibly interpreted as holding that *all* non-moral (heteronomous) action is motivated by the desire for personal pleasure or happiness. I do not see this as Kant's view, however; even though I agree that he was a type of psychological hedonist.

or displeasure. So I think Kant qualifies as a psychological hedonist in this broad sense. Someone rejects this sense of psychological hedonism, as I see it, in saying that human beings do not require feelings of pleasure in order to act. Later in this chapter we shall look briefly at the view of John Searle. He rejects psychological hedonism, construed broadly, because he insists that a feeling of pleasure is not necessary for rational action; and he criticizes Kant for having said the opposite.

Psychological hedonism need not be accompanied by the assumption that good and bad are ultimately based on sources of pleasure and displeasure. That assumption can be called *normative* hedonism. Kant was not a normative hedonist. He did not think that the distinctions between right and wrong, and virtue and vice, necessarily follow the distinction between pleasure and displeasure. He did not think that the basis for moral justification is anything felt, or empirical. There is ample textual evidence for this. Yet it seems that Kant nevertheless supposed that pleasure plays a role in the explanation of all maxim-based action. This includes action on moral maxims; and this is why I think he can be classified as a type of psychological hedonist.

Psychological hedonism need not imply that our desires are for nothing but pleasure. In fact, it would be consistent with psychological hedonism, broadly construed, to say that pleasure is something we cannot desire. Here is how. It is plausible to say that the psychological function of pleasures and pains felt in the experience of objects is to cause us to desire or be averse to them; and that without such feelings we could never desire or be averse to anything. So it is plausible to say that in order to form a desire for pleasure we would have to experience pleasure *with pleasure;* and it is also plausible to say that we cannot do that. Whether we can do that or not is beside the point at present. The present point is just that it is consistent to hold that all human motivation and action depends on feelings of pleasure, while also denying that our actions are ever motivated by the desire for pleasure. So a psychological hedonist, as I see it, need not assume that we desire nothing but pleasure, or that we act for no purpose but to feel pleasure. I think Kant was a type of psychological hedonist, but I do not think he assumed these things.

Because "psychological hedonism" has been construed in different ways in the literature on Kant's theory of action, I think it best to start fresh and say that Kant was what I call a "motivational hedonist." I think of motivational hedonism as the doctrine that human beings cannot act without feelings of pleasure or displeasure forming part of their motivation, or that feelings of pleasure and displeasure are explanatory for all human actions. Motivational hedonism is an element of the doctrine of psychological hedonism, broadly construed, and I think it would be held by all psychological hedonists. So by classifying Kant as a motivational hedonist I do not intend to deny that he was a psychological hedonist. I intend merely to focus on the aspect of the theory of action in virtue of which I think Kant can be classified as a psychological hedonist.

Several points have already been made in support of interpreting Kant as a motivational hedonist. Not the least of these points is that he claimed that reason is practical only by means of "interest," and he defined interest in terms of pleasure. A passage quoted above from *The Metaphysics of Morals* also presented Kant's view of all human motivation as consistent with the doctrine I call motivational hedonism. In that passage he compared motivation and action in the non-moral case with the moral case, and he distinguished the different roles played by pleasure in each case. I think he committed himself unequivocally to motivational hedonism when he wrote that, "*Every* determination of choice proceeds from the representation of a possible action *to* the deed *through the feeling of pleasure or displeasure*, taking an *interest* in the action or its effect" (201/6:399, emphasis added). This is a relatively late statement, however; one published in his last book (1797). But here is a similarly hedonistic statement from an early lecture (*c.*1770): "If we take away the faculty of pleasure and displeasure from all rational beings, and enlarge their faculty of cognition however much, then they would cognize all objects without being moved by them; everything would be the same to them, for they would lack the faculty for being affected by objects" (*Lectures on Metaphysics*, 62/28:246). Human motivation depends upon feelings of pleasure and displeasure, in Kant's view. So if there is a kind of human motivation that does not depend on *sense-based* feelings of pleasure, it must depend on some other feeling of pleasure, an intellect-based feeling.

2.10 Moral Feeling

There will be some resistance to interpreting Kant's theory of human motivation as any kind of psychological hedonism, even as motivational hedonism. It will come from those convinced that he categorically denied that moral motivation can depend on any feelings of pleasure whatsoever (6.1). The sentences just quoted belie that conviction, however. But the interpretation that is being developed here is based on more than those pieces of textual evidence just quoted. This section presents several more texts that support interpreting Kant as having held a hedonistic view of human motivation, even of moral motivation.

We may begin with another passage from the lectures. There, in discussing moral motivation, he seems convinced that feelings of pleasure are essential, even though he is frustrated in his attempts to explain their role. "One is to cognize [moral] good through the understanding," he said,

> and yet have a feeling for it. This is obviously something that cannot be properly understood. . . . I am supposed to have a feeling of that which is not an object of feeling, but rather which I cognize objectively through the understanding. Thus there is always a contradiction hidden in here. For if we are supposed to do the good through a feeling, then we do it because it is agreeable. But this cannot be, for the good cannot at all affect our senses. But we call the pleasure in the good a feeling because we cannot otherwise express the subjective driving power of objective practical necessitation.   (72−3/28:258)

Here Kant appears perplexed about a "contradiction" lurking in his view. But he insists in the end that "pleasure in the good" refers to an action-explaining force coordinated with intellect-based, moral justification. This pleasure is, he says, "the subjective driving power of objective practical necessitation."

At about the same time Kant replied to a letter from Marcus Herz, who was a former student and who was then working on a book in practical philosophy. He advised his student that "The highest ground of morality . . . must itself be pleasing in the highest degree. For it is no mere speculative idea; it must have the power to move. Therefore, though the highest ground of morality is intellectual, it must nevertheless have a direct relation to the primary springs of the will."[25] In this statement, the

---

[25] Immanuel Kant, *Correspondence*, trans. and ed. Arnulf Zwieg (Cambridge: Cambridge University Press, 1999), 140/10:145. The date of the letter to Herz is late 1773; in it Kant related to his former student that he was expecting, just after Easter, to complete a book that he hoped would give philosophy a "durable form, a different and—for religion and morality—a more favorable turn." The

connection in Kant's mind between pleasure and "the power to move" the will, even in moral action, could hardly be clearer. Some years later, following his own advice to his student, Kant wrote in the *Groundwork* that: "In order for a sensibly affected rational being to will that for which reason alone prescribes the 'ought,' it is admittedly required that his reason have the capacity to *induce a feeling of pleasure* or delight in the fulfillment of duty...." (64/4:460).

A chapter of the second *Critique* is entitled "On the Incentives of Pure Practical Reason." Here Kant explicitly endorsed the idea that "feeling" plays an essential role in moral motivation. But he did not claim unambiguously that it is the feeling of pleasure. The feeling necessary for moral motivation is called "moral feeling," and it is identified as the feeling of respect (6.2). Commenting on the "causality of reason to determine sensibility" referenced just above in the quotation from the *Groundwork*, Kant claimed in the second *Critique* that "This feeling (under the name of moral feeling) is.... produced solely by reason. It does not serve for appraising actions ... but only as an incentive to make [the moral law] its maxim."[26] Here he also expressed the same view of moral feeling presented years earlier in the lecture, as the subjective, action-explaining counterpart of moral justification: "Thus the moral law, since it is a formal determining ground of action through practical pure reason ... is also a subjective determining ground—that is, an incentive—to this action inasmuch as it has influence on the sensibility of the subject and effects *a feeling conducive to the influence of the law upon the will*" (65/5:75, emphasis added).

The final passage to be consulted here comes from *The Metaphysics of Morals*. In that text Kant claimed, as we saw, that we always go from the thought of a possible action to performance of it "through the feeling of pleasure or displeasure, taking an interest in the action or its effect." Then, several lines after identifying moral feeling as that which can only follow upon a representation of the moral law, Kant added that there can be no duty to *acquire* moral feeling. This is because no moral agent

prediction turned out to be too optimistic, since the book, his *Critique of Pure Reason*, did not appear until 1781.

[26] 65/5:76. On the next page he wrote: "*So little* is respect a feeling of *pleasure* that we give way to it only reluctantly with regard to a human being" (66/5:77). This comment reflects his more nuanced treatment of moral feeling in the second *Critique*. There he presented it as in part negative and humiliating, but also as positive and elevating.

lacks it. "Obligation with regard to moral feeling," he wrote, "can be only to *cultivate* it and to strengthen it through wonder at its inscrutable source" (201/6:399). This point signifies that from a moral point of view the strength of moral feeling matters. It tells us that as Kant understood moral feeling, it is morally better to have stronger moral feeling(s). This is presumably because stronger feelings of moral pleasure or displeasure provide more effective motivation to action. They constitute stronger moral interests in doing the right and avoiding the wrong.[27] Stronger feelings of moral pleasure and displeasure account for what Kant called, in the passage quoted above from the lectures, the "subjective driving power of objective practical necessitation."

2.11 The Classical Model

Above we noted that John Searle has criticized Kant's theory of action for his view of pleasure and motivation. Kant's motivational hedonism can be further clarified in this final section of the chapter by responding to Searle's objection. This will also help set up the main line of argument in the chapter to follow.

Searle is in complete agreement with Kant's view that we can be moved to action independently of sense-based desires. He thinks, with Kant, that we can be motivated by "desire-independent reasons." But he criticizes Kant for having insisted that a feeling of pleasure is necessary in order for us to act as reason would dictate, as he did at *Groundwork*, 64/4:460. Searle objects: "I think we can perform many actions in which there is no 'feeling of pleasure,' only the recognition that we have a valid reason for doing them. I no more have to have a 'feeling of pleasure' when I have to get my tooth drilled than I have to have a feeling of pleasure when I keep my promises."[28]

The response I'll offer here to Searle's objection will be that Kant would agree that a feeling of pleasure is not necessary in order to *justify* actions; but he didn't think that justifying an action suffices to *explain*

---

[27] To avoid being misunderstood Kant sometimes claimed explicitly that moral feeling would not be required for judging or understanding what is right or wrong. See, for example, *Lectures on Ethics*, 65–7/27:274–6.

[28] John R. Searle, *Rationality in Action* (Cambridge, MA: MIT Press, 2001), 191.

it. He thought that a feeling of pleasure would be necessary for the explanation of action; and that is why, unlike Searle, he was a motivational hedonist.

Searle rejects what he believes is a confusion in Kant's theory of action, and what he sees as a fallacy in what he calls the whole tradition of the "Classical Model of Rationality." He explains this fallacy as follows:

> If every action is the expression of a desire to perform that action, and every successful action results in the satisfaction of desire, then it seems that the only thing that can motivate an action is desire satisfaction, that is, a feeling of pleasure. But this is a fallacy. From the fact that every action is indeed the expression of a desire to perform that action, it does not follow that every action is done for the *purpose* of satisfying the desire, nor does it follow that actions can be motivated only by desire satisfaction, in the sense of a feeling of pleasure.   (192–3)

Searle's objection here seems to be the following. Just because satisfying desires may be pleasant, this doesn't mean that we always act *for* the pleasure of satisfying desires. It doesn't mean that we are motivated to act only by pleasure. Kant and the whole classical tradition of practical rationality went wrong right here, as Searle sees it. He thinks Kant and others, including Hume, assumed that a rational agent cannot have a reason why he ought to act unless there is some feeling of pleasure to be gotten from the action. Searle thinks Kant assumed, fallaciously, that an action is always an expression of a desire for the pleasant feeling of desire satisfaction. Yet that makes no sense, as Searle sees it; and about that part, at least, I think Searle is exactly right.

But to say that human motivation and action always *depend on* feelings of pleasures (or displeasure) is not to say that our desires are *for* feelings of pleasure. Nor is it to say that we act for the purpose of *feeling satisfied*. As pointed out above, a psychological hedonist is not forced to accept the view that desires are always for feelings of pleasure. A psychological hedonist can deny this, and be a motivational hedonist. It has been explained above how in Kant's view a feeling of pleasure in the sense-experience of an object would cause a desire for it. But there is no reason to suppose he thought that a desire caused in this way would be a desire for pleasure. The experience of a pleasing object may cause a desire for that object, which could justify the agent's acting in order to re-experience it. Yet justification for an action could also come from the recognition that it is morally required. In the latter case, Kant thought, no pleasant experience is needed in order to justify the agent's acting.

Accordingly then, Searle might now ask: So why assume that a feeling of pleasure is necessary in order for us to be motivated? Why not assume that all that is required is justification? Justification for action might sometimes depend upon a prior experience of pleasure, but it need not. Either way, the work of motivating action can be done by justification; a feeling of pleasure is not necessary.

I think Kant's response to this line of thinking might be to say that Searle is correct, provided we are talking about agents for whom an action's being rationally justified is sufficient to explain it. But human beings are not like that. Kant wrote about his concepts of "incentive," "interest," and "maxim" that "they all presuppose a limitation on the nature of a being, in that the subjective constitution of its choice [*Willkür*] does not of itself accord with the objective law of a practical reason; they presuppose *a need to be impelled to activity by something* because an internal obstacle is opposed to it" (*Practical Reason*, 68/5:79, emphasis added). The point is that, for us, justification does not explain action. We can, after all, recognize that we are justified in acting one way, and yet do the opposite. The example of moral weakness presented above (2.3) shows this quite well. Kant thought that feelings of pleasure may often be involved in the justification of action. But he did not see pleasure as necessary for justification. He saw pleasure as necessary for explanation, however. This makes him what I am calling a motivational hedonist.

If we think of the feeling of pleasure as every desire's object—in the way Searle seems to characterize the thinking of those who adhere to what he calls the Classical Model—then psychological hedonism is implausible. For people clearly do desire things other than pleasure. But if we think of pleasure's role in human motivation as at least partly constitutive of the psychological state of desire, then hedonism is not so implausible. This was a view of the relation between pleasure and desire that was well known to Kant and his contemporaries. It is found in Locke, for example. In attempting to say *"what is it that determines the Will in regard to our Actions?"* Locke answered: a feeling of "uneasiness."

This *Uneasiness* we may call, as it is, *Desire*; which is an *uneasiness* of the Mind for want of some absent good. All pain of the body of what sort soever, and disquiet of the mind, is *uneasiness*: And with this is always join'd Desire, equal to the pain or uneasiness felt; and is scarce distinguishable from it. For *desire* being nothing but an *uneasiness* in the want of an absent good, in reference to any felt pain, ease is that absent good; and till that ease be attained we may call it *desire*, [there being] no body feeling pain, that he wishes not to be eased of, with a desire equal to that pain, and inseparable from it. Besides this desire of ease from pain, there is another of absent positive good, and here also the desire and *uneasiness* is equal. As much as we desire any absent good, so much are we in pain for it.[29]

Three points can be noted here about Locke's view of determination of the will. The first is that all desires, hence all motivational states, are "inseparable" from a feeling. Locke here emphasized the negative character of the feeling, as uneasiness. But its positive character, as pleasure, is implicit in his statement that "in reference to felt pain, ease is that absent good." We can consider uneasiness in bodily pain, or in absent good, as equivalent to agreeableness or pleasure arising from the relief of pain, or from the arrival of a recognized good. In other words, saying that I feel bad because I lack something is equivalent to saying that I expect to feel good if I get it. Kant wrote in the second *Critique* that it is "the agreeableness, the gratification expected from the object, which impels activity to produce it" (21/5:23). His claim there would not be substantively different if, like Locke, he had written that uneasiness or disagreeableness in the absence of the object is what impels the activity to produce it.[30]

Second, Locke may seem to tell us here that all desire is therefore only for "ease," for relief of uneasiness, or only for a feeling of satisfaction. But he is careful to add that besides desires for relief of bodily pain, there are also desires for "absent positive good." Even if desires are feelings of uneasiness from which we crave relief, they can still have (good) objects that are different from their relief or satisfaction. These would be objects, absent goods, it is our purpose to obtain in acting to satisfy our uneasy desires. There is no reason to attribute to Locke the fallacy Searle seems to

---

[29] John Locke, *An Essay Concerning Human Understanding*, ed. Peter H. Nidditch (Oxford: Clarendon Press, 1975), 2.21.31.

[30] Kant seems to make a similar point about pleasure and pain algebraically: "With respect to pleasure and pain there is a . . . middle term, whereby pleasure $= a$, pain $= -a$, and the state in which neither of the two obtains is indifference, $= 0$" (*Religion*, 48n./6:22n.). From this statement it seems to follow that a state of pain partly relieved counts also as an increase in pleasure. If for my headache $(= -10)$ I take aspirin and later feel almost fine $(= -1)$, then the change $(= +9)$ can be considered an increase in pleasure.

find in the Classical Model: that "every action is done for the *purpose* of satisfying the desire."

Third, and finally, Locke acknowledged that there is a proportionality between the feeling of uneasiness and the desire inseparable from it.[31] "As much as we desire any absent good, so much are we in pain for it." In other words, the stronger the feeling, the stronger the desire.

It is not unreasonable to attribute to Kant a view of human motivation similar to Locke's. If we do, we can account for his comments to the effect that a feeling of pleasure or displeasure is always required, even for moral action justified by pure practical reason. We can say that the subjective dimension of having a justification for acting is, in Lockean terms, "an *uneasiness* of the Mind for want of some absent good." In positive and somewhat more Kantian terms, it is a feeling of "pleasure in the reality of the object," or "interest." Its role is to "impel activity" in an imperfectly rational agent, the kind of agent whose action depends on incentives, interests, and maxims, since an "internal obstacle is opposed to it." The internal obstacle is a psychological obstacle. It is a desire for acting otherwise, related to another "pleasure in the reality of [an] object." The feeling of pleasure is required in order to explain how the agent could overcome the internal obstacle and act. In the example that Kant cited from Romans 7, the Apostle acted on inclination rather than as he believed he ought to act, because the incentive for the latter, moral action, was weaker. The inclination posed an internal obstacle that, in this case, was too strong.

It is commonly held, nevertheless, that Kant did not think action can be explained in terms of the psychological forces desire, or of pleasures or displeasures. It is said that as Kant understood human action, the strengths of such desires or feelings cannot cause us to act one way or another (see 3.1). Rather, we *freely choose* to act one way or another; and we can do that independently of any feelings of pleasure or displeasure, by our "power of free choice" (*Willkür*). According to most of Kant's recent interpreters, actions cannot be explained by any psychologically forceful feelings unless they are first incorporated into a maxim. In that case, however, the maxim

---

[31] The proportionality is not between the goodness of the object and the desire, he adds; since he thinks it possible to recognize absent good and not desire it. "But here all absent goodness does not, according to the greatness it has, or is acknowledg'd to have, cause pain equal to that greatness...." (*Essay*, 2.21.31, cf., 2.21.35).

would have explanatory power. Or the choice to incorporate the incentive into the maxim would have explanatory power. The feeling would not explain the action, it is said.

In the next chapter we explore the reasons for this more usual way of interpreting Kant's theory of action. His emphasis on freedom of the will, especially in his moral theory, certainly lends credence to the usual interpretation—especially because of the deterministic implications of actions causally explained by psychological forces. Some often-quoted passages in his published texts support the more usual interpretation also. These passages will be examined in the following chapter. Then in Chapters 4 and 5 we explore Kant's conception of human freedom, which, as he himself said, is supposed to be compatible with thoroughgoing determinism.

The present chapter, on incentives, has laid the groundwork for understanding how practical reason can explain the actions it justifies. We have seen here how incentives can be regarded either objectively or subjectively. Regarded objectively they are objects or conditions "incorporated" into the maxims of practical reasoning, just by being recognized as good. Regarded subjectively, as claimed here, incentives are psychological forces with explanatory power. They are either sense-based (*stimuli*) or intellect-based (*motiva*), and they are identical with what Kant called "practical pleasures." The greater the pleasure, the stronger the incentive's explanatory power. So the idea, in summary, is that maxims are principles of practical reasoning, by which actions are justified, and incentives incorporated into maxims have explanatory power for the actions their maxims justify.

3

Free Choice

What I have called the problem of justification and explanation seems relatively easy to solve. We need only assume that in acting on maxims our actions are explained by psychological forces. These are the causal forces of incentives "incorporated" into our maxims (2.2), which are conveyed from our maxims to our actions by inferences of practical reasoning. This assumption can solve the problem. But it also implies something that few seem to accept. It implies that, according to Kant's theory of action, our free actions can be causally determined by psychological forces.

This chapter defends the controversial interpretation of Kant's theory of action so far developed, against objections likely to arise over the explanatory power of psychological forces. We begin by exploring different commentator's views on whether Kant rejected the doctrine of "psychological determinism." Then we turn to examine a couple of texts often cited as evidence that he did reject it. The first is a statement found in *The Metaphysics of Morals,* where Kant appears to deny, explicitly, that psychological forces causally determine human choices. The second is the so-called "Incorporation Thesis," from *Religion within the Boundaries of Mere Reason.* Not all of the arguments presented in this chapter will focus on the interpretation of texts, however. A few, near the end, will be concerned with conceptual issues related to the explanatory power of free choice. In the last two sections we consider the merits of an alternative, "free-choice solution" to the problem of justification and explanation. The chapter will then close with another look at some texts in which Kant characterizes what he calls "free choice" (*freie Willkür, arbitrium liberum*).

3.1 Psychological Determinism

A principal thesis of Kant's *Critique of Pure Reason* was that belief in the thoroughgoing causal determinism of nature does not contradict belief in free will. Yet many now assume that belief in the thoroughgoing *psychological* determinism of our actions actually does contradict belief in free will. I do not agree, however. I think that solving the problem of justification and explanation *requires* belief in psychological determinism. I think it requires assuming that our acting on one maxim rather than another is causally determined by the relative strengths of psychological forces incorporated into our maxims.[1] Most recent interpreters believe that Kant rejected this kind of determinism, however. And in order to show that this is the case, I shall devote this opening section of the chapter to examining others' views on Kant's attitude toward psychological determinism.

Some think he rejected psychological determinism because it is incompatible with his view of human freedom. Others think that he rejected psychological determinism, or that he should have rejected it, because he rejected scientific psychology. Here I'll begin exploring several views along these lines with an example of someone who thinks that Kant actually embraced psychological determinism, and who criticizes him for having done so, because he does not believe that psychological determinism is compatible with Kant's understanding of self-determining choice. Jay Wallace writes:

If, as I suppose, transcendental freedom in Kant's sense involves the power of self-determining choice—the capacity, in his terms, to take an incentive into one's maxim—then it seems that we cannot have that power at all if the version of psychological determinism Kant himself embraces for theoretical purposes is correct. We possess the capacity for choosing independently of our desires only if it is not the case that what we do is determined by those desires.[2]

---

[1] Here I do not mean that the action is explained by our thought or belief that the one was stronger than the other. I mean that the one desire, through its psychological force, and not through our belief in the same, causes us to act on it, rather than on another desire.

[2] R. Jay Wallace, "Moral Responsibility and the Practical Point of View," in *Normativity and the Will: Selected Papers on Moral Psychology and Practical Reason* (Oxford: Oxford University Press, 2006), 144–64 at 161. Westphal also sees a tension between Kantian freedom and psychological determinism. See Kenneth Westphal, "Noumenal Causality Reconsidered: Affection, Agency and Meaning in Kant," *Canadian Journal of Philosophy* 27 (June 1997): 209–45 at 239.

Wallace defines psychological determinism in this context as "the characteristically empiricist assumption that human action is causally determined
by states of belief and desire to which persons are subject, and with respect
to which they are basically passive" (146).

Most recent commentators on Kant's practical philosophy seem to agree
with Wallace in thinking that freedom of choice would be incompatible
with psychological determinism. But few agree with his assumption that
Kant intended to embrace them both. Onora O'Neill is representative of
this group. She does not see Kant as holding that, as Wallace puts it, we
are "basically passive" with respect to forceful desires or motives. O'Neill
once cautioned that,

it is easy to think of motives as sorts of pushes or pulls which can never fail to be
at least partially determining. But this is to forget Kant's view on human freedom
and the role of motives. Motives, in Kant's sense, are something we choose to
determine our action. We are not impelled by them. Even when "impulsion" is
determining, it is we who have chosen to make it so.[3]

I take the following as sufficient for denying that Kant accepted psychological determinism. This is denied when someone attributes to him
the view that the motives, desires, inclinations, or incentives that affect
us through their psychological forces are incapable of causing us to act
one way rather than another. I see views like this as ruling out psychological *determinism*. But I do not see them as precluding our actions' being
caused by desires. Those two conditions are subtly different. I see the
view just stated by O'Neill, for instance, as both denying psychological determinism and agreeing that a desire can determine action through
its psychological force, by "impulsion." The view she has expressed
allows that a desire may causally determine action, only provided we
first do whatever is supposed to be necessary for freely choosing to
act on the desire.[4] And the desire could not causally determine our
doing *that*.

    [3] Onora Nell (O'Neill), *Acting on Principle* (New York: Columbia University Press, 1975), 118.
See also eid., *Constructions of Reason*, 71; and see Marcia Baron, *Kantian Ethics Almost Without Apology*
(Ithaca, NY: Cornell University Press, 1995), 89; Andrews Reath, "Kant's Theory of Moral Sensibility:
Respect for the Moral Law and the Influence of Inclination," *Kant-Studien* 80 (1989): 284–302 at 290;
and Yirmiyahu Yovel, "Kant's Practical Reason as Will: Interest, Recognition, Judgment and Choice,"
The Review of Metaphysics 52 (December 1998): 267–94 at 289.
    [4] But I do not think it is psychologically sound to assume that the forces of motives or desires can
be expected to work this way (see below, 3.7).

For this reason I think that Henry Allison has also denied that Kant was a psychological determinist. He has done this in his various characterizations of what he calls Kant's "Incorporation Thesis."[5] It was Kant's view, according to Allison, that "an incentive (or motive) is denied any causal efficacy apart from the adoption of a maxim by an agent to act on the basis of that incentive . . . . Moreover . . . this act of adoption or incorporation is not itself causally conditioned" (189). Allison denied that it was Kant's view "that motives or incentives are distinct psychic forces that can move an agent either singly or in cooperation with one another" (117). He denied further that Kant adopted "a conflict-of-forces conception of agency" where "inclinations directly determine the will by exerting an affective force on it," so that "if the [moral] law is to determine the will instead (. . .), it can do so only by exerting a stronger and contrary affective force" (126). To these statements we may add Allison's claim that, in Kant's view, "a rational agent is not regarded as being determined [, even in the case of inclination-based actions,] in a quasi-mechanistic fashion by the strongest desire (roughly the Leibniz–Hume model)" (39).

I think also that Christine Korsgaard denied that Kant accepted psychological determinism, in writing the following: "[T]he reflective mind must endorse the desire before it can act on it, it must say to itself that the desire is a reason. As Kant puts it, we must *make it our maxim* to act on the desire. Then although we may do what the desire bids us, we do it freely."[6] Her concluding point here seems to indicate her belief that psychological determinism, or our being "basically passive" with respect to the bidding of desires, would interfere with our capacity to act freely.

[5] Allison acknowledges that Kant intended to embrace psychological determinism "at the empirical level." But like Wallace, he regards this intention as raising problems for Kant's conception of freedom. Allison suggests that Kant actually rejected psychological determinism with his recognition that psychological states of desire are "not so determining" that they preclude spontaneous free choice (see *Kant's Theory of Freedom*, 31–2, 39, esp. 45, 49–50, 51–3). This also means, according to Allison, that human rational agents enjoy "independence from the causal principle of the Second Analogy," which "involves all of the problems connected with a contracausal conception of freedom" (52). Later (5.2) we shall look briefly at how Allison supposes Kant attempted to deal with these problems: "by considering [free agents] from two points of view." Guyer and Wood have also embraced some version of The Incorporation Thesis, as it is explained by Allison. See Paul Guyer, *Kant on Freedom, Law and Happiness* (Cambridge: Cambridge University Press, 2000), 293, and Allen Wood, *Kant's Ethical Thought*, 53. Guyer, I think, comes closer than any other recent interpreter to appreciating Kant's psychological determinism. But I do not see his interpretation as supporting this doctrine in a completely consistent way.

[6] *Sources of Normativity*, 94.

Just prior to this passage Korsgaard provided a narrative indicating what she means by "endorsing" a desire, or saying that it is a reason. "I desire and I find myself with a powerful impulse to act. But I back up and bring that impulse into view and then I have a certain distance. Now the impulse doesn't dominate me and now I have a problem. Shall I act? Is this desire really a *reason* to act?" (93). This narrative appears to serve as Korsgaard's description of what we must do in order to act freely on a psychologically forceful desire. Or it may be only an example of something we must do. In any case, what she says here implies that we would not act freely if a desire or incentive were to cause us, by its impelling force, to endorse it, or to make it our maxim to act on it, or to act on *it* rather than on another desire or incentive.[7] For these reasons it seems to me that Korsgaard sees psychological determinism as a threat to Kantian freedom of choice.[8]

Other commentators offer a completely different reason why Kant should not be interpreted as having accepted psychological determinism. They point to his rejection of scientific psychology.[9] Kenneth Westphal represents this view when he argues that Kant's belief in the impossibility of identifying psychological substances implies that "we cannot ... justify any determinate causal judgments in psychology. Hence determinism is in principle insupportable, unjustified, in the psychological realm. Consequently, for good Critical reasons we must be theoretically agnostic about psychological determinism."[10]

---

[7] I think this is implicit in her claim, elsewhere, that "If you feel that the desire impelled you into the act, you do not regard the act as a product of your will, but as involuntary" (*Creating the Kingdom of Ends*, 162).

[8] There is a complication that should be noted here, however. I do not think Korsgaard believes that her interpretation of Kant's theory of action rules out psychological determinism absolutely. In her view, there are two perspectives we can take on human action (see *Creating the Kingdom of Ends*, 173, 203–4; *Sources of Normativity*, 94–7). In one perspective it would be possible to accept psychological determinism. We can look at actions with the purpose of explaining how they come about, like a scientist or an empirical psychologist. But we can also look at the world practically, with the purpose of deciding what to do. According to Korsgaard, Kant's view rejects psychological determinism for the latter, practical perspective, where freedom is presupposed. So in this sense she regards psychological determinism as a threat to Kantian freedom. To her mind, it would be self-contradictory to say of one's action that it is both free and caused by the psychological force of a desire, unless one shifts perspectives in mid-sentence. And then it is a good question whether the subject of predication, the action, is the same in both perspectives. Korsgaard's perspectivism will be a subject of discussion later (see 5.2 and 5.4).

[9] See Immanuel Kant, *Metaphysical Foundations of Natural Science*, trans. Michael Friedman, in *Theoretical Philosophy after 1781*, ed. Henry Allison and Peter Heath (Cambridge: Cambridge University Press, 2002), 186/4:471.

[10] Kenneth Westphal, *Kant's Transcendental Proof of Realism* (Cambridge: Cambridge University Press, 2004), 231. Hanna argues, for similar reasons, that "for Kant psychological laws *cannot be deterministic*."

I think the different types of explanations and arguments just presented show that skepticism about Kant's having accepted psychological determinism is well represented in recent secondary literature. And for that reason we can expect a fair amount of resistance to the solution I have proposed here for the problem of justification and explanation: that our actions are explained by the psychological forces of incentives. Yet, despite what may be more commonly believed, there are a number of passages in Kant's published texts that actually seem to confirm that he accepted psychological determinism.

This seems to be confirmed in his claim, for example, that: "[I]f it were possible for us to have such deep insight into a human being's cast of mind ... that we would know every incentive to action ... we could calculate a human being's conduct for the future with as much certainty as a lunar or solar eclipse .... " (*Practical Reason*, 83/5:99, see also *Pure Reason*, A549–50/B577–8). This passage affirms the possibility, in principle, of predictive certainty regarding human conduct: a certainty based on "deep insight" into psychological incentives to action. And that possibility, I think, requires the assumption of psychological determinism. Worth pointing out here too is that in the same statement Kant also affirmed his belief in human freedom. The quoted sentence ends with: " ... and could nevertheless maintain that the human being's conduct is free." So he does not seem to have recognized any incompatibility between psychological determinism and human freedom, as his more recent interpreters have.

Passages like the above confirm Kant's belief in psychological determinism, at least indirectly. Yet there is a passage in which he as much as said that psychological phenomena are subject to the same causal determinism as physical phenomena. In his *Prolegomena to Any Future Metaphysics* he referred to "universal natural science in the strict sense." This is natural science construed broadly, as science dealing with the objects of outer sense as well as the objects of inner sense; or as Kant wrote in this passage, "the objects of physics as well as psychology." He said there that two

See Robert Hanna, *Kant, Science and Human Nature* (Oxford: Oxford University Press, 2006), 440. But I do not see why Kant should have to reject or remain agnostic about psychological determinism just because he denied the scientific status of psychology. It seems to me perfectly consistent to deny scientific status to meteorology, for example, while still believing that weather phenomena are causally determined. I agree with Allison, who points out that Kant also denied scientific status to the chemistry of his day, though it is hard to believe that he would have been agnostic about determinism in chemical processes (see *Kant's Theory of Freedom*, 34).

general, a priori principles of the sciences of physics and psychology are that "*substance remains* and persists, and that *everything that happens* always previously *is determined by a cause* according to constant laws."[11] So Kant claimed there, unequivocally, that determinism is presupposed in psychology in the same way it is presupposed in physics. The only difference is that the phenomena under investigation are "inner" in psychology and "outer" in physics. It seems to me that Kant's embracing psychological determinism here is consistent with his also having denied that we can ever discover any psychological laws through experience.[12] Our inability to make scientifically useful observations in psychology would not imply that psychological phenomena are exempt from causal determinism. And I do not think Kant supposed otherwise.

3.2 Affected but Not Determined

Those who deny that Kant accepted psychological determinism, because it would be incompatible with human freedom, have passages of their own to cite. In different texts Kant seems to have claimed that psychological forces explain the actions of unfree animals, but not of free human beings.[13] A passage from *The Metaphysics of Morals* can be taken as representative of these claims:

That choice [*Willkür*] which can be determined by *pure reason* is called free choice. That which can be determined only by *inclination* (sensible impulse, *stimulus*) would be animal choice (*arbitrium brutum*). Human choice, however, is a capacity for choice that can indeed be *affected* but not *determined* by impulses, and is therefore of itself (apart from any acquired aptitude of reason) not pure but can still be determined to actions by pure will. *Freedom* of choice is this independence from being determined by sensible impulses. . . . (42/6:213)

[11] Immanuel Kant, *Prolegomena to Any Future Metaphysics that will be Able to Come Forward as Science*, trans. Gary Hatfield, in *Theoretical Philosophy after 1781*, ed. Henry Allison and Peter Heath (Cambridge: Cambridge University Press, 2002), 90/4:295.

[12] I think Westphal misses this point and, as a consequence, draws an invalid inference. He writes: "If we have no [empirical] evidence of a substantial self, then we cannot . . . justify any determinate causal judgments in psychology. Hence determinism is in principle insupportable, unjustified, in the psychological realm" (*Kant's Transcendental Proof of Realism*, 231). Only if psychological determinism were an empirical hypothesis would Westphal's conclusion follow.

[13] See *Pure Reason*, A534/B562, A802/B830; *Practical Reason*, 29/5:32, and *Lectures on Metaphysics*, 263/29:896.

Passages like this seem to discredit the idea that Kant assumed psychological forces can explain our choices to act one way rather than another. But here everything depends on what he meant in writing that the human capacity for choice is "*affected* but not *determined* by impulses." If in interpreting this phrase we equate "impulses" with the psychological forces of incentives, of any kind, then what Kant claims here seems very clearly to repudiate psychological determinism. For in that case the passage seems to say that our free choices cannot be determined by impulsive psychological forces. But there are three textual points to observe about what Kant wrote here: three points besides the fact of Kant's also having claimed, a number of times, that incentive forces are the causes of choice (2.5).

The first point is that it is not clear that in the passage quoted we should equate his term "impulses" with incentive forces of any kind. Kant had used the word "impulse" in the sentence just preceding the one in which "*affected* but not *determined* by impulses" appears. And he used it there in referring to a "stimulus."[14] But as we have seen, he was accustomed to distinguishing between "*stimuli*" and "*motiva*" as sense-based and intellect-based incentives respectively (2.4). So it does not seem correct to interpret what he wrote here as denying that the choices of human beings can be determined by incentive forces *of any kind*.

The second point, which is related to the first, is that in the sentence preceding the phrase "*affected* but not *determined* by impulses" Kant also wrote that animal choice "can be determined *only* by inclination" (emphasis altered). The use of "only" here is not an apt qualification if his point was that human choice is completely free of determination by incentive forces of any kind. For saying that animal choices can be determined *only* by inclinational incentives expresses a limitation. It suggests that human choices, by comparison, may be determinable by inclinational incentives as well as by other kinds of incentives. This seems to be what he meant when he compared animal and human choice years earlier, in the first *Critique*: "A faculty of choice ... is merely animal (*arbitrium brutum*) which cannot be determined other than through sensible impulses. ... However, one which can be determined independently of sensory impulses, thus through motives [*Bewegursachen*, moving causes] that can only be represented by

---

[14] See *Practical Reason*, 29/5:32, where Kant uses "pathologically affected" but "not thereby determined"; and *Pure Reason*, A534/B562, where he compares pathological affection with pathological "necessitation."

reason, is called free choice (*arbitrium liberum*). . . ." (A802/B830). Here the comparison between animal choice and free choice is between choice that cannot be determined by anything other than sense-impulses, and choice that can be determined by something other than sense-impulses, like the psychological forces of intellect-based incentives (*motiva*). So, again, it is likely that in writing that human choice is "*affected* but not *determined* by impulses" Kant did not intend to deny that human choices are causally determinable by the psychological forces of incentives. He may have intended to deny, instead, that our free choices are determinable by inclinational incentives *only*.

The third point is that in the sentence in which "*affected* but not *determined* by impulses" appears, Kant wrote that human choice is "not pure but can still be determined to actions by pure will." Two sentences preceding he had also written: "That choice which can be determined by *pure reason* is called free choice." These statements suggest that Kant did not intend to deny that human free choice is *determinable* by something. Yet he apparently did not see pure will, or pure reason, as the sole determinant of human free choice. In each of the above statements, from *The Metaphysics of Morals* and from the first *Critique,* he wrote merely that choice *can be* so determined (*bestimmt werden kann*). This suggests that our free choices can also *fail* to be determined by pure reason or will, in which case they would be determinable by impulses of sensibility (*stimuli*). In the final section of this chapter we shall look more closely at some other ways Kant described free choice and its relation to incentive impulses.

Kant's having claimed that human free choice is "*affected* but not *determined* by impulses" has seemed to imply that our choices and actions cannot be explained by the psychological forces of incentives. But the preceding three points of textual interpretation show that this is not necessarily what he meant. Moreover, reading Kant's phrase "*affected* but not *determined* by impulses" as if it does deny the action-explaining role of incentive forces raises a philosophical problem. For if that is what Kant meant to deny here, then it is hard to understand why he would have claimed that incentive impulses can even *affect* what they cannot determine. To affect something is, after all, to determine it, or to determine it to some degree.

Consider what it would mean for a causal force to affect something without determining it. It would presumably mean that the force in question would be effective in some way, but not fully effective, or not effective to the degree that might be expected. A rolling billiard ball might *affect* a stationary ball with which it collides by merely nudging it into a cushion. It might *affect* it in this way without *determining* it to roll, as might ordinarily be expected from a collision of two billiard balls. A rolling ball might glance off another rolling ball and *affect* its trajectory, without *determining* it to roll along its own trajectory. In these cases of affection falling short of determination, in some sense, that which affects could in principle still determine what it affects; but that is what Kant is usually supposed to have denied. The only way to express the idea that sensible impulses cannot determine free human choices, in principle, seems to require denying that they can even affect human choices. But Kant does not deny this.[15]

The conceptual difficulty raised by this last observation is the problem of how one thing can be *affected* by another, without being capable of being *determined* by it. In view of this problem, it seems likely that all Kant meant to deny in the passage from *The Metaphysics of Morals* is that sense-based incentives are the *only possible* determinants of how we choose, as is the case with animals.[16]

---

[15] It should be acknowledged that another way to think of affection falling short of determination would be to distinguish between the object affected and the object determined. It might be imagined that here Kant meant to say that *human agents* are affected in some way by incentive impulses, but *human choices* are not determined by them. This is not what he wrote, however. What he wrote implies that the same thing, *human choice,* is affected but not determined by impulsive stimuli.

[16] Here it is worth quoting two sentences from the first *Critique* seeming to suggest that the conflict between sensible impulses and the incentive of pure reason is a contest for the *determination* of human choice. Kant wrote:

It is easy to see that if all causality in the world of sense were mere nature, then every occurrence would be determined in time by another in accord with necessary laws, and hence—since appearances, insofar as they determine the power of choice, would have to render every action necessary as their natural consequence—the abolition of transcendental freedom would also simultaneously eliminate all practical freedom. For the latter presupposes that although something has not happened, it nevertheless *ought* to have happened, and its cause in appearance was thus *not so determining* that there is not a causality in our power of choice such that, independently of those natural causes and even opposed to their power and influence, it might produce something determined in the temporal order in accord with empirical laws, and hence begin a series of occurrences *entirely from itself.* (A534/B562, emphasis added)

Kant seems to have said here that the sensible impulses that causally determine choice are "not so determining" that they rule out the possibility of another causality, of reason, capable of determining the choice instead. In the language of *The Metaphysics of Morals*, this seems to mean that the affecting impulses which determine the choice in the case in question are not the only possible determinants of choice, as they would be in the case of animal agents.

3.3 The Incorporation Thesis

Another passage related to free choice and the psychological forces of incentives comes from Kant's *Religion within the Boundaries of Mere Reason*. It has led many influential commentators to think that Kant viewed human choices as free of causal determination by incentive forces of any kind. Though this passage from *Religion* is often quoted in interpretive arguments, the sentence containing it is almost never quoted in its entirety. This is because it begins with references to ideas discussed in the surrounding text. The complete sentence is:

On the rigorist's criteria, the answer to the question just posed is based on the morally important observation that [*quotations usually begin here*] freedom of the power of choice has the characteristic, entirely peculiar to it, that it cannot be determined to action through any incentive *except so far as the human being has incorporated it into his maxim* (has made it into a universal rule for himself, according to which he wills to conduct himself); only in this way can an incentive, whatever it may be, coexist with the absolute spontaneity of the power of choice (freedom). (48–9/6:23–24)

In the analysis of this passage to follow I shall attempt to explain both the significance that recent interpreters have attached to it, and the context in which Kant wrote it. Part of what I want to show here is that the context of the passage does not support the significance usually attached to it. Additionally, I want to show how conceptual, philosophical difficulties arise for the theory of action that results when the passage is interpreted as denying that incentive forces cause us to choose one way or another. I think both of these lines of argument, taken together, should raise grave doubts about the propriety of interpreting this passage from *Religion* in the way it is now usually interpreted.

Henry Allison referred to the passage quoted above as "The Incorporation Thesis" when he called it the "centerpiece of Kant's conception of rational agency."[17] Other recent commentators seem either to have endorsed Allison's interpretation of the passage in question, or to have offered variations on it. These include Christine Korsgaard, Paul Guyer,

---

[17] *Kant's Theory of Freedom*, 5, 89.

and Allen Wood.[18] Earlier writers interpreting the passage similarly include
Gerold Prauss, John Rawls, and John Silber.[19] With the possible exception
of Silber, all these interpreters seem to agree that the passage from Kant's
Religion demonstrates his beliefs that,

- (*a*) in practical deliberation, our objective is ordinarily to choose which
  of our available incentives we shall incorporate into our maxim, or,
  which maxim (incorporating an incentive) we shall adopt;
- (*b*) though they may affect us with strong psychological forces, because
  of our freedom of choice incentives are incapable of causing us
  to choose to act on them, and of causing us to adopt maxims
  incorporating them;[20] hence,
- (*c*) in deliberating between alternative courses of action, or between
  alternative incentives unequal in their psychological forces, it is
  always possible for us to choose to incorporate a weaker incentive
  into our maxim, and act on it.

One further point about the action-explaining forces of incentives should be
made, or noted as a reminder, before we proceed to explore the context of
the passage quoted above from *Religion*. That passage is usually interpreted
as denying that psychologically forceful incentives, of any kind, can causally
determine free choices and actions. But no one, as far as I know, takes it to
deny that psychological forces of incorporated incentives can explain actions
after they have been freely incorporated into maxims, or *after* one freely
chooses to act on them. Allison seems to have this "post-choice" causality
of incentives in mind when he writes that "insofar as we are moved by
inclination, it is because we, as it were, allow ourselves to be so moved."[21]

---

[18] See Korsgaard, *Creating the Kingdom of Ends*, 162, 165; and *Sources of Normativity*, 94; Paul Guyer, *Kant on Freedom, Law and Happiness*, 293–4; and Wood, *Kant's Ethical Thought*, 51–3. See also Andrews Reath, *Agency and Autonomy in Kant's Moral Theory* (Oxford: Oxford University Press, 2006), 154.

[19] See Gerold Prauss, *Kant über Freiheit als Autonomie* (Frankfurt am Main: Vittorio Kolstermann, 1983), 93–4; John Rawls, *Lectures in the History of Moral Philosophy*, ed. Barbara Herman (Cambridge, MA: Harvard University Press, 2000), 294, and John R. Silber, "The Ethical Significance of Kant's *Religion*," in Immanuel Kant, *Religion within the Limits of Reason Alone*, trans. Theodore M. Greene and Hoyt H. Hudson (New York: Harper & Row, 1960), lxxix–cxxxiv, esp. xcv–xcvi.

[20] Silber's interpretation was that we are caused to choose by the force of incentives, though it is ultimately we who freely choose their relative strengths (see xcv).

[21] *Kant's Theory of Freedom*, 189. Korsgaard seems to express a similar view of the force of desire when she writes, "If you feel that [a] desire impelled you into [an] act, you do not regard the act as a product of your will, but as involuntary" (*Creating the Kingdom of Ends*, 162). She seems here

In this way of seeing the causality of incentive forces, an incentive's being incorporated into a maxim, by a freely chosen "act of incorporation," may indeed causally explain one's acting on it. The psychological force of the incentive would become effective, once this is allowed, upon its being freely incorporated into a maxim. But an incentive's force cannot causally explain the choice to incorporate it. Nor can an incentive's force explain the choice to incorporate and act on it rather than on another, competing incentive.

3.4 The Question Just Posed

The Incorporation Thesis is said to be the centerpiece of Kant's theory of action. But if this is so, Kant chose a very odd context in which to write the sentence expressing it. As can be seen from the seldom quoted beginning of the sentence, it was written in answer to a question having something to do with "rigorist criteria." At this point in the text of *Religion* Kant was attempting to demonstrate why human beings are evil by nature. A central premise offered for this conclusion is the doctrine of "rigorism": the doctrine that there is no intermediate position between moral good and evil. The rigorist judges by the criterion that a moral agent who is not wholly good must be wholly evil. But to this doctrine, as Kant recognized, some would object that it poses a false dilemma. Some would undoubtedly say that it ignores the possibility of a person's being partly good and partly evil (or neither good nor evil). So the question posed in the text just preceding the sentence expressing The Incorporation Thesis is, roughly, why is there no alternative to being by nature either wholly good or wholly evil? This is the question Kant intended that sentence to provide a basis for answering.

Before showing how it answers that question we must concentrate a bit more on its context. Kant's doctrine of the evil nature of humanity is his version of the Christian doctrine of original sin ("*peccatum originarium*," see 55/6:31). But unlike Christianity's tracing the original sin of humanity to

---

to envision a desire's forcefully causing an action without the agent's consent or free choice. So it seems she would agree that a desire would be capable of impelling action subsequent to a choice to act on it.

the primordial sin of Adam, Kant indicted each human being for the moral shortcomings of his or her own nature. We are each our own Adams, as Kant saw it, having each corrupted our own natures by a primordial misdeed (see 64/6:42–43). Here by "nature" he meant: "the subjective ground—wherever it may lie—of the exercise of the human being's freedom in general (. . .) *antecedent to every deed that falls within the scope of the senses*" (46/6:21, emphasis added; cf. also 64/6:42–3).

From the context of Kant's sentence about the incorporation of incentives into maxims we can see that what he meant by it is this: that whether we are good or evil by nature depends upon a free choice we make *antecedent* to moral experience. The choice at that point to incorporate the moral incentive into a maxim would result in a nature that is morally good. Otherwise, if a different maxim is incorporated also, or instead, the result is a nature that is evil. This is because the criterion for a good nature is so rigorous. A person must incorporate the moral incentive into what Kant's sentence calls "a *universal* rule for himself, according to which he wills to conduct himself" in perpetuity. Anyone who would make his or her nature good in this way, in that primordial choice, would never deviate from moral principles, throughout the entire course of moral experience. He or she would always obey the moral law, and the moral incentive incorporated into his or her maxim would explain every action in obedience to the law. Failure to make one's nature good in just this way results, therefore, in an evil nature.

So that is Kant's answer to the question just posed about the rigorist's criterion; the question, Why is it impossible to be partly good and partly evil? And from the rigoristic doctrine it follows easily that we are all evil by nature as soon as we add the simple, empirical observation that all human beings are morally imperfect.[22] Any transgression of the moral law within the course of a person's moral experience shows that in his primordial free choice he has not incorporated only the incentive of the moral law into the universal rule (maxim) of his or her nature. So by examining its context we see that the sentence expressing The Incorporation Thesis is about the incorporation of incentives in a unique free choice, antecedent to experience. There is little reason, therefore, to suppose that the sentence was intended to be the centerpiece of a theory

---

[22] "[A]ccording to the cognition we have of the human being from experience, he cannot be judged otherwise" (*Religion*, 56/6:32).

of human rational agency. There is little reason to interpret it as implying points (a)–(c) listed above.

In the next pair of chapters we shall explore the conditions for the original freedom of choice, antecedent to experience, through which each human being becomes evil. We shall see why someone making a free choice under those conditions would not be affected by stronger or weaker forces of incentives at all. That original choice would be, as the context of Kant's sentence shows, a singular choice of a universal rule for one's conduct. But as we shall also see, it would be a choice of the relative strengths of the incentive forces that explain choices and actions in experience. Reading Kant's sentence in this way can actually harmonize the freedom of choice we expect to find in his theory of action with the causal, action-explaining role of the psychological forces of incentives. This is helpful, of course, for solving the problem of justification and explanation in a way that does not threaten Kant's theory of human freedom.

3.5 Adopting Maxims

The preceding section offered a text-based argument raising doubts about the usual reading of the sentence referred to as The Incorporation Thesis. This is the reading that presents the passage found in *Religion* as denying that psychological forces of incentives causally determine our free choices. When read in light of its context, that passage seems to say, instead, that antecedent to experience we freely choose the incentives that will causally determine our choices throughout experience. In this section, and in the pair of sections that follow, some more philosophically oriented arguments will be offered against the usual reading of the passage from *Religion*. It will be shown in these sections that interpreting Kant's theory of action in line with The Incorporation Thesis generates conceptual problems. And these problems will provide a good reason for thinking that Kant would not have endorsed that Thesis.

The present section raises difficulties I have raised elsewhere, about how to understand the relation between free choices to adopt maxims, and free choices to act on them.[23] The argument below will take two steps. First, it

---

[23] See "The Maxims Problem," *The Journal of Philosophy* 99 (January 2002): 29–44.

will show why The Incorporation Thesis implies that a free choice must be a choice *to adopt* a maxim, and cannot be a choice *to act on* an adopted maxim. Second, based on that result, the argument will then show why The Incorporation Thesis implies that in making a free choice an agent would commit herself always to act the same way in the same circumstances. The following arguments will also employ a conception of maxims, and consequently of acting on maxims, that differs from what was explained earlier, in Chapter 1. This shift is required in order to understand The Incorporation Thesis. For the same reason, we shall also presuppose a conception of incentives that differs from what was spelled out earlier, in Chapter 2. Advocates of The Incorporation Thesis typically regard maxims as conditional policies of action that are adopted by free choice; and they see incentives as states of desire or inclination.[24] So maxims are thought of as rules or policies of action to which we freely commit ourselves, often in order to satisfy desires or inclinations. They are seldom seen by advocates of The Incorporation Thesis as thoughts or representations that something is good—as desires, that is. Allison, for example, writes that "a maxim may be characterized as a self-imposed, practical principle or rule of action of the form: When in S-type situations, perform A-type actions."[25] One is thought to "incorporate" an incentive into such a maxim by "adopting" it as a rule of action for oneself, in order to satisfy the incentive. The usual reading of the sentence supporting The Incorporation Thesis suggests then that *choosing is adopting a maxim*.

In fact, that sentence from *Religion* is usually interpreted as virtually defining the procedure we follow in making our everyday free choices, whether we are conscious of it or not. The usual assumption is that, in Kant's view, freely choosing to act is selecting from a set of available alternatives, a (psychologically forceful) incentive as the basis for our adopting a maxim—a maxim that either already does, or will, incorporate it. This is supposed to ensure that the incentive's psychological force does not causally determine how we act. It ensures that *we* determine, by our own free choice, the effectiveness of our chosen incentive for causally explaining our action; that *we* make the incentive into our reason for acting, ensuring that when we act on the basis of the incentive we act freely.

---

[24]   The moral incentive of respect for the moral law is also presumed to be available for incorporation into a maxim.

[25]   *Kant's Theory of Freedom*, 89–90.

But with the procedure for freely choosing so defined, it will not make sense to presume that once we have adopted a maxim we must then choose again, whether to act on it. It will not make sense even to presume that once we have adopted a maxim we *may* then choose again, whether to act on it. This is because choosing *to adopt* a maxim would be a different mental operation from choosing *to act* on an adopted maxim. If the procedure for selecting an incentive and adopting a maxim that incorporates it is identical with freely choosing—if that is what it means to choose freely—then deciding subsequently to act on the maxim is not choosing freely. So from the definition of choosing implied by The Incorporation Thesis it follows that once we have adopted a maxim we have no choice but to act on it. Our action on the maxim must be assumed to follow "automatically," so to speak. Adopting a maxim in a free choice would be like "programming" oneself to act on the maxim. It would be like setting one's will to act a certain way, under certain conditions. Again, there is no free choice whether to act on a maxim or not, because a free choice is just the incorporation of an incentive into a maxim, or just the adoption of a maxim.

It might be thought that the definition of free choice implied by The Incorporation Thesis need not be so restrictive. Perhaps the idea of a free choice as defined by that Thesis can be expanded somehow to include also choosing whether to act on an adopted maxim. It may at least seem plausible to say that Kant could have understood free choice disjunctively: to choose freely is *either* to adopt a maxim *or* to decide whether to act on an adopted maxim. So after we have freely adopted a maxim, the logic of choosing will not preclude our then freely choosing again, whether to act on it.

This disjunctive expansion of the definition of free choice would be inadvisable, however. As we are about to see, it will place a peculiar restriction on free choice. Note first of all that if freely choosing is defined as *doing either* X *or* Y, then there can be no free choice *between* doing X or Y. Since deciding between them is doing neither X nor Y, it will not fit the expanded, disjunctive definition of a free choice. Consequently, if we define freely choosing as *either* adopting a maxim (X) *or* deciding to act on an adopted maxim (Y), then by definition we will not be able to choose between them.[26]

---

[26] To address this problem, suppose we expand the disjunctive definition of freely choosing even further, to include: adopting a maxim, or acting on a maxim, or freely choosing between them. This

But would we ever need to choose between adopting a maxim and deciding whether to act on an adopted maxim? It seems that this would be a very common need. Suppose, for example, that a moment ago I adopted the maxim of making a lying promise in order to get out of a financial bind. Yet now I am hesitant to go ahead with that plan of action. Suppose the categorical imperative has shown me that acting on my adopted lying-promise maxim would be wrong. Or suppose I now see that making a lying promise would ruin my credit. Either of these considerations may have brought me to the point of trying to decide now whether to adopt a different maxim for my situation, or to go ahead and act on my adopted maxim. But by the proposed, disjunctive definition of free choice, I will not be able to choose here. My decision *between* adopting another maxim (X) and deciding to act on my already adopted maxim (Y) will not fall under the expanded definition of freely choosing. So I cannot choose my way out of this impasse.

The preceding difficulty shows, I think, that if we follow The Incorporation Thesis, it is better to define freely choosing strictly as adopting a maxim. It is best to assume that action follows from the adoption of the maxim "automatically." It is best to think that in choosing to adopt a maxim we choose, in effect, to take the action the maxim would call for. It is like choosing to board the west-bound train, by which we, in effect, choose to travel westward.

So let us suppose that to choose would be just to adopt a maxim. Now another problem emerges. It is that since maxims are general principles of action, adopting any maxim should entail *always* acting as indicated in the maxim. We should not be thought capable of choosing to take action on our freely adopted maxims, as just shown. So if someone makes it her maxim (always) to borrow money with a lying promise when she needs cash, then, since that is how she "programs" herself, in those circumstances she will automatically act that way, by her own free choice, of course. It should be recalled that in the sentence supposed to support The Incorporation Thesis, Kant wrote about an agent's incorporating an incentive into a maxim as a "*universal* rule for himself, according to which he wills to conduct himself." Here "universal" would mean for all time, not for all agents. So

---

will not help if we shall ever have to decide among doing any of the three, since doing *that* will not fall under this further expanded definition of freely choosing.

this would imply that the agent adopting the lying-promise maxim would set herself *always* to borrow money with a lying promise when she needs cash. Once she is self-programmed to act this way she can never choose to do otherwise. For again, there is no free choice whether to act, or not to act, on one's freely adopted maxims.

This result seems to pose a serious problem for Kant's theory of action. And it will not do to insist in response to it that because of our freedom we should have the option of discarding our previously adopted maxims, so as to avoid having always to act on them.[27] This will be impossible because to adopt a maxim is to do one thing, and to discard a maxim is to do something else. Since freely choosing is defined as adopting a maxim, we cannot, by a free choice, discard a maxim. Nor, for reasons similar to those explained above, is it advisable to expand the definition of freely choosing to include either adopting a maxim (X) or discarding a maxim (Y).

But someone might now offer the following response to the present difficulty: that there is no reason why we cannot simply adopt new maxims, or make new resolutions, to replace our old maxims. It might be suggested that if a free agent has adopted the lying-promise maxim, all she need do to prevent herself from acting on it, at any time, would be to adopt a maxim of never making lying promises. She can simply adopt this new maxim to "overwrite" her old maxim. Why wouldn't this allow us to define freely choosing as adopting a maxim, without locking agents into acting on their adopted maxims in perpetuity?

The answer, in short, is that this suggestion fails to take seriously the generality of adopted maxims. It implies that adopting a maxim is not, as Kant himself wrote, adopting a universal rule for oneself. If adopting a maxim is setting oneself to act on a rule that is truly universal, then it should not be possible ever to act contrary to that maxim. Nor should it be possible later to reset oneself to act on a contrary maxim. If that is possible, then the first rule adopted was not universal. The suggestion that new maxims can be adopted to overwrite old ones implies that an adopted maxim has the force of an effective "policy" only so long as one allows it to last. It implies also that one need not ever allow an adopted "policy" to last even long enough to act on it twice. So on this proposal, it would be

---

[27] "It is a corollary of Kant's conception of human freedom that we can adopt *or discard* maxims. . . ." (O'Neill, *Constructions of Reason*, 106, emphasis added).

possible to act always on adopted maxims, and never act the same way in the same circumstances. But that possibility would make nonsense of what Kant wrote: that by incorporating an incentive into a maxim one makes it into a universal rule according to which he wills to conduct himself. It would also make it difficult to understand what is meant by characterizing maxims as personal "policies." How is something my policy if I can change it any time I choose, even every time I choose?

Common sense suggests, of course, that adopting, revising, and violating personal policies are among the easiest things in the world to do. But common sense does not also *define* freely choosing as adopting a personal policy. The overall argument here is that when choosing is defined as adopting a maxim, understood as a general or universal rule of conduct, of the form *When in S-type situations do A-type actions,* then to make a free choice is not just to make up one's mind to do something. It is to determine oneself to follow such a rule of conduct in perpetuity.

I do not believe it was Kant's assumption that in everyday life, whenever we make a free choice to do something, we set ourselves to act always in the same way in the same circumstances. Yet I think this is an unavoidable implication of his sentence in *Religion* when it is interpreted as his explicit denial that free choices are caused by the psychological forces of incentives.

3.6 Incentive Strength

The sentence upon which The Incorporation Thesis is based has been interpreted as denying that incentives causally determine our choices through their psychological forces.[28] But as indicated earlier, some advocates of that thesis grant that the psychological forces of incentives can explain

---

[28] See some of the statements quoted above from Allison (3.1). Rawls, who acknowledged that "all of our desires have psychological strength," expressed a similar idea when he said that: "as ideally reasonable persons, we have the capacity to stand above and to assess our object-dependent desires. This gives us an elective power to determine from which of those desires, if any, we shall act." We exercise this power, he wrote, "by incorporating the desire into the maxim from which we propose to act" (*Lectures*, 151–2). A common assumption of these and other interpreters is that although incentives for action are forceful psychological states, we have a power of free choice that makes us exempt from their determining forces, allowing us to choose whether any of their forces will influence our conduct. They assume that without such a power of free choice we would be constantly controlled by the psychological forces of incentives.

actions. They say these forces can cause actions after the incentives are incorporated into maxims, by free choice. So what is actually denied here, or what advocates of The Incorporation Thesis claim that Kant denied, is that the psychological forces of incentives, through their relative strengths, can explain *choices*.

In this section and the one that follows I want to focus mainly on this purported denial. I want to raise what I see as a logical problem for anyone who makes this denial, while also agreeing that incentive forces are stronger or weaker, as ordinarily understood. I shall argue that acknowledging that incentives are stronger or weaker psychological forces, in the usual sense of stronger or weaker desires, implies that they causally determine our choices: that through their strengths they causally determine us to act one way rather than another. So here my point will be, overall, that The Incorporation Thesis attributes to Kant an inconsistent view of the strength of desire. It is inconsistent, I think, to acknowledge that incentives are stronger or weaker, in the sense of having greater or less psychological force, while denying that they causally determine our choices.

It will be helpful to indicate at the beginning of this argument that Kant himself recognized incentives as stronger or weaker psychological forces, in the ordinary sense of stronger or weaker desires. He referred to the strength or weakness of incentives in contexts where their strength or weakness seems directly relevant to acting one way rather than another. In the second *Critique,* for example, he wrote that the representation of the observance of duty, or of "pure virtue,"

can have *more power* over the human mind and can provide a far stronger incentive to effect even [the] legality of actions and to bring forth stronger resolutions to prefer the law to every other consideration, from pure respect for it, than all the deceptive allurements of enjoyment and, in general, everything that may be counted as happiness, or even all threats of pain and troubles can produce. (125/5:151)

Another example of the same type of reference to incentive strength is found in the discussion of weakness of will, in *Religion*. Kant there attributed the Apostle's failure to do what he acknowledged as good to do to the subjective weakness of "the law" as an incentive, compared with inclination (2.3). In *The Metaphysics of Morals* he later claimed that our duty with respect to the incentive of moral feeling is "to strengthen it through wonder at its inscrutable source." We earlier concluded from this passage that Kant must have assumed that the strength of the moral incentive *matters* for moral conduct (2.10). To confirm this further we can now add more evidence found in the second *Critique*. Kant referred there to the moral feeling of respect for the law as an "intellectual cause" of action, and he noted that it sometimes "fails to express its effect in actions only because subjective (pathological) causes hinder it" (68/5:79). That is, sometimes it is too weak in comparison with the causal forces of non-moral incentives. Kant's analysis of the example of the Apostle explained his lamented failure to do the good through moral weakness in just this way.[29]

In his many comments on incentives throughout his psychology lectures and in his published texts Kant seems never to have made any attempt to alert his students and his readers that by the "strength" of an incentive he meant something other than what would ordinarily be understood as the strength of a desire. An incentive, technically speaking, is not a desire (2.4). But we have seen that an incentive, which is either a sensible stimulus or an intellectual motive, is either a desire's cause, or its effect. We have also seen that an incentive's strength can be presumed to explain the strength of a desire.[30] Moreover, as a representation of some object or course of action "as good," a maxim would count as a desire (1.5). So an incentive incorporated into a maxim would, subjectively, constitute the psychological strength of a maxim.[31] For these reasons we need not distinguish here between incentive strength and desire strength, as the action-explaining, psychological force of a maxim. We can be confident that by the strength or weakness of incentives Kant meant virtually the same as what most of his contemporary audience, and most of us today, would recognize as desire strength. And it is worth reiterating that he never offered any indication to his audience that his use of "strength" in comments about incentives should be understood differently from the way people commonly understand desire strength.

---

[29] Kant makes references to incentive strength also at *Groundwork*, 46/4:439, *Practical Reason*, 125/5:151 and *Lectures on Metaphysics*, 262/29:895.

[30] It needs to be borne in mind here that at least in the case of the moral incentive of respect for law, the causality goes the other way: a desire, a "determination" of the faculty of desire, is the cause of this incentive (see Table 2:1). It is nevertheless stronger or weaker in effecting actions, as Kant said, or implied, in the passages just quoted.

[31] Cf. *Metaphysics of Morals*, 197/6:394, where Kant defined "virtue" in terms of the strength of maxims of duty.

3.7 Strength of Desire

It is now time to ask what "strength of desire" can *mean* if, as advocates of The Incorporation Thesis say, desire or incentive strength cannot causally determine our choices. I think everyone will grant that if desires can be strong at all then their strength is their ability *to do something*. So, if our desires cannot cause us to act one way rather than another, then what would a strong desire be capable of doing, by means of its strength, that a weaker one would be incapable of doing, because of its weakness?

In this section I shall consider two of the most plausible-sounding proposals for answering such a question. But each will be found to deviate significantly from what ordinary people usually understand by the concept of desire strength. And for that reason, I think, it will be fair to say that advocates of The Incorporation Thesis cannot provide a plausible account of what "strength of desire" is supposed to signify.

Let us first consider the proposal that the strength of a desire would be its potential to cause a freely chosen action. This is the same as to say that desire strength is not a choice-causing force, but only an action-causing force. The idea would be that an incentive we freely incorporate into our maxim can be expected to exercise its psychological force in causing action on that maxim. But the incentive's force would not explain our choice to incorporate it into the maxim, or to adopt the maxim that incorporates it. So the force of the incentive could not explain why we choose to adopt or act on that maxim rather than on another maxim.[32] Hence, by a free choice undetermined by any incentive force, we choose, in effect, to unleash the psychological force of an incentive that will cause our action on our adopted maxim. An incentive incorporated into a maxim might therefore be compared to the engine in a taxi. If we choose to take the taxi the engine's horsepower will drive us where we intend to go. But the

---

[32] Some who endorse The Incorporation Thesis actually do seem to think of the force of an incentive as something capable of causing free agents' chosen actions. Allison, for example, interprets the sentence from Kant's *Religion* as implying that "insofar as we are moved by inclination, it is because we, as it were, allow ourselves to be so moved" (*Kant's Theory of Freedom*, 189). Korsgaard, as has been noted before, expresses a similar view of the force of desire when she writes, "If you feel that [a] desire impelled you into [an] act, you do not regard the act as a product of your will, but as involuntary" (*Creating the Kingdom of Ends*, 162). Here she seems to attribute an impelling, action-causing force to a desire, although in her example the agent does not choose to deploy the desire's force, it operates independently.

engine's horsepower does not, of course, or does not usually, cause our choosing to take the taxi.

There is a problem with proposals for understanding incentive or desire strength as just an action–causing force, however. It is that they make desire strength indistinguishable from body strength. For on these proposals, nothing can show that a person's desire is strong enough for an action, while her body is too weak to perform it. Nothing can indicate that a person's failure to accomplish some action can be put down to weakness in his desire, rather than to weakness in his body. When we think of a desire's strength as its potential to cause something external to the mind, its strength is then seen as a measure of effectiveness in causing action in the world. But when desire strength is seen this way, then all external obstacles to the action, and therefore to the body's movement in the world, become obstacles to the desire's strength.

To see why this is so, it should be observed first that the strength of a desire, in general, cannot be understood apart from potential obstacles to its effectiveness. Something is strong or weak only in relation to something that could prevent it from causing an expected result. This goes for desires as well as for muscles and limbs. Therefore, second, if a desire's strength is its potential to cause action in the world subsequent to the choice to act on it, then a desire is strong or weak in relation to, and only in relation to, any obstacle that would impede the action. From this it follows, third, that since obstacles to bodily movement (or to intentional immobility) are the obstacles to action in the world, they are also the obstacles to the effectiveness of desire. Therefore, fourth, the obstacles to desire strength are the same as the obstacles to body strength. And if the very same obstacles that provide the basis for understanding desire strength also give meaning to the idea of body strength, then these strengths have to be the same. Consequently, there must be no difference between strength of desire and strength of body.

No one sees it this way, however. So something is wrong with the assumption that the strength of a desire or incentive is the strength that would cause our action once we freely choose to act on the maxim incorporating it. Consider the following example. Suppose I desire to raise my right hand, and suppose I choose to engage this desire's strength to cause this action while I am in a rocket having just blasted off the launch pad. Because I will then experience a G-force several times earth gravity,

I will not be able to accomplish my chosen action. But is this because my desire is too weak against the multiplied G-force, or is it due to weakness in the muscles of my scrawny arm? My contention is that if we assume the strength of a desire is the strength of an action-causing force, then there is no way to tell. For under that assumption, nothing could show that my desire's strength would be sufficient to cause the action, but my arm is too weak. Nor, I think, could anything show the opposite. This is because any obstacle that could test the strength of my desire's action-causing force would also be an obstacle for testing the strength of my arm. Accordingly, strength of desire understood as an action-causing force cannot be distinguished from strength of body. From this it follows also, as an incredible corollary, that a strong man is a man of strong desire.

We may take this result as refuting the idea that in Kant's various references to the strength of incentives quoted in the previous section he was thinking of their strength as an action-causing force whose effectiveness we trigger by adopting a maxim. The argument just above is only conceptual, of course. It does not show that Kant did not think of desire or incentive strength this way. But if this way of thinking is as problematic as we have just seen, then it is best to avoid attributing it to him, if we can.

Let us next consider the proposal that Kant's many references to the relative strengths of incentives and desires can be interpreted as referring to the psychological force with which they are felt, rather than to any action-causing force. A desire's strength may be thought of as its ability to dominate consciousness, or to hold attention; nothing more. So here the obstacles against which desires would prove their strengths are only internal. They are other desires, or other mental states. This will prevent problems like the one we have just seen from arising. For now the strength of a desire can, in principle, be measured independently of the strength of muscles or limbs.

But the difficulty that arises for this proposal is that there is no natural way to connect these merely phenomenological aspects of desires with ordinary conceptions of desire strength. Why would a desire that is merely felt strongly be a hard desire to resist acting on? Why would a desire's being felt weakly, almost imperceptibly, be closely associated with half-heartedness?[33]

---

[33] Freud was not making a logical mistake in assuming that unconscious desires can be strong. Hume insightfully distinguished between strength and violence in passions and weakness and calmness

Stronger or weaker feelings of desires would be comparable, as phenomena, to their longer or shorter durations. Kant would include both among the phenomena of "inner sense." But we do not ordinarily associate a desire's being old or long-held with its being hard to resist acting on. We do not commonly associate a new desire with lassitude, or near indifference to an object. Why then should we so naturally associate a desire felt strongly with devotion and ardor, and a desire felt weakly with half-heartedness?

The argument here emphasizes arbitrariness. Any correlation between a desire's strength as just a phenomenon of inner sense and its being difficult to resist acting on would be purely arbitrary. Suppose we grant that a desire's strength is not its potential to cause us to choose to act one way rather than another, but is just the way it feels. In that case it is perfectly conceivable for someone to have to struggle to resist acting on only her faintest, weakest desires. To someone having failed to act through weakness of will, it would be perfectly meaningful to ask him whether the desire that got the better of him was strong or weak. It would be no less meaningful than asking him whether the desire was long-held or came on all of a sudden. So the proposal that desire strength is only phenomenological, and not effective in determining how we choose to act, seems not to match ordinary, common-sense notions of desire strength. Nor does it offer any plausible explanation why Kant would have recognized a moral obligation to cultivate the strength of the moral incentive (*Metaphysics of Morals*, 201/6:399). What would be morally good about our having stronger moral feelings of respect for law unless a stronger feeling or incentive here would be more effective in determining us to act morally rather than otherwise?

Here we first considered the proposal that a stronger desire is one with a greater potential to cause action as some effect outside the mind. We next considered the proposal that a stronger desirer is one with a greater potential to make some internal, merely phenomenological difference. These two seem to me to be the only plausible ways to understand desire strength if we are committed to The Incorporation Thesis. But neither proposal

(*Treatise* 2.3.3.8–10). The former in each pair refers to our desires' effectiveness in causing choices to act, the latter, to their phenomenology. He acknowledged that a phenomenologically violent desire could be motivationally weaker than a phenomenologically calm one. He thought even that the calm passions are generally stronger, more likely to cause action, than the violent. So Hume rightly saw no obvious connection between a phenomenologically weak desire and a desire not likely to be acted upon.

seems to approximate what we should think Kant had in mind in referring to the relative strength or weakness of desires and incentives. That thesis rules out the idea that an incentive's strength is a measure of its potential effectiveness in causing a choice to act one way rather than another. But apart from that idea I cannot see how the concept of desire strength would have gotten the meaning ordinarily associated with it. So I do not see how The Incorporation Thesis is consistent with ordinary conceptions of desire strength. And since it seems that Kant's conception of desire or incentive strength is ordinary, I think that to attribute The Incorporation Thesis to him is to attribute to him an inconsistent conception of the strength of desire.

3.8 Two Types of Choice

Solving the problem of justification and explanation requires showing how practical reasoning that justifies action can also explain it. In this chapter and the one before it I have attempted to clarify and defend a solution to this problem. It is, again, that actions can be explained by forceful incentives incorporated into maxims of practical reasoning—maxims from which justifications for action can be derived. This solution presents human actions as the effects of psychological forces; and it implies that we are always caused to act one way rather than another, that is, on one maxim rather than another, by the relative strengths of those forces. A central methodological assumption here is that all things being equal, the strongest incentive, which is to say, the strongest force of desire, causes (explains) action.

   It is time now to begin facing more directly the main obstacle to acceptance of the solution I am offering. This obstacle is a widely held conviction that explanation of action in terms of psychological forces is incompatible with Kant's theory of freedom. Our freedom of choice, many insist, precludes our being caused to act one way rather than another—especially in purely moral action.[34] It is thought that as Kant

---

[34] I think Reath expresses this conviction in a compelling form:

consider a model [of moral motivation] on which the recognition of the Moral Law motivated by exerting a force on the will. Reason might still determine the will, but it is difficult to see how it does

conceived of rational human agents, our "power of free choice" (*Willkür*) enables us to determine for ourselves how we will act on our desires. So we are not basically passive with respect to them. We are not caused to act by their psychological forces. In the following section, however, I want to raise a problem for this more usual understanding of Kant's view of free choice. I want to show why it fails to provide an adequate solution to the problem of justification and explanation. In preparation for that argument it will be helpful, in this section, to clarify a couple of different roles that free choice can be imagined to play in the explanation of action.

Sometimes we offer explanations of action that merely cite what seems to have been the reason upon which the agent acted. An example of this type of explanation that is well known from Kant's moral theory is his explanation of "morally worthy" action as done purely for duty's sake. This type of action-explanation is not always to our purpose, however. For other times we want to present the agent not merely as having acted on a certain reason, like for the sake of duty, or for the sake of inclination, but as having acted on one reason rather than another. It seems that the concept of "choice" would play different roles in these two types of explanation. So in what follows I shall designate these roles, respectively, as *executive choice* and *elective choice*.

We may sometimes explain someone's action merely by citing her reason for doing it, by saying, for example, that she recognized that it was her duty. That type of explanation can be sufficient for some purposes. But it conceals an explanatory gap. As has been pointed out several times now, for us imperfectly rational human beings, just recognizing the justification for an action will not suffice for our doing it. So although we may say that someone recognized that a certain action was justified, by some reason or other, our saying this is no explanation of the action. It does not explain why it occurred. Hence, it may seem that the role of free choice in human action is to fill an explanatory gap: the gap between the agent's recognized justification, and her execution of the justified action. "Executive choice," as I call it, seems to explain someone's acting on a reason she recognizes as

---

so through a choice by the individual. The moral motive would still be one psychological force among others, which is effective when it is the strongest, or when favored by the balance of psychological forces. What is missing from this model is the idea that the subject's action stems ultimately from a choice made on the basis of reasons.   ("Kant's Theory of Moral Sensibility," 291)

justifying her action. She moves from the recognition of the justification, to the justified action, by means of her "executive choice." Here her choice is the choice to act on her recognized justification. This way of thinking about choice therefore suggests that it would be suitable for filling the explanatory gap between recognized justification and action on that justification. Hence, we can think of the capacity for "executive choice" as simply the capacity to act on a recognized justification for action. This is one way the concept of choice is understood, and sometimes discussed.

Yet when we want to emphasize someone's choosing to act one way rather than another, we apparently have a different conception of choice in mind. The above example of doing one's duty for duty's sake can be adapted to illustrate this point. For it is possible that someone who does her duty for duty's sake recognizes one or more additional, inclinational justifications for doing the same thing; and she probably also recognizes one or more inclinational justifications for doing something else instead. An explanation of her action as having been freely chosen (executed) for duty's sake will tell us why she did it, or the reason upon which she acted. But a more complete explanation of a choice can tell us something about an agent's priorities; and from this information we can sometimes draw inferences about her character. This is evident when it is explained, for example, that a person chose to keep a promise despite being very strongly tempted to break it.[35]

The choice that seems to explain action here would not be the same type as identified previously (executive choice). Here the idea is not just that a choice would explain action on a justification. It is rather that a choice explains why action occurs on one justification rather than an available, alternative justification. I call this type of choice "elective choice." The capacity for "elective choice" would be the capacity of selecting the justification upon which one will act, from among a set of alternatives. For

---

[35] Henson, in writing on Kant's moral theory, emphasizes two types of moral appraisal that seem to correspond roughly with the distinction between these two types of action-explanation. Sometimes the evaluation of an action as morally worthy is a "fitness report," he says, indicating that the reason why the agent executed the action is the fit or proper motive. But other times ascriptions of moral worth are like what he calls "battle citations," where what is to be emphasized is the motive of duty's triumph, in the agent's elective choice, over contrary motives. See Richard G. Henson, "What Kant Might Have Said: Moral Worth and the Overdetermination of Dutiful Action," *Philosophical Review* 88 (1979): 39–54.

example, the agent saw a reason why she ought to return the borrowed book on the day she promised to return it, and she also saw a reason why she ought to keep the book another day. She chose, by elective choice, to keep her promise rather than to break it. This is another way the concept of choice can be understood, and is sometimes discussed.

So the two ways the concept of choice is applicable in action-explanation are executive choice and elective choice. The former might be seen as indicating, roughly, that the agent performed an action *voluntarily*. She did it for a reason she recognized, and by her own volition. The latter might be seen then as indicating, again, roughly, that the agent performed an action *deliberately*. That is, she did it after weighing her options, or did it despite the recognition that something else would have been good to do also, and may even have been better to do.

But some might now argue that so-called elective choice is a phantom, or that in theory we can get along without it. Their argument may turn on the following premise: that a rational human being cannot act without rational justification, and this is always *all-things-considered* justification. The idea would be that no one can ever have alternative justifications for action at the same time. There may perhaps be alternative *considerations* that suggest multiple justifications for action. But the rational agent cannot act on any of these as mere *considerations*. She can act only by first seeing a consideration as providing a justification (all things considered) for acting. Hence, it may be said, what was above called "electing" whether to act one way rather than another, or on one justification rather than another, is not a type of free choice. It is only making a decision about which of several alternative considerations is a justification. So there is no "*elective* choice." A free choice is nothing but the rational agent's choice to execute an action she recognizes as all-things-considered justified for her circumstances.[36]

I do not find the reduction of all free choice to "executive choice" plausible for Kant's theory of action, however. He provided an example of someone who fails through weakness of will to act as he recognized he ought to act, all things considered; and in that example the agent

---

[36] An idea like this may be behind Korsgaard's explanation of incorporating incentives into maxims. See *Creating the Kingdom of Ends*, 165. There she seems to explain all incentives as mere "candidate reasons," which do not become reasons for action until they are incorporated into a maxim. This is like saying that we never act except by executive choice, on our all-things-considered justifications. To carry out the metaphor, we cannot choose to act on a candidate reason unless we elect the candidate, by deciding that it is the way we ought to act.

seems nevertheless to act with some justification or other (see 2.3). This would be impossible if all justification for action were all-things-considered justification. So the reduction of all choice to executive choice to act on an all-things-considered justification does not seem consistent with Kant's example of weakness of will. Granted, there is some kind of irrationality in examples of weakness of will. It is of course irrational in some way to acknowledge that, all things considered, one ought to do something, and then do something else instead. But I do not see any good reason for committing Kant to the view that when someone fails through weakness of will, the irrationality of his action consists in its lacking *any* justification. It must be borne in mind here that Kant would think of at least some examples of morally wrong action as having occurred through weakness of will. From his moral theory we know this implies that in such cases the agent acts on a maxim of a certain form: on a maxim that cannot become a universal law. From his theory of action, further, we know this implies that the agent is capable of deriving a justification for his morally wrong action from its maxim (see 1.9). So it does not seem plausible to think that Kant assumed human beings can never act except on reasons they take as justifying their actions *all things considered*. Hence, the argument for eliminating all "elective choice" in favor of "executive choice" is not convincing. Nor, as we are about to see, would it help bolster the case against the explanatory power of incentives.

3.9 Choice and Explanation

Those skeptical about the solution I have offered for the problem of justification and explanation will likely propose an alternative solution. They can be expected to say that, in Kant's view, actions for which we can be held responsible, technically, *deeds* (1.1), are not explainable by the psychological forces of incentives. These actions are explainable only by our free choices to act on reasons, or on rational justifications. They are operations of what Kant often called *"freie Willkür,"* or *"arbitrium liberum,"* now often referred to as "the power of free choice." It will be added, also, that our ability to choose to act on rational justifications is what enables practical reasoning to explain human actions. There has to be something to fill the explanatory gap between recognition of a justifying principle of action and the agent's performance of the action. And free choice is what fills that gap. We act as we believe we are justified in acting, because we freely choose to do so.

But I want now to offer an argument for rejecting this proposal for solving the problem, which I'll call "the free-choice solution." I want to examine each of the two types of free choice distinguished in the previous section, and show that neither would serve to explain action in the way that is required, in order to solve the problem of justification and explanation. I'll show first why what was above called "executive" free choice can play no role whatsoever in the explanation of action. Then I'll turn to "elective" free choice, showing why it, also, is unsuitable for explaining action. This will show, I think, that there is no adequate free-choice solution to the problem of justification and explanation. But before proceeding I want to post one clarificatory note about the preceding distinction between executive choice and elective choice. It is that these should not be thought of as referring to two types of choices free agents can make.[37] They are rather two ways we may think about and discuss choice, as possibly explanatory for action.

It will be easiest to show first why so-called executive choice can play no role in the explanation of action—why it cannot fill the explanatory gap. Executive choice would be, simply, the execution of an action on a recognized justification for acting. It can play no role in the explanation of action because, in Kant's theory of action, nothing counts as a human action, a *deed*, unless it is executed by choice. An executive choice, therefore, would be logically implied in the very concept of an action; so it cannot explain an action.[38] Choice in this sense is not explanatory; it is

---

[37] This way of seeing the two types of choice would pose a real difficulty whenever it comes to choosing between them. Because some third type of choice would be required, and so on.

[38] Wood seems to have action-explanation by "executive choice" in mind in discussing what he calls "normative law explanations." These types of explanations, he writes, "are highly appropriate to voluntary, rational actions because rational actions are by their very concept freely chosen and norm-guided" (*Kant's Ethical Thought*, 173). But it seems to me that these so-called "explanations" merely cite the maxim upon which the agent acts. They do not offer any enlightenment at all regarding the agent's acting on that maxim rather than another. How would citing the "maxim of respect for law" explain the moral action of someone who was tempted to act otherwise? Note that someone's acting on that maxim rather than another is consistent with his acting on that maxim by sheer chance; and in that case there would be no explanation for his action apart from saying that he acted on the moral maxim.

part of what needs to be explained.[39] What needs to be explained is an agent's executing an action, by choice, on a recognized justification for action.

So those who offer the free-choice solution must say that what explains action on a justification is the agent's *election*.[40] What explains, they must say, is a choice of the justification upon which to act, from among a set of recognized, alternative justifications.[41] The set of alternatives might consist of different reasons justifying the same action, or of different reasons justifying different actions, or even of some mix. It may help here if we briefly review what these alternative justifications are supposed to be.

We have explained that practical reason justifies actions through imperatives, either hypothetical or categorical (1.9). For any action justified by a hypothetical imperative, the agent is understood to desire the object that the commanded action can be expected to bring about. In having a desire for the object, it should be recalled, the agent thinks of the object as good (1.5). This is to say also that she has a maxim that incorporates the object as an incentive (2.2). The subjective, psychological force of this incentive constitutes the force of the agent's desire for the object (2.8–11, 3.7). From these basic elements of Kant's theory of action something important follows about the relation between imperatives and maxims. It is that one cannot recognize a hypothetical imperative's justification for an action without already having a maxim. The maxim presupposed by a hypothetical imperative's justification for an action would be the maxim upon which one would act in acting on that justification, in acting on that hypothetical

---

[39] If we say that the occurrence of an effect is explained by its cause, we make a similar mistake. The occurrence of an *event* is explained by its cause, of course. But the occurrence of an *effect* logically implies the action of a cause. So the occurrence of an effect is not thereby explained. That a man is a bachelor implies that he has no wife. But his having no wife does not explain his bachelorhood. The latter is explained by whatever explains his having no wife.

[40] Something like this seems to be assumed by many of Kant's interpreters who see actions as explained by rational agents' free choices of what they call alternative "principles of choice," "practical laws," or "practical principles." These are sometimes represented as alternative principles of either heteronomy or of autonomy. See, for example, Reath, "Hedonism, Heteronomy and Kant's Principle of Happiness," 50–62; Onora O'Neill, "Autonomy: The Emperor's New Clothes," *Proceedings of the Aristotelian Society* (suppl.) 77 (2003): 1–21 at 7–11; and Allison, *Kant's Theory of Freedom*, 39, 49, 51, 189.

[41] If there are no alternative justifications from which to choose, then the choice in question can be nothing other than an executive choice. Any time I can see only one justification for doing something, and no justification for doing anything else, my choice to do it will be part of the action to be explained. So my choice cannot explain the action of which it is a part.

imperative.[42] The same would be true in the case of a categorical imperative also. The moral maxim supporting the categorical imperative would be the maxim upon which we act, if we choose to follow the moral law, just for morality's sake. The crucial difference between hypothetical imperatives and categorical imperatives lies not in how we act on them. It lies rather in whether the object that is our incentive is something empirical, to be brought about in the world as a consequence of our action, or whether the incentive object is something purely intellectual; that is, duty, or the moral law (1.9).

Proponents of the free-choice solution will insist that we are not caused to choose (elect) to act upon one rational justification rather than another by any psychological forces. They will say that which justification we act upon must be always up to us. But now there is this difficulty. It is hard to see how our acting upon one justification rather than another can be up to us if we can never know whether we have succeeded in acting upon a justification upon which we have chosen to act. And Kant's view, acknowledged as uncontroversial by almost all interpreters, is that which justification we act upon is impossible to know. In Kant's moral theory, for example, it is possible for us to recognize a moral justification for an action at the same time we recognize a non-moral justification for doing it. That is, a categorical imperative and a hypothetical imperative can in some situations command the very same action. In these cases, Kant also claimed, we can execute that action without ever knowing which of these alternative justifications we end up acting on. We may think that we have acted in observance of the categorical imperative, or on a maxim of duty. But there is no way we can know. This limitation on our knowledge implies, I think, that in Kant's view we cannot control, by a free choice, the justifications upon which we execute our actions.

Therefore, it seems to me, either of the following pair of conditions is true. Either we do not freely choose (elect) the justification upon which we execute our action, because this is not under our control; or, we do make such elective choices, but in doing so we are causally determined by something we do not know, and that we do not control. Neither of these results can be tolerated by those who offer the free-choice solution,

---

[42] I think it is commonly supposed, to the contrary, that an imperative justification always prompts us to adopt a maxim.

however. For in neither case is free choice explanatory. Not in the first case, since, by hypothesis, there is no free choice. Not in the second case, since the action is explained by something we do not control, which causally explains our choice.

Kant's view about the outcome of choices where multiple justifications for the same action are present seems consistent with the explanatory power of psychological forces. Something must determine which justification we act upon: something about which we are, and remain, ignorant. From Kant's own description of the "opacity" of our true intentions in such cases it is hard to draw any other conclusion:

It is absolutely impossible by means of experience to make out with complete certainty a single case in which the maxim of an action otherwise in conformity with duty rested simply on moral grounds and on the representations of one's duty. It is indeed sometimes the case that with the keenest self-examination we find nothing besides the moral ground of duty that could have been *powerful enough to move us* to this or that good action and to so great a sacrifice; but from this it cannot be inferred with certainty that no covert impulse of self-love, under the mere pretense of that idea, was not actually *the real determining cause of the will;* for we like to flatter ourselves by falsely attributing to ourselves a nobler motive, whereas in fact we can never, even by the most strenuous self-examination, get entirely behind our covert incentives. . . .   (*Groundwork,* 19–20/4:407, emphasis added)

Kant here indicated that our action in these special circumstances might be attributable to the *moving power* of the moral ground of duty. But he insisted that we can never know whether this power is the *real determining cause* of the choice to act. Yet whether we choose to act from duty or from a "covert impulse of self-love" is something we would have to be capable of knowing if this were under our control, as the free-choice solution implies.[43] So it appears that, in Kant's view, an elective free choice

---

[43] Some may see the preceding passage as implicating the ever-present possibility of self-deception. But here Kant refers instead to "self-flattery." Self-flattery would be more appropriate for situations where the facts simply cannot be known by any thorough, empirical investigation. Self-deception, on the other hand, suggests that one could get the facts straight, and that normal people not subject to idiosyncratic delusions usually do get them straight. The point of interest here, nevertheless, is that if it is always impossible for us to know which of two recognized justifications for action we have ended up acting upon, then it is impossible for us to control which justification we act upon. How will we ever know whether what we are doing in attempting to control our choice to act on the one justification instead of the other has worked?

between alternative rational justifications is not what would explain action on a moral justification.

But some might be tempted here to regard the moral case as merely a special exception to the principle that free choice explains action. They might think that all Kant has denied in the passage above is that because of the uniqueness of the moral incentive it is always impossible to tell whether we have acted on it. This would not be so for any other incentive, they may say; so free elective choice could well be supposed to explain most other types of action. Yet it is worth noting that the free-choice solution is in trouble if our actions, in moral cases, could never be explainable by an elective choice. For in view of the emphasis Kant placed upon the concept of freedom in moral action, it seems that free choice would have to be explanatory in a moral choice, if it is explanatory anywhere. Moreover, it seems that even when we do not recognize any specifically moral justification among our alternatives, our action is still not explained by an elective free choice between two or more non-moral justifications. In these cases, it seems, we are still not able to be certain about the precise justification, or structure of justifications, upon which we act. We do not know whether we elect to act on all non-moral justifications we may have for the same action, or only on some. So as far as the "opacity" of our true intentions goes, it seems not to matter whether the available justifications for our actions are moral or not.

When we recognize two or more alternative justifications for the same action, and execute that action, the justification upon which we act remains unknown, even to us. But this could not be so if our acting upon one justification rather than another is always under our control, as the free-choice solution implies. So this type of solution does not seem adequate for solving the problem of justification and explanation.

3.10 Another Look at "*Willkür*"

In this final section on free choice we return to the interpretation of Kant's term, "*Willkür*." For this term he sometimes substituted the Latin equivalent, "*arbitrium*," and their most popular English translations today are "choice," and "power of choice." The reason for returning now to this textual basis for interpreting Kant's views of free choice is the following. In many of the preceding arguments we have pointed out conceptual difficulties that arise when we deny that the psychological forces of incentives are not explanatory. And some might well agree that these arguments pose interesting and serious challenges to the Kantian account of freedom of choice. But they might say that, nevertheless, these arguments do not tell us that Kant must actually have believed that whenever we choose to act our actions are caused by the psychological forces of incentives. Very much of his moral theory, it will be said, depends on the idea that we are truly active, or "autonomous," when by our own free choice, and independently of any psychological forces, we choose to obey the objective moral law. So to say that we are basically passive in our moral actions, because even here we are causally determined to act by psychological force, is to deny a doctrine that Kant, in his moral theory, at least, was in no position to deny.

I am not convinced this is so, however. I believe that much here depends upon how we interpret the meaning of Kant's terms *"Willkür"* and *"arbitrium."* And I do not believe we are correct in thinking that these terms are well translated by English "choice," in the sense of selection or decision: the mental act that brings deliberation to a close. Let me begin by noting that in German Kant had available to him another word corresponding to English "choice," and he sometimes used it in referring to moral choice. Here is a good example of his use of *"Wählen"* and *"Wahl,"* instead of *"Willkür."*

Autonomy of the will is the property of the will by which it is a law to itself (independently of any property of the objects of volition). The principle of autonomy is, therefore, to choose [*Wählen*] only in such a way that the maxims of your choice [*Wahl*] are also included as universal law in the same volition.[44]

I have pointed out that Kant used *"Willkür"* in a seemingly peculiar way in *The Metaphysics of Morals,* when in defining the concept he contrasted

---

[44] *Groundwork,* 47/4:440. It might be supposed that this passage, from Kant's *Groundwork,* reflects his uncertainty or confusion over "choice," as distinct from "will"—a confusion cleared up finally when, in *The Metaphysics of Morals,* he made a clear distinction between *Wille* and *Willkür.* But this line of thinking perpetuates a myth surrounding Kant's thoughts on the will. The truth is that Kant understood and employed the concept of *Willkür* often in his lectures prior to publication of the *Groundwork,* and some claims about *Willkür* found late in *The Metaphysics of Morals* are also found in the first *Critique.* Moreover, the distinction between *Wille* and *Willkür* was familiar to Kant and his audience already from the psychology of Christian Wolff.

it with "wish" (1.7). But this relatively late definition signals no change in Kant's understanding of *Willkür*, since long before then, in his lectures, he had often contrasted these concepts similarly. The difference between *Willkür* and wish is just that in the latter case one lacks consciousness of how to act in order to achieve the object desired. So in contrast with wish, "*Willkür*" would presumably not translate straightforwardly as "choice," in the sense of selection or decision. As I have indicated previously, Kant sometimes explicitly characterized "*Willkür*" and wish as different types of desire state. The same appears in other contexts, also, even where Kant emphasizes the freedom of moral *Willkür*; and we shall turn to some examples momentarily. In these cases it will be seen that the freedom of *Willkür* is very implausibly construed as the freedom to choose one course of action over another, independently of any causally determining influence of psychological impulses.

In many of Kant's published comments on *Willkür* he distinguishes between "human" or "free" *Willkür* and "animal" *Willkür*. This looks like a straightforward distinction between the way free humans choose, and the way unfree animals choose—if we allow that they "choose."[45] But outside of Kant's published texts there is another distinction to be found in his comments on *Willkür*. Or perhaps it is the same distinction, in different terms. This is his distinction between "intellectual" and "sensible" *Willkür*, which is sometimes stated in terms of "higher" and "lower" *Willkür*. Kant is recorded as having said in an early psychology lecture that "The human power of choice [*arbitium humanum*] is free, be it sensitive or intellectual";[46] and that "The more a human being has power, by means of the higher power of choice, to suppress the lower power of choice, the freer he is" (71/28:256). Here we find that the faculty of choice in human beings divides, like the more general faculty of desire, into

[45] Some interpreters have expressed puzzlement about Kant's even having allowed that animals "choose," and thus about the plausibility of his frequent contrasts between human and animal choice. I think, with them, that Kant really should not think of animals' choosing if his terms "*Willkür*" and "*arbitrium*" refer to deciding between conflicting forces of desire. See Meerbote, "*Wille* and *Willkür* in Kant's Theory of Action," 82n.1; and see Onora O'Neill, "Agency and Anthropology in Kant's *Groundwork*," in Yirmiyahu Yovel, ed., *Kant's Practical Philosophy Reconsidered* (Dordrecht: Kluwer Academic Publishers, 1989), 63–82 at 69; and Hud Hudson, "Wille, Willkür, and the Imputability of Immoral Actions," *Kant-Studien* 82 (1991):179–96 at 185.

[46] *Lectures on Metaphysics,* 70/28:255. Here and in what follows I quote the translator's mechanical substitution of "power of choice" for "*Willkür*" or "*arbitrium*," as the case may be (see my earlier remarks on why this translation is unadvisable, 1.8).

higher and lower divisions (1.6). Later, a few years beyond publication of the first *Critique*, where Kant had distinguished between human and animal choice as *arbitrium liberum* and *brutum*, his lectures again clarified the two divisions within human choice, in this way: "The power of choice [*arbitrium, Willkür*] is either sensitive, which represents things to us that are agreeable to the senses, [or] intellectual—things which the understanding approves."[47] In the same set of lectures we also find the comment that "Freedom is merely the capacity for acting according to the intellectual power of choice [*arbitrio intellectuali*], and not the power of choice itself [*arbitrium*]" (265/29:898). We are not free just because we have a faculty of choice, according to this comment. Rather, we are free because of our ability to act on higher, intellect-based choice.

If we attend to just his published comments on the concept of choice, we fail to recognize that all along Kant thought of *Willkür* as divided.[48] The lectures he gave for over twenty-five years show that he did not think of *Willkür* as the unified faculty by which human beings freely decide between alternative desires or incentives. We may think of it as either human or animal, where the former is our faculty of free choice and the latter is the determination of animal actions by sense-impulses alone. But if we interpret Kant's terms this way, then the distinction between intellectual and sensitive choice poses at least a question for us. How are we to understand the difference between the so-called "lower," "sensible power of choice," which human beings are supposed to have, and animal choice? Wouldn't they both be determinable by sensible incentives only?

In a set of ethics lectures given in 1793, the same year Kant published *Religion within the Boundaries of Mere Reason,* he again emphasized the causal

---

[47] Ibid., *263/29:896*. Subsequent to publication of the third *Critique*, and just prior to publication of the first part of *Religion*, Kant explained to his metaphysics students that "The free power of choice [*arbitrium liberum*] is either sensitive or intellectual" (348–9/28:588). Even as late as the mid–1790s, only a few years prior to publication of *The Metaphysics of Morals*, notes from Kant's psychology lectures confirm the same distinction within human choice. "Thus arises the division of the concept into *the higher or rational power of choice* [*arbitrium*], i.e., the faculty of desiring through motives, or will or the power of choosing from an impelling intellectual cause, and sensitive power of choice, the faculty of desiring through stimuli" (484/29:1014–15). Here, as elsewhere (cf. 378/28:677, early 1790s), the distinction between intellectual and sense-based choices can be seen as grounded in the distinction between intellectual and sense-based incentives; that is, between the causal operations of "motives" and "stimuli."

[48] "[P]art sensual, in part intellectual," as Kant puts it in lectures around 1794–95 (*Lectures on Metaphysics*, 485/29:1016).

role of incentives for determining choices, and he again confirmed the divided nature of *Willkür-arbitrium*. "[E]very *causa implusliva* or trigger of the mind to action is called, *in genere, elater animi*. . . . This motivating cause is called either *motivum* or *stimulus*. A distinction well worth noting, in view of the dual nature of man. For he has [*sic.*] both a natural being and a free being" (*Lectures on Ethics*, 262/27:493). From here Kant went on to indicate that a *motivum* is a "*moral causa impulsiva*," which determines choice (*arbitrium*) insofar as the latter is free. But a *stimulus,* which is a sensory impulse, determines choice according to the laws of nature.[49] It is peculiar that he would here allow that sensory impulses "determine" choice for human beings, according to laws of nature. For in published texts, as we saw earlier in this chapter, he seems to have denied that human free choice is determined by sensible impulses. He wrote that human choice can be "*affected* but not *determined*" by them. And in this very lecture, in fact, just a few paragraphs later, he said it again: "Man can only be affected by the stimulus, never determined to action" (262/17:494). So there seems to be an inconsistency. On the one hand, choice in human beings, when it is "sensitive," is determined, causally, by sensible impulses (*stimuli*) according to the laws of nature. On the other hand, human choice cannot be determined by sense impulses; it can only be "affected."

There is a way to reconcile this apparent inconsistency: a way which seems also to give us clearer insight into what Kant might have meant by the expression "free choice" (*freie Willkür*). Intellectual choice, "higher," free, moral choice, can be equated with "human choice." Sensible and "lower" choice, choice determined by sensible impulses, can be equated with "animal choice." And we can see the human agent as capable of each type of choice. So when we act to satisfy our inclinations, we are acting by animal (sensitive) choice. But when we act morally, determined to action by intellectual motives of reason, we are acting by human (intellectual) choice. Here we must read "choice" not as decision or selection, but as a type of desire, comparable to a wish, but effective in action. A human, "higher" choice so understood cannot therefore be "determined" by sensible impulses. It can be affected by them, however, in the following

---

[49] "We call it a natural cause, or inclination, when, for example, a person is brought by hunger and physical hardship to obey his parents, or to be diligent. Even among animals, these *casuae determinantes* operate to possible ends, for taming them, and man is like them in that respect" (262/27:493).

way. The motive cause of the intellectual incentive that would causally determine free, human choice, can be opposed by, and so can even be defeated by, sensible incentives of inclination. Kant's saying that human free choice *cannot be determined* by sensible impulses would therefore mean that it is not sensibility, not inclination, that determines us to, motivates us to, moral action. And his saying that human choice nevertheless *can be affected* by inclinational impulse would mean that intellectual, moral motivation can be opposed by inclination, and may well be defeated by it.

Consider the following explanation Kant provided on this point: "As a natural being, man can be affected *per stimulum*, though as a free being this means is altogether fruitless. Hence man, insofar as sensory drives are operative upon him, is also quite passive . . . . Conversely, motives occur only insofar as man is considered a free being; they contain his activity. . . ." A bit later Kant concluded: "The stimulus may therefore be called *arbitrium brutum,* and the motive, on the other hand, *arbitrium liberum.*" Note here how he actually collapsed the distinction between the stimulus-incentive and the "animal" choice, on the one hand, and the motive-incentive and the free choice, on the other. The incentive is the cause of choice (2.5), in the sense of effective desire (1.7). So the intellectual incentive is the cause of "higher," intellectual choice, and the sensible incentive is the cause of "lower," animal choice. In some contexts this cause and effect need not even be distinguished. So we can be truly active insofar as our choices are (caused by) intellectual incentives of reason and understanding; and we are passive insofar as our choices are (caused by) sensible incentives. Here, "choice" (*arbitrium*) is not any kind of neutral arbiter among conflicting incentives. *Abritria libera* and *bruta* are, rather, the conflicting incentives.

Would this imply, then, that we are free only when we act morally, whereas when we act in order to satisfy our inclinations we are passive, and so unfree? Not necessarily, I think. If we are moved by, or at least influenced by, an intellectual motive-incentive, then we are free. In this case something determining our so-called "choice" cannot be understood in terms of prior natural causes, according to the law of nature. It does not matter if a stimulus-incentive of inclination also stands in opposition to our intellectual "choice." Nor would it matter if the stimulus-incentive prevails, and causes us to act in order to satisfy the inclination. Freedom of "choice" here is the independence of determination by a natural cause;

the determining influence of the intellectual incentive need not go so far as to cause action, in order for us to be free. So we are still free, in the end, even if we act to satisfy inclination; even if we are so strongly affected by sensible incentives that they overpower our intellectual, "free choice."

This interpretation of Kant's remarks on "human free choice" raises further questions, of course. How, for instance, are we to understand the "freedom" guaranteed by the intellect-based motive—especially if it would be expected to move a human being to act in a world where every event is determined by natural causes, according to laws? We turn next to this important feature of Kant's theory of action, in Chapter 4, where we explain his view on the "two worlds" in which we act.

In this chapter I have responded to an anticipated line of objection to the solution I have offered for the problem and justification and explanation. I presented the views of other commentators who deny an assumption that is central to my solution: the assumption that Kant embraced psychological determinism. I then discussed two passages from his texts that are usually interpreted as denying that actions can be explained by the psychological forces of incentives. In one, Kant wrote that human choices are "*affected* but not *determined*" by impulses. In the other, he wrote that a human being with free choice "cannot be determined to action through any incentive *except sofar as [he] has incorporated it into his maxim*." I have offered both text-based and conceptual arguments showing why these statements should not be read as denying that our free actions can be explained by psychological forces. After these interpretive arguments I then presented a critique of an alternative solution to the problem of justification and explanation. This is the "free-choice solution," which says that actions are not explained by psychological forces, but by the free agent's choice. In arguing against this proposal, I first distinguished two types of choice: "executive" and "elective" choice. The former is the choice to execute action on a recognized justification for action. The latter is the choice between alternative justifications upon which to execute action. I argued that neither type of choice would be explanatory. Part of my argument appealed to Kant's well-known agnosticism about actions' "moral worth." He claimed, quite plausibly it seems to me, that when we freely choose between alternative justifications for the same action, we can never know which one really explains our action. I think this implies that something other than our free choice would be, as he put it, "the real determining cause of the will.'' As the chapter concluded we saw how Kant would characterize the freedom of "human choice," and the passivity of "animal choice," in terms of the freedom and passivity of the incentives that would cause them. Free choice (*freie Willkür*) seems not to be, in his view, a mental power by which we decide between competing incentives or reasons for action.

4

Acting in Two Worlds

Kant's wider philosophy employs what is called a "transcendental distinction," between things as they appear in human experience, and as they are in themselves. He sometimes presented this distinction as the basis for distinguishing between two worlds. One would be the familiar *sensible world*, where things appear under the conditions of space and time. The other would be an *intellectual* or *intelligible world*, where things are thought to exist apart from those conditions.

This chapter shows how Kant's transcendental distinction enables us to think of our actions as both psychologically determined, and as free. Everything we do here in the sensible world is causally determined through psychological forces. But if we belong to an intelligible world, our actions there would be free of all prior, causal determination. For there we would not act in time. And if everything we do here is an appearance of what we do there, then our actions here are both causally determined and free. This "two-worlds" interpretation of Kant's transcendental distinction makes it possible to answer critics of the solution that I have proposed for the problem of justification and explanation: critics who say that the solution eliminates our freedom of choice. We can assume that our actions in this world are explained by the psychological forces of incentives; that our choices to act one way rather than another are caused by our strongest desires: by the relative strengths of incentive forces. Yet we need not deny that we act freely, or that we are morally responsible for what we do.

This is a controversial interpretation of Kant's philosophy, however. To defend it here I shall begin by exploring some of the background assumptions of his "rational cosmology." This will require introducing the special concept of a "world," and showing how the sensible world of appearances can be distinguished from the intelligible world of things in themselves. From there I'll proceed to explain how Kant understood the compatibility of acting freely in the intelligible world, with the causal determinism of actions in the sensible world. But this will raise several questions: questions about the legitimacy of the idea of timeless action or causation, especially in Kant's own philosophy; and questions about personal identity, or about the relation between ourselves as subject to determinism by psychological forces, and ourselves as acting freely in the intelligible world. These and some related issues will be subjects of the later sections of the chapter.

4.1 Causation in Time

The main argument of the chapter should begin with an explanation of the importance, in Kant's view, of causal determination for all events occurring in time. As we shall see below, that importance comes roughly to this: that without strict and thoroughgoing causal determination among events in the sequence of time, there would be no sequence of time.

Kant's transcendental distinction between things as they appear and as they are in themselves, or between *phenomena* and *noumena,* is crucial for understanding his theory of freedom. He claimed that those who ignore this distinction, and mistake appearances for things in themselves, cannot hope to solve the problem of freedom and determinism.[1] If they do not recognize the transcendental distinction they will face the following dilemma: either our actions are necessary effects of prior causes, and so, given the antecedent states of the world we could not have done otherwise; or, our actions are lawless events, unconnected to any prior conditions of the agent or the world, and may well initiate a whole new world whenever they occur.[2]

As Kant explained, it is not possible to think of something's happening without thinking of a prior time. This is because a happening is a change, and it is not possible to think of a change without thinking about a prior

---

[1] Cf. *Pure Reason,* A536/B564; and *Practical Reason,* 78–80/5:94. See also *Lectures on Metaphysics,* 412/28:773.

[2] One might imagine a middle position: many actions and events are determined through causal laws, but some are not. The difficulty here will lie in specifying the determination of even the supposedly lawful actions and events. Unless we can be confident that every action and event is causally determined, we have no way of knowing whether the many that appear to be so determined really are. In other words, if we cannot rule out chance occurrences in the empirical world, then we cannot be confident that ice, which always melts above $0°C$, does so according to law or always just by chance.

time. Nor can we think about a prior time without imagining something happening in it. We cannot think of an empty time (cf. *Pure Reason*, A191–2/B236–7). Kant took this to mean that all events, including our everyday actions, not only *occur* in time, but must also be *connected* with events in prior time. The alternative to this idea is to think of events or actions as if what preceded them is unrelated, and makes no difference to their occurrence. But to think this way, Kant supposed, would be to think of events as changes in things in themselves.[3] And that would make it impossible to discover how any such things could be connected as causes and effects.

Here we have in mind a view of events in time that can be attributed to Hume. He argued that no object, *A*, considered just in itself, could stand in any "necessary connection" with any subsequent object, *B*. That is, considering *A* just in itself, the later occurrence of *B* is neither called for, nor do we have any reason to expect it. So considering them as things in themselves, *B* could have occurred in the world in exactly the same way even if *A* had not occurred. As Hume saw it, when we recognize cause-effect connections between things, we are not recognizing anything about the things *in themselves*. We are noticing instead nothing other than connections between them *in ourselves*. We are noticing only connections in our own thinking, which are made possible through repeated experience and habituation. This means that from Hume's point of view we are fortunate that there are so many regular, habituating sequences of objects in our experience. Because there have been so many objectively unconnected events occurring in recognizable sequences, we have formed the habit of expecting every event to have a cause. This, according to Hume, is "Why a Cause is Always Necessary."[4] Without so much recognizable regularity we might have been able to see only very few things as connected in causal relations. And then we would have had almost no disposition to believe that events happening in our experience are always caused.

Kant's transcendental distinction between appearances and things in themselves allows us to see connections between things in the world

---

[3] Kant himself would not think of events or objects in time as things in themselves, because he understood time in such a way that events or objects in time can be nothing other than appearances. But those who mistake appearances for things in themselves *do* see things occurring in time as things in themselves.

[4] *Treatise*, 1.4.3; see also Lorne Falkenstein, "Hume's Answer to Kant," *Noûs* 32 (1998): 331–60.

differently. For he thought a cause would be necessary for every event, even if human beings were not able to recognize so much regularity in the world. His view was that the way human understanding works, we are required to understand each event in the worlds as causally determined by some prior event, in accordance with a law. This holds for human actions as well, *deeds* included. We are required to understand everything that happens in the world as causally connected with a prior event because there is no other way to see their sequence as belonging to the same course of time, and so to the same world.

Suppose, for instance, that what we imagine to be an earlier state of a person, A, could be followed immediately by an action, B, but not through any causal connection. Assume that the person's action, B, was uncaused, so that it could have been otherwise, even though its immediately preceding condition, A, had remained exactly the same. If this were so, then A and B could belong to, and might well have to belong to, different worlds. During the interval we imagine between A and B, the world in which A occurred could have been annihilated, and replaced by a world that begins with B.[5] A could have been the last event in the time-series of one world, and B the first event in the time-series of some other world.

To this point it might be objected that there simply can be no endings or beginnings in time-series. Therefore, if states A and B of an object or a person are events, they must belong to the same series of time, even if they may lack any causal connection. So it is ridiculous to think, it may be said, that the occurrence of an action, B, that is not causally necessitated by a prior condition of the agent, A, could entail the end of one world and the beginning of another.

There is something right about this objection, but we can respond to it here with an explanation similar to the one provided above. We can replace events A and B with the different moments in time at which they occur. Supposing that t_A and t_B are different moments, what could possibly join them in the same series of time? What third thing could require us to take t_A and t_B as parts of one series? The only answer we can have for this question, as Kant saw it, is that this third thing is the law-governed, causal connection between events A and B occurring at t_A

---

[5] I say "the interval we *imagine* between A and B," because without assuming the continuity of the same time-series in which both occur, there could be no interval of time between them (cf. *Pure Reason*, A201/B246).

and t_B. Connection by causal laws is the common element that accounts for the continuity even of the time-series in which moments t_A and t_B occur. Hence, it also accounts for the temporal continuity of the world in which they occur.[6] In other words, we have no criterion for a sequence of events occurring in the same world, in the same course of time, apart from their connection through causal laws governing events in the same series of time. It may seem easy to conceive of some sequence of events occurring without being causally connected. But Kant's view would be that we cannot think of those events in a temporal sequence, and so as events in the same world, unless we see them as joined by something. The joining of events in time is the work of causal laws.[7] That is why the relation of causal connection has been aptly called "the cement of the universe."[8]

4.2 Cause and World

The preceding account of Kant's view of causation in time enables us to draw a conclusion about human action. It is that assuming human beings' freely chosen actions are "underdetermined" by their prior psychological conditions implies that worlds could end and begin with every free choice. That seems like a drastic and absurd consequence of admitting freedom of choice, however. Why couldn't the temporal continuity of the world, and so the sequence of time itself, be preserved just so long as *some* series of its events unfolds in a continuous causal sequence? Why wouldn't it be sufficient for preserving the world's temporal continuity that successive states of physical substances are strictly determined by causal laws? That

---

    [6] Kant wrote: Now if it is a necessary law of our sensibility, thus a *formal condition* of all perceptions, that the preceding time necessarily determines the following time (in that I cannot arrive at the following time except by passing through the preceding one), then it is also an indispensable *law of the empirical representation* of the temporal series that the appearances of the past time [causally] determine every existence in the following time, and that these, as occurrences, do not take place except insofar as the former [causally] determine their existence in time, i.e., establish it in accordance with a [causal] rule. *For only in the appearances can we empirically cognize this continuity of the connection* of times.   (*Pure Reason*, A199/B244)

    [7] This is a point taken from critical thinking about Humean empiricism. It is standardly put this way: that a sequence of impressions is not the impression of a sequence. In other words, there is more in the idea of a sequence than the events following in the sequence. It is for this reason posed as a challenge to Humean empiricism to explain the idea of a sequence.

    [8] See J. L. Mackie, *The Cement of the Universe* (Oxford: Clarendon Press, 1974).

way, the free actions of human beings could belong to the same, continuing world without being set in the causal cement of the universe.

This prospect is ruled out, in part, by Kant's concept of a "world." He defined a world as a whole of substances, in which each part stands in interaction ("community," "commerce") with every other part.[9] He also recognized mental substances as parts of the empirical world, and therefore as interacting with the world's physical substances.[10] Consequently, he could not exempt the psychological states of minds from the same rule of law that governs physical events.[11]

It is helpful in understanding Kant's conception of a world to note that God and creation do not together constitute a world. This is because the causal relation between them is not reciprocal: the created world does not affect the creator (cf. *Lectures on Metaphysics*, 20/28:196). Substances constitute a world just insofar as each participates in the same community, where "participating" means making a difference for every other substance in the world. In any world we can think of, therefore, what Kant called a "ground-consequence" relation holds between each and every coexisting substance. Each, as a ground, makes some difference or "determination," as a consequence, for every other substance. This principle applies equally well for both material and mental substances. And the connections between grounds and consequences here are causal. The idea is that a substance participates in a world community by making some difference for every other substance, in accordance with causal laws. So not only are causal laws necessary for the unity of a time sequence, they are necessary also for the unity of a world.

The same world cannot therefore accommodate a series of causally determined events, plus a number of causally underdetermined, "free"

---

[9] Cf. *Lectures on Metaphysics*, 19–21/28:195–7; 207–11/29:849–54.

[10] Kant accepted substance-dualism in his metaphysics of the phenomenal world. He addressed the Cartesian problem of mind–body interaction ("community") by assuming that substances actively cause their determinations, or their accidents; including material substances. He held that a physical substance is extended in space not by definition, as Descartes assumed, but by exercising its own power to extend itself. Every material and mental substance, by exercising its own power, directly or indirectly affects every other coexisting substance in the world. Phenomenal minds, mental substances, must be causally connected with all physical substances if mind and body are to belong to the same world. (See ibid., 90–1/28:280, 273/29:908, 386/28:685, 399/28:758, 477/29:1008.)

[11] Kant did not assume, though it may have been open to him to do so, that the psychological attributes of phenomenal minds are mere epiphenomena, and so not part of the causal interaction of mind and body. The strongest evidence that he did not assume this is his definition of the faculty of desire in terms of the concept of causality (1.5), and his insistence on the causal efficacy of incentives (2.4, and 3.6).

actions that, given their antecedent conditions, could still have been otherwise. The dilemma that would arise if we think otherwise is this: that the free actions we might suppose to be underdetermined by the causal series of the world will either make a difference in that series, or they will not. But if they do, then the continuity of that world-series will be threatened: its cement will crumble if human actions make "contra-causal" differences, or differences in violation of causal laws. Or if they do not, that is, if human actions do not make any difference in the temporal sequence of the physical world, then they must belong to a different world.[12]

Finding neither horn of this dilemma acceptable, Kant wholeheartedly embraced what is usually called "determinism" in his theory of action.[13] It is the idea that a human action in the temporal sequence of experience is an event causally connected with other, prior events, in such a way that the action could have been different only if other, prior events had been different. Kant assumed that human actions that would not be bound by causal laws—actions whose occurrences would not be causally necessitated by antecedent psychological conditions of the agent—simply cannot belong to the empirical world-series (cf. *Pure Reason,* A544/B572). Yet free actions could, he supposed, belong to a different, "noumenal" world, of things in themselves. That is why Kant insisted that only by distinguishing between a world of things in themselves and a world of appearances can we preserve the prospect of free actions not causally determined by prior events. But understanding how our free actions might occur in a world apart from this world, and yet *make a difference* in this world, is the central difficulty of his theory of freedom. It is, understandably, the main reason Kant's critics reject his theory of freedom and attempt to make do with alternatives. It is probably also the main reason many otherwise sympathetic interpreters have misconstrued his theory of freedom, and with it, his theory of action.

At first it seems bizarre to suggest that our free, causally undetermined actions belong to a different world from the one we experience. It can even seem bizarre to entertain the prospect of there being more than one world.[14] But Kant's argument for multiple worlds turns on the ideality

---

[12] The difference here is not between the empirical world and a non-empirical world, but between a physical empirical world and a psychological empirical world.

[13] Cf. *Lectures on Metaphysics,* 489–90/29:1021.

[14] For Kant's thinking on multiple worlds see Immanuel Kant, *On the Form and Principles of the Sensible and Intelligible World* [*Inaugural Dissertation*], in *Theoretical Philosophy, 1755–1770,* trans. and ed.

of space and time. Multiple worlds cannot coexist in space, since such worlds, like the planets, would properly count only as causally connected parts of a larger, cosmological whole: solar system, galaxy, universe. The prospect of worlds succeeding one another in the course of one time-series should be impossible also, for similar reasons. If they belong to the same series of time then they will have to be connected by common causal laws. They will belong to the same developing, cosmological whole. The unities of space and time connect everything that can appear in them, and hence they preclude the possibility of there being more than one space-time world. But space and time need not be thought of as objective containers of everything that can exist. They can instead be what Kant called "formal conditions" of things as they appear to our sense experience. When space and time are seen in this way, then their unities preclude only the possibility of there being more than one world of appearance.[15] They do not cancel the prospect of there being other worlds that do not appear in space and time: such as the world Kant called "noumenal" or "intelligible." If actions appearing in the empirical world must be without exception the necessary effects of prior causes, this need not be the case for actions in the intelligible world. In such a world, it would be conceivable for agents to act independently of any prior conditions that would be causally determining.

4.3 Noumenal Action

How then shall we understand the prospect of our freely acting in a world apart from the world we experience? In order to make this easier to imagine, we may begin by assuming that everything experienced in space and time has a counterpart entity in a world of things in themselves. (We shall see later why we must give up this assumption. But it can be a useful hypothesis at the beginning.) We may imagine also that this world of appearances and that world of things in themselves are related roughly in

David Walford and Ralf Meerbote (Cambridge: Cambridge University Press, 1992), 402–5/2:407–10; cf. also *Lectures on Metaphysics*, 210–11/29:853–4.

[15] "Only one sensible world is possible, and two times cannot take place together, for there is only one space and one time, but both can make up the ground of the interaction of all substances in the sensible world, so again, only one sensible world is possible" (*Lectures on Metaphysics*, 211/29:854).

the way the world of shadow images appearing on the cave wall in Plato's allegory is related to the world of the real objects that cast the shadows. The prisoners confined to the cave in Plato's allegory think the objects in the projected shadow-world they perceive are causally related to one another. But their keepers behind them understand that the things that cast the shadows on the cave wall are the true relata of the shadowy cause-effect relations appearing to the prisoners.

This allegory complicates our thinking about causation, however. It presents for our consideration causal relations among objects casting shadows, causal relations between those objects and their shadows, and, from the prisoners' perspective, causal relations among those shadows. By comparison, in Kant's two-worlds metaphysics we may think of causal relations holding among things in themselves in the noumenal world, between those things and their appearances in the sensible world, and lastly, among those appearances. The latter are supposed to be the causal relations of our everyday, space-time experience. The causal relations of things in the noumenal world would not require space and time, of course. We may suppose nevertheless that each thing in itself *acts* in the noumenal world, insofar as its membership in that community implies its making a difference there for everything else.

Our first quotation from Kant, in Chapter 1, contained his definition of action in general as "the determination of the power of a substance as a cause of a certain accident" (1.1). This definition would apply to human beings and other things acting in the world of space and time, as well as to all the substances of an intelligible world. Substances, whether noumenal or phenomenal, affect other substances existing in the world to which they belong by altering or "determining" differences in their accidents. In doing this they *act,* according to Kant's theory of action.[16]

It follows that belonging to a noumenal world would imply acting, as well as acting independently of the conditions of space and time. A noumenal substance does not, therefore, act consequent upon any temporally prior actions of other substances. So the communal activity of noumenal substances is not interaction in the sense of action and subsequent reaction. It is rather activity as mutual determination, where the action of each noumenal agent affects the action of every other. Accordingly, the

---

[16] See *Lectures on Metaphysics,* 327–9/28:562–5.

substances in the noumenal world would be active as well as passive.[17] Each would be active in the exercise of its power(s). But each is also passive in regard to the resistance or hindrance posed by the other's exercise of power(s). By analogy, I am active in lifting a heavy weight. But I am at the same time passive in not being able to raise it over my head. I exert my power on the weight, as the weight exerts its power on me. It is not that I act on the weight and then suffer from its subsequent response to my lifting it. It is rather that our relation is one of mutual causal determination, in which we are together both active and passive.

The noumenal world of things in themselves would be the "ground" of appearances in our phenomenal world. For this reason, events in the space-time world of experience would be dependent upon differences made by things in themselves, in the noumenal world. But note that there would be no causal relations going back the other way. The reason why God is not a member of the created world, it will be recalled, is that God and the world do not stand in the relation of causal interaction. The relation between the noumenal world and the world of appearance is similar. We may suppose that substances in the noumenal world are causally responsible for their appearances in the sensible world, but without being affected by their appearances. That is why we are entitled to distinguish the noumenal *world* from the phenomenal *world*.

Supposing therefore that we are free in our actions in a noumenal world, the difference we make by acting freely there can appear in this world as so many free actions causally determined in time. In this way, Kant's theory of freedom allows us to attribute both freedom and causal determination to our actions in this world.

4.4 Timeless Causation

Critics have charged that as interesting as this account of the possibility of human freedom may be, it cannot really have been Kant's; or if it was, it should not have been. Beginning with this section I devote the rest of this chapter to considering several objections likely to be raised against this

---

[17] "Every substance is active insofar as its accidents inhere, but also passive, insofar as they inhere through an external power, this is not self-contradictory" (ibid., 181/29:823).

account of the freedom of human actions. Some of these objections have been posed even by writers sympathetic to Kant's wider philosophy.

A familiar line of critique is that talk of actions or causes in a noumenal world runs counter to Kant's own conception of causality, which is applicable only to objects appearing in time. As is sometimes pointed out, the categories of the understanding in Kant's system, including the relational categories of *substance, cause* and *community*, are legitimately employed only under temporal conditions. So this restriction seems to make the foregoing interpretation of his theory of freedom illegitimate on two counts. First, insofar as it assumes that things in themselves are *substantial*, and enter into *causal* and *communal* relations, this interpretation would set them in temporal relations with one another, which is absurd. Second, by assuming that things in themselves cause their appearances to us in the world of sense it supposes that they would operate on our senses in time, which is likewise absurd.

Understanding the relation between phenomena and noumena, between appearances and things in themselves, has been an obstacle to acceptance of transcendental idealism since critics first reacted to Kant's *Critique of Pure Reason*.[18] Here we cannot make very much headway in addressing the sizeable critical literature on this topic.[19] But we can nevertheless raise a few points suggesting that Kant's usual characterization of noumena and phenomena as causally related is defensible. The first point is that although he denied that the categories are applicable for *knowing* anything apart from space and time, he nevertheless acknowledged the "transcendental significance" of these concepts.[20] He allowed, that is, that we can at least

[18] For simplicity's sake, I here equate phenomena and noumena with appearances and things in themselves. For arguments against this equation see Arthur W. Collins, *Possible Experience* (Berkeley, CA: University of California Press, 1999), 26–30.

[19] For a good start on some of this literature see Westphal, "Noumenal Causality Reconsidered"; and Lucy Allais, "Kant's One World: Interpreting 'Transcendental Idealism,'" *British Journal for the History of Philosophy* 12 (2004): 655–84.

[20] "It may therefore be advisable to express ourselves thus: The pure categories, without formal conditions of sensibility, have merely transcendental significance, but are not of any transcendental use...." "[T]hey do not have any use at all if they are separated from all sensibility...rather they are merely the pure form of the use of the understanding in regard to objects in general and of thinking, yet without any sort of object being able to be thought or determined through them alone" (*Pure Reason*, A248/B305, cf. also A254/B309). But see also the second *Critique*, where Kant argues explicitly that application of the categories can be extended to things in themselves for practical purposes in, "On the Warrant of Pure Reason in Its Practical Use to an Extension which is not Possible to It in Its Speculative Use," *Practical Reason*, 44–50/5:55–8.

think of something that is not an appearance in space and time as a *substance* and a *cause* in a world *community*.[21] What we cannot do is know "determinate" properties of noumenal substances, including any causal properties (cf. *Pure Reason*, A295–6/B351–3).

Kant's technical use of "determinate" and "determination" is relevant here. He once explained in a lecture that "Determination is [the application of] a synthetic predicate. E.g. a body is extended. It is not yet determined by this. A learned human being is determined, for learnedness does not lie in the concept of a human being."[22] Following this use of the adjective "determinate," Kant's denial that we can know any determinate properties of things in themselves does not mean that we cannot speak intelligibly about them through analytic judgments. In his system we are allowed to claim that an atemporal thing in itself is the cause of its appearance in the temporal world. We just have to bear in mind that in doing so we understand the thing in itself as nothing more than the whatever-it-is, the "transcendental object = x," that is the cause of the appearance. Kant allowed such "pure" or "transcendental" uses of the categories as this when he wrote: "Now through [the use of] a pure category, in which abstraction is made from any condition of sensible intuition[, including time,] . . . no object is determined, rather only the thought of an object in general is expressed. . . ." (*Pure Reason*, A247/B304). In describing a thing in itself as causing the appearance of a table or a chair we therefore refer merely to an "object in general." It is the whatever-it-is that we think of as the cause, without "determining" anything about it. Like saying that a body is extended, saying that the noumenal counterpart of the table *causes* its appearance in sensation adds nothing more than we already think in conceiving of it as the table's noumenal counterpart.

As a consequence of this point we must now withdraw an assumption invoked above for purposes of illustration. We assumed earlier that each object in the world of appearance would have its counterpart thing in itself in the noumenal world. But it must be acknowledged now that we are incapable of knowing whether this would be so. We can know that space

---

[21] "To *think* of an object and to *cognize* it are . . . not the same. For two components belong to cognition: first, the concept, through which an object is thought at all (the category), and second, the intuition, through which it is given; for if an intuition corresponding to the concept could not be given at all, then it would be a thought as far as its form is concerned, but without any object. . . ." (*Pure Reason*, B146).

[22] *Lectures on Metaphysics*, 173/29:819; cf. also *Pure Reason*, A598/B626.

and time are the forms of human perceptual experience. So we can know
that anything experienced by human beings is an appearance in space and
time of something not known through those forms of perception, and so is
not part of the world of space and time. But it would be an unjustifiable,
"determinate" use of the category of cause to say that the appearance of the
table is caused by the noumenal table, and that the appearance of the chair
is caused by the noumenal chair. We can distinguish the table from the
chair as appearances. But since we are permitted to think of the noumenal
cause of each appearance only indeterminately, we cannot, strictly speaking,
distinguish the noumenal causes of these appearances. The whatever-it-is
that we think of as causing the appearance of the table might be different
from the cause of the appearance of the chair, or it might be the same. We
would need more knowledge of the noumenal world than Kant's system
allows us in order to distinguish or identify these causes. For this reason,
employment of categories like *substance* and *cause* outside the appearance-
world should not ordinarily allow us to distinguish any specific noumenal
substances as causes of this world's objects or events. Since we cannot make
any determinate, numerical causal judgments about noumena, moreover,
we should never be justified in thinking that there is even more than one
noumenal cause of all phenomena. Noumenal solipsism, which Kant called
"metaphysical egoism," is an option here.[23] So also is Spinozism. Both of
these hypotheses would deny the existence of a noumenal *world*. As long as
we do not venture out of what Kant called speculative philosophy, we can
never justifiably say whether or not I myself, as a noumenon, am causally
responsible for the entire world of appearance. We can never confidently
affirm the existence of a noumenal world. Convincing arguments against
noumenal solipsism, and for free actions in a noumenal world, can come
from practical philosophy alone.

We can say then, in summary, that Kant's transcendental idealism allows
meaningful application of categories like *substance, cause*, and *community*
apart from conditions of space and time. But unless we are operating
under assumptions of practical philosophy, in ways to be identified in what
follows, we are not justified in using the categories for any determinate,

---

[23] Wolff raises an objection to Kant's practical philosophy that presupposes solipsism in speculative
philosophy, see Robert Paul Wolff, "Remarks on the Relation of the Critique of Pure Reason to
Kant's Ethical Theory," in Bernard den Ouden and Marcia Moen, eds., *New Essays on Kant* (New
York: Peter Lang, 1987), 139–53.

synthetic judgments about things in themselves. Kant's system allows us to think of things in themselves as noumenal causes of appearances in this world.[24] It allows us also to think of noumenal substances as joining with and affecting other members of a noumenal world community, provided we have grounds for thinking there is one. But time need not be presumed to be a feature of a noumenal world just because it is a community of substances in causal interaction. Nor need there be any interval of time, nor even any simultaneity, between a noumenal thing's action in the intelligible world and its appearance to human beings in the world of sense experience.

4.5 Personal Identity

So far we have seen how the two worlds of Kant's wider philosophy can accommodate the prospect that human actions are both free and subject to psychological determinism. But in order to solve the problem of freedom and determinism in a manner suitable for making reasonable judgments of praise and blame, something more needs to be added. Kant's theory of freedom as represented here must also confirm that we act as the same, self-identical agent in each of the two worlds. It must show, that is, that each of us appearing as an agent in the world of experience bears a suitable relation of identity with a freely acting, noumenal agent. This stage of Kant's solution to the problem of human freedom surfaced in his *Groundwork of the Metaphysics of Morals* (cf. 55–8/4:450–3), and especially in the *Critique*

---

[24] Hanna argues against the two-worlds or metaphysical reading of Kant's transcendental distinction on the basis of its presupposition that our experiences would have to have both noumenal and phenomenal causes (see *Kant, Science and Human Nature,* 422–3). To his mind this entails causal overdetermination, which is, he says, "rationally unacceptable." From the context of his argument it seems that he may be confusing the distinction between mental and physical causation, both in time, with the distinction between timeless noumenal and temporal phenomenal causation. In any case, his objection is that on the two-worlds interpretation, things in the noumenal world are assumed to cause our experiences of them; and yet we must also trace the causes of those experiences to the phenomena of the empirical world. So there are evidently two causes for any experience. But we can reply to this objection by pointing out that the relation of causal overdetermination requires a plurality of efficient causes, *each of which would be by itself sufficient for the same effect.* Yet the two-worlds interpretation does not say that a noumenon is by itself causally sufficient for an appearance that is attributable also to a by-itself causally sufficient phenomenon. In the second *Critique,* Kant points out that it is a contradiction to say even that God creates phenomenal effects (appearances) through his noumenal causality (see 86/5:102). In the first *Critique* he presents noumenal and empirical causality as related in this way: the effect of a noumenal cause is not an empirical object, but empirical *causality* (see A544/B572).

of Practical Reason (cf. 41–2/5:47). But before we can present a complete account of his solution to the problem of noumenal-phenomenal personal identity, one remaining, cosmological point must be mentioned.

A plausible solution to the metaphysical problem of freedom and determinism could present the phenomenal world as grounded in, caused by, a community of active, noumenal things in themselves. Yet we can also imagine the existence of a plurality of things in themselves that do not interact to form a world community. This shows that something must be added to our bare conception of things in themselves if they are to be conceived as members of a community of interacting substances. At the very least, some cosmological principle of unity, analogous to the space-time of the phenomenal world, would be required in order for the plurality of noumena we are imagining to form a community.[25]

This principle can be derived, in Kant's view, from the concept of the creator of the noumenal world. He explained that noumenal substances are capable of interacting to form a world because of their common dependence upon their creator. Just as, in the phenomenal world, there is one space-time that makes it possible for everything here to be causally related, so in the noumenal world there is a divine condition of its unity. "Every world," Kant said in a lecture, "presupposes a primordial being, for no interaction is possible except insofar as they are all there through One."[26] So if we assume that the phenomenal world is the appearance of a noumenal *world,* then we seem committed to the existence of three classes of substances or entities: God; the world of created things in themselves; and the appearing substances of the phenomenal world. It is possible, moreover, that God created the things in themselves interacting in the noumenal world in such a way that we human beings appearing in the phenomenal world would be personally identical with noumenal counterparts. If we assume that God did this, then we can also assume that our phenomenal actions, though they are caused by psychological forces, are nevertheless appearances of what we ourselves

---

[25] A charge Kant raised against Christian Wolff is that mere existence of objects is not enough to ground their interaction; see *Lectures on Metaphysics,* 34/28:212–13. In one place Kant treats Newtonian space as a suitable, phenomenal analog for noumenal space: "The concept of space accomplishes in the sensible world what the divine omnipresence does in the noumenal world, and one can perhaps call [space] as it were a phenomenon of the divine omnipresence. Perhaps God wanted thereby to make his omnipresence sensibly cognizable to us. Newton called it the seat of the senses [*sensorium*] of the divine omnipresence" (ibid., 236/29:866). Cf. also Westphal, "Noumenal Causality Reconsidered," 231.

[26] *Lectures on Metaphysics,* 35/28:213, see also 236/29:866.

do freely in the noumenal world.[27] Making the concept of freedom *practically* adequate in this way, for judgments of moral responsibility, requires making theological assumptions similar to these. And speculative metaphysics, which cannot apply its concepts in any determinate manner to the noumenal world, is in no position to deny them.

Kant gave two kinds of practical arguments, which may ultimately collapse into one, for thinking that phenomenal human beings may be personally identical with freely acting noumenal counterparts. One is an argument from "I," the pronoun of self-identity; another is an argument from practical rationality. The self or soul participating in a noumenal world community would be a created being, since the community of which it is a member would have to be grounded in some primordial being that would account for its unity. This, however, would naturally raise a question about the freedom of a created, noumenal soul. "If it is assumed that the soul has a cause, that it is a dependent being, is an effect of another, then the question is here: whether absolute spontaneity can be attributed to the soul, as a being which has a cause."[28] We cannot conceive how a thing could be created by another and yet remain absolutely free in its actions. But, as Kant pointed out, neither can we say it is impossible. What justifies us in thinking the created soul is free, he argued, is the "I think," more specifically, the "I do." In notes from a metaphysics lecture we read: "I am conscious to myself that I can say: I do; therefore I am conscious of [the absence of causal] determination in me, and thus I act *absolutely freely*. Were I not free, but rather only a means by which the other does something immediately in me, that I do, then I could not say: I do."[29]

---

[27] This need not mean that someone's telling a lie to his business partner on Monday would be the appearance of his freely telling a lie to his partner in the noumenal world. It could be instead just that something he freely does in the noumenal world makes its appearance here, in the phenomenal world, in the lie told on Monday.

[28] Ibid., 80–1/28:268; cf. also *Practical Reason*, 84–6/5:100–3.

[29] *Lectures on Metaphysics*, 81/28:269. This appears to be the only record of Kant's arguing for freedom from the ability to say "I do." He may have later recognized the argument as question-begging, since what is at issue is nothing more than whether in saying "I do" we are deluded. It seems an equally strong argument to say that I must be free because I am conscious of "feeling free"; to which Spinoza famously responded by saying that a rock in flight would feel the same if it were conscious. Later, Kant argued that creation does not make us mere means of divine causality, a view identified with Spinozism, because God creates only noumena; and these, in turn, would be causally responsible for their actions as appearances in the sensible world (see *Practical Reason*, 85–6/5:102).

This classroom argument, whatever its merits, implies that the phenomenal agent who can consciously say "I do" must be self-identical with a noumenal agent acting independently of both divine and natural causal determination.

Following immediately upon this argument for the freedom of the created soul is another one, or possibly an extension of the same argument. It emphasizes rational imperatives as evidence for freedom: "there are such imperatives according to which I should do something; therefore all practical propositions, problematic as well as pragmatic and moral, must presuppose a freedom in me; consequently I must be the *first cause* of all [my] actions" (*Lectures on Metaphysics,* 82/28:269). This line of argument is familiar from the work of recent Kantian writers.[30] It suggests that to the extent that our phenomenal actions can be justified (and explained) by practical reasoning, we must be self-identical with an agent enjoying noumenal freedom. It suggests, in other words, that if the justifying imperatives of practical reasoning are relevant for our conduct, then we are the same as a noumenal agent who acts as a *"first cause."* This is so even if, as merely phenomenal agents, we cannot be the first causes of anything.

The difference made by practical reason in the self-consciousness and conduct of phenomenal human beings would be what justifies us, in practical philosophy, in attributing the actions of each one to a unique, self-identical agent acting freely in the noumenal world. Again, speculative philosophy would overstep its limits in any attempt to repudiate this practical justification of the noumenal freedom of human agents. It would have to apply concepts like *substance* and *cause* determinately in order to do so. There is no contradiction in the idea that a noumenal agent identical to me is the cause of my actions as appearances in this, phenomenal world. Consequently, to show that this is not the case, speculative philosophy would have to demonstrate that there is no identity relation between a noumenal substance and myself as a phenomenal being. And it cannot do this. Speculative philosophy cannot employ the category of *substance* in the required, determinate way apart from the conditions of space and time.

---

[30] See for example Korsgaard, *Creating the Kingdom of Ends,* 377–8.

4.6 Metaphysical Egoism

But do we have any practical grounds for thinking there is a noumenal *world*? Suppose we concede to Kant that there is a difference between appearances and things in themselves. Still, if our knowledge cannot extend beyond appearances, then why should we think there is a plurality of things in themselves united in a world community? And if it must be granted, for practical purposes, that I am personally identical with a noumenal agent, then what grounds do I have for thinking there is anything noumenal other than myself? The fact that there appear to be causal agents different from myself does not establish anything about the noumenal basis of those appearances. So it does not convince me that ultimately, there is something other than I, who say "I do."

This is the position Kant labeled "metaphysical egoism." There are no grounds for believing it, although we should be able to find grounds for rejecting it. "I cannot refute the egoist by experience," Kant said, "for this instructs us immediately only of our own existence." It will therefore be necessary to respond to the challenge of egoism with what he called "moral proofs." His example of such a proof was: "the human being is limited, thus contingent. Accordingly he must have a cause.... Thus it cannot be assumed that one is here all alone" (*Lectures on Metaphysics, 226/29:927–8*). The strength of this argument depends upon the strength of the grounds for believing that one is finite and contingent, and these, if we are honest, seem rather strong. They include the undeniable fact that things in the world of experience do not always turn out the way we want them to.

Closely related to the hypothesis of egoism is the doctrine Kant called "empirical idealism." This idealism, familiar from Berkeley, stops short of egoism by conceding the reality of minds and agents other than oneself. This idealist says that there are other minds, but no "bodies," no things outside minds to which our experiences of tables and chairs, for example, correspond. The reason this view is presently of interest to us is that Kant argued against it, and believed that the argument he offered would also refute egoism.[31] By showing grounds for believing, against the idealist, that some objects of experience are outside the mind, Kant supposed he had

---

[31] See *Lectures on Metaphysics*, 382–3/28:680–1; 410–11/28:771–2.

demonstrated that the egoist must concede the reality of something other than himself.

His refutation of Berkeley's idealism works this way: it shows that we cannot have confidence in our enduring existence without having confidence in the existence of something (spatially) external to us (see *Pure Reason*, B274–9). The key premise is that time is one-dimensional. It has no "breadth," as Kant said (*Lectures on Metaphysics*, 382/28:681). By this he meant that everything in time appears only in the moment. Hence, if time alone is the formal condition of experience, and if space is illusory, as the idealist thinks, then there could be no experience of any real duration. I could not then consider even myself as really enduring from moment to moment. For to perceive myself as enduring I need an external object I think of as persisting through my subsequent self-experiences. And that object's existence must be determined in some other form besides one-dimensional, moment-to-moment, time. That is, I must ground my endurance as a continuing self upon the endurance of an object that is in space as well as in time. So I contradict myself, Kant suggested, if I believe that I really endure through time, and that there are no objects extended in space outside me. For our present purposes, what interests us here is that the egoist must therefore admit that, since he continues to exist through time, he is not alone in the empirical world.

But it may not be obvious how this proof would defeat *metaphysical* egoism. The egoist might concede that space and time are conditions of the possibility of all things presented in his sensory experience. So he would not doubt that there are empirical objects outside him in space. But he might still believe that he alone is the noumenal reality behind all that appears to him in space and time. So although he must admit there is an empirical world outside him, he may not see why he must admit that the noumenal ground of the entire empirical world is anything other than himself. Still, his belief that he alone is the noumenal reality must be based on the "I do" as he applies it in the empirical world. That is, he could think "I do" in regard to his noumenal self only by analogy from the "I do" of his empirical self, or from the things he does in the world of space and time. And Kant's refutation of idealism shows that he must admit that as a condition of his enduring existence as an empirical agent there must be other things outside him that are equally real, and that affect him. So besides recognizing the noumenal significance of "I do," he must also recognize the noumenal significance of "It does," for some empirical reality outside of himself. And this means that the grounds he would have for believing that he is identical with a noumenal agent are as strong as the grounds he would have for believing in another noumenal agent. If he will take "I do" as proof of his causal responsibility for appearances, then he must take "It does" as proof that he is not the only noumenal agent. Therefore, since he cannot believe he is an enduring agent without recognizing that something outside him is also active, he must believe in a plurality of noumena, and in a noumenal world.[32]

4.7 Panlibertarianism

Let us assume, then, that our actions in the phenomenal world are appearances of what we do freely, independent of prior causal determination, in a noumenal world. Presumably, everything else in the noumenal world would act in the same way: independent of prior causal determination. So why doesn't everything in the phenomenal world enjoy the same freedom we enjoy? Arthur Schopenhauer not only admired Kant's solution to the problem of freedom and determinism, but even embraced "panlibertarianism" as its logical consequence. He wrote:

But the shocking, indeed revolting, thing about this inevitable and irrefutable view of the [phenomenal world as a purposeless, and therefore incomprehensible, play of an eternal, causal necessity] cannot be thoroughly eliminated by any assumption except the one that, as every being in the world is on the one hand phenomenon and is necessarily determined by the laws of the phenomenon, it is on the other hand in itself *will*, indeed absolutely *free will*.[33]

This panlibertarian implication of the theory of noumenal freedom was evidently understood by Kant as well. For he appears to have acknowledged

---

[32] It may be suggested that the only other noumenal agent he needs to acknowledge could be God. He need not then be in a noumenal world, if only he and God exist. Kant has an argument against this, however. It is that God does not cause appearances directly, but creates only things in themselves. Hence, if he is affected by something else in the empirical world, and if this must be taken as evidence that he is not the only noumenon, then besides God and him there must be yet another thing in itself. See *Practical Reason*, 85–6/5:102.

[33] Arthur Schopenhauer, *The World as Will and Representation*, vol. II, trans. E. F. J. Payne (New York: Dover, 1958), 320.

it in a lecture, not long after publication of the *Critique of Pure Reason*. "When we look upon the appearances," he said,

they all fit together according to the laws of nature. But still all appearances also have a transcendental cause which we do not know, e.g., body is composite, i.e., an appearance. But there must still be a transcendental cause that contains the ground from which this appearance arises. This cause is unknown to us; but because it does not belong to the sensible world, it also cannot be determined by other causes in it, consequently it likewise does not stand under the laws of nature or of the sensible world and is thus transcendentally free.   (*Lectures on Metaphysics*, 217–18/29:861)

Not surprisingly, a number of commentators have considered the panlibertarian implication of Kant's theory of freedom to pose a serious problem. Lewis Beck, for example, wrote that "If by 'freedom' we mean noumenal causation and assert that we know no noumena, then there is no justifiable way, in the study of phenomena, to decide that it is permissible in application to some but not others of them to use the concept of freedom."[34]

But the two practical arguments presented just above, for noumenal-phenomenal personal identity, can be enlisted also against the charge of panlibertarianism. One argument suggests that to the substantive difference between the class of phenomenal beings that can think "I do," and the class of those that cannot, there could correspond a difference between noumenal beings who act freely in the noumenal world, and those whose causality in that world is divinely determined. In the passage from Kant's metaphysics lectures quoted just above he seems to have claimed that the noumenal, "transcendental cause" of phenomenal bodies (matter) would be "transcendentally free." So he seems to embrace panlibertarianism. But there he may have meant only that the creator of the noumenal ground of the material bodies that appear in the phenomenal world must be

---

[34] *A Commentary on Kant's Critique of Practical Reason*, 192; cf. 188. Another commentator nicely capsulized this objection to explaining Kantian freedom in terms of timeless, noumenal activity: "Noumenality, however vaguely understood, proves too much if it proves anything"; Ralf Meerbote, "Kant on the Nondeterminate Character of Human Actions," in William L. Harper and Ralf Meerbote, eds., *Kant on Causality, Freedom, and Objectivity* (Minneapolis: University of Minnesota Press, 1984), 138–63 at 160. See also Jonathan Bennett, "Kant's Theory of Freedom" in Allen W. Wood, ed., *Self and Nature in Kant's Philosophy* (Ithaca, NY: Cornell University Press, 1984), 102–12, esp. 106–7; C. D. Broad, *Kant: an Introduction* (Cambridge: University Press, 1978), 277; and Hud Hudson, *Kant's Compatibilism* (Ithaca, NY: Cornell University Press, 1994), 27–8.

transcendentally free; not that the action of every noumenon appearing as a phenomenal body is free.[35]

The other line of argument, from practical reason, suggests that this faculty would be suitable as a distinguishing mark of noumenal freedom. In writing on this point in the first *Critique* Kant emphasized human reason's transcendence of sensible conditions:

In the case of lifeless nature and nature having merely animal life, we find no ground for thinking of any faculty which is other than sensibly conditioned. Yet the human being, who is otherwise acquainted with the whole of nature solely through sense, knows himself also through pure apperception, and indeed in actions and inner determinations which cannot be accounted at all among impressions of sense; he obviously is in one part phenomenon, but in another part, namely in regard to certain faculties, he is a merely intelligible object, because the actions of this object cannot at all be ascribed to the receptivity of sensibility. We call these faculties understanding and reason. . . .[36]

It appears that practical reasoning cannot explain the actions of animals and lifeless phenomenal beings, and so its imperatives are irrelevant to their conduct. This provides a suitable basis for distinguishing phenomenal beings to whom we are entitled to apply the concept of freedom, from all the others.

4.8 Timeless Agency

The idea of timeless noumenal agency has not been well received by Kant's critics. Even some of his more sympathetic commentators have had trouble with the idea. Philosophical objections to the idea that we are timeless free agents in some literal sense abound. At least two forms of this type of objection can be found in recent literature.

---

[35] Statements from Kant's lectures are not as reliable as indicators of his views as statements found in his published texts. This is especially true when a comment from a lecture seems controversial in light of what we find in the published texts *and* when there are no corroborating comments in other lectures. In this case I have not been able to find any other statements in the lectures that corroborate Kant's endorsing panlibertarianism.

[36] A546–7/B574–5. A few sentences later Kant added, "Now that this reason has causality, or that we can at least represent something of the sort in it, is clear from the *imperatives* that we propose as rules to our powers of execution in everything practical."

(a) Timeless agency simply makes no sense. Jonathan Bennett capsulized this objection as follows: "When Kant says of a noumenon that 'nothing happens in it' and yet that it 'of itself begins its effects in the sensible world' (B569), he implies that there is a making-to-begin which is not a happening; and I cannot understand that as anything but a contradiction."[37]

(b) Timeless agency interrupts natural causation. This objection is that timeless, noumenal agency really cannot be made consistent with thoroughgoing determinism in the phenomenal world. For it is incompatible with the way Kant explained causation in the *Critique of Pure Reason*'s Second Analogy of Experience. Ralf Meerbote writes, "According to the Critical Kant, it is a necessary condition of the empirical knowability of temporal, natural events that whatever causes them be itself temporal. Since some of the effects of [free, human agency] are temporal and empirically knowable, this agency must then itself be temporal."[38]

In objection (*a*) Bennett cites a passage from the first *Critique,* where Kant draws a distinction between a noumenon's beginning something in the sensible world *from itself,* and something's beginning *in it.* Here Kant denies that for the noumenal agent something needs to begin *in it,* in order for it to begin something *from itself.* But this is where Bennett objects, not seeing how that can be so. How can a noumenon begin something in the sensible world, *from itself,* without this beginning's counting as a "happening," or as a beginning *in it*?

I think the answer to this question depends on all the assumptions it was necessary to make in order to place the noumenal being in a noumenal world. Some of these assumptions are required by practical philosophy;

[37] "Kant's Theory of Freedom," 102. Cf. also Meerbote: "The notion of [a timeless free choice] is intrinsically puzzling, since it is the notion of something coming about in an agent, but timelessly so. We normally view any coming-about as temporal, and we normally take any reason from which an agent acts to obtain temporally before or during his (temporal) performance." Ralf Meerbote, "Which Freedom?" in Predrag Cicvacki, ed., *Kant's Legacy: Essays in Honor of Lewis White Beck* (Rochester, NY: University of Rochester Press, 2001), 197–225 at 207. Kemp Smith writes about Kant's resolution of the Third Antinomy: "A solution is rendered impossible by the very terms in which he formulates the problem. If the spiritual and the natural be opposed to one another as the timeless and the temporal, and if the natural be further viewed as a unitary system, individual moral freedom is no longer defensible." Norman Kemp Smith, *A Commentary to 'Kant's Critique of Pure Reason'* (New York: Humanities Press, 1962), 518. Cf. also Paton, *Categorical Imperative,* 274.

[38] Meerbote, "Which Freedom?" 208. Here Meerbote credits and cites Hudson, *Kant's Compatibilism,* 25.

like, for instance, the denial of solipsism or "metaphysical egoism." But the question's answer seems to depend also upon the meaning of a "beginning" in the sensible world.[39] That, too, it seems, is a concept that must be determined practically, like the beginning of a new day, or of a life. A sensible beginning would be an event, at the very least. As such it would be connected to prior events by causal laws.[40] Depending on the contents of those laws, the event we presume to mark a phenomenal beginning may come out one way or another, given the same prior conditions. So suppose a phenomenal beginning is a man's decision to quit smoking, made in a moment of calm reflection upon a friend's recent death from lung cancer. The difference he makes by acting as an agent in the noumenal world could determine the contents of the causal laws governing how, as a phenomenal agent, he is affected by the death of his friend. If so, then as a noumenal agent he would *from himself* act in a way that can, practically speaking, be said to begin a new course of action in the sensible world. But he would do this without anything's beginning *in him* as a noumenal agent. It seems that Bennett, in his objection, may have assumed that the sense in which Kant supposed that the noumenon begins something *from itself* is the same sense of "begins" he used when he denied that something begins *in it*. But when we keep these senses of "begins" properly distinct, when we do not confuse noumenal action with a phenomenal beginning, the contradiction Bennett finds does not arise.

In objection (*b*) Meerbote challenged the timelessness of free agency based on a requirement of Kant's epistemology: that whatever causes an event in this world has to be a prior, temporal event. Unless this requirement can be met, Meerbote suggests, nature cannot be known to be thoroughly law-governed, in the way Kant supposed. Yet we may reply to this objection by pointing out that there is no reason to think the *effects* of noumenal actions, in the world of appearance, lack prior temporal causes. Our free actions as events in this world can be seen as caused both by our timeless, noumenal agency, and by prior, temporal events. Imagine God's timelessly creating a temporal world in which all *B*-type events are lawfully preceded by, that is, caused by, *A*-type events. This would imply that all occurrences of *B*-events have both a cause independent of time, which is

---

[39] Cf. *Religion*, 61–2/6:39–40.

[40] It should be noted that here I do not see that it is necessary, in employing a practical concept like "beginning" in the phenomenal world, to assume that a beginning is not caused.

God, and natural causes that are temporally prior, namely: A-events. In the case of our free actions, the difference we make in the noumenal world can be understood also on the model of timeless creation of law-governed sequences of events. Through a timeless, free contribution to the noumenal world an agent can appear in the phenomenal world as someone for whom A-type psychological events characteristically cause her to perform B-type actions. When human freedom is understood this way, we can see how a B-type action can follow from of a prior, A-type condition, through both natural causality and the causality of timeless agency. The prospect of timeless free agency need not, therefore, threaten the principles of Kant's epistemology, as he himself believed (cf. *Pure Reason,* A536–7/B564–5).

These replies to the preceding objections to timeless agency understandably raise further questions. They provoke inquiries about what kind of difference the free agent's noumenal action can be expected to make in the phenomenal world. As we shall see in the next chapter, noumenal freedom is consistent with psychological determinism provided our free actions in the noumenal world are supposed to determine the contents of our characters as empirical agents (5.5–6).

In this chapter my aim has been to show how, in Kant's view, our actions can be free even if they are always causally determined by psychological forces of incentives. As we saw near the beginning of the previous chapter, a number of recent interpreters have denied that in Kant's theory of action we are "basically passive" in regard to the psychological forces of our desires. Most have assumed that actions explained by psychological forces could not be free. But I have attempted to show here that our freedom is not threatened by this psychological determinism. Our actions can be both free and psychologically determined provided, first, we act freely in another, intelligible world, and second, what we do in that world appears as what we do in this world. In this chapter I have laid the metaphysical groundwork for this by explaining Kant's conceptions of a "world," and of causation and action in a world without time. I showed also how Kant supposed we can see ourselves as personally identical with agents acting freely in a world without time.

5

Character from Two Standpoints

The previous chapter introduced Kant's doctrine of the two worlds. This doctrine, he wrote, gives a rational being "two standpoints from which he can regard himself and cognize laws . . . for all his actions" (*Groundwork,* 57/4:452). The first standpoint, he said, is the one from which we regard ourselves as belonging to the world of sense, and see ourselves as subject to the laws of nature. But from the second standpoint, we regard ourselves as belonging to the intelligible world, and as subject to "laws which, being independent of nature, are not empirical but grounded merely in reason." This chapter offers an interpretation of those two standpoints as they relate to the two worlds, and as they relate to Kant's double conception of character.

The most popular interpretations of Kant's transcendental distinction today treat it as merely an epistemological, or methodological distinction. It is said that Kant's terms "phenomena" and "noumena" should not be understood as referring to ontologically distinct objects, in different worlds. They are better seen as referring to different aspects of things in *this* world—different aspects that depend upon our considering them from either a phenomenal or a noumenal standpoint. It is easy to see why this ontologically leaner, "two-standpoints" interpretation of the transcendental distinction would be more attractive than the robust, and seemingly fantastic, two-worlds interpretation. Yet I think that only the latter captures what Kant himself intended. I also think the former interpretation introduces insurmountable difficulties.

The first sections of this chapter present an extended argument against "two-standpoints" interpretations of the distinction between appearances and things in themselves. It will probably come as no surprise that I think these interpretations cannot solve the problem of justification and explanation. The positive contribution of this chapter will then appear in the middle sections, where the focus will be on another, related distinction that Kant makes. This is his distinction between empirical and intelligible *character*; and it helps to clarify how our phenomenal actions, which are causally determined by psychological forces, relate to our free, noumenal actions. The former are determined through the causal laws of our empirical characters, which are our maxims. The latter are our free actions, which determine our having the maxims that we have. But some may see this two-part structure of human action as implying a kind of fatalism. There may also be concerns about Kant's famous slogan: "'ought' implies 'can'." How, after all, *can* we do what we recognize we *ought* to do, if all we ever *can* do in the empirical world is psychologically determined? As we shall see near the end, Kant's "two-standpoints" language will help us respond to questions about fatalism and the significance of "'ought' implies 'can'." The final section of the chapter will then deal with objections to the idea of timeless free agency that raise moral questions: including the question of our moral responsibility for our empirical characters.

5.1 Standpoints

The "two-worlds" interpretation of Kant's theory of action presented in the previous chapter has not been favored by commentators in recent years. In this section I'll clarify a couple of different approaches to the more popular alternative: the "two-standpoints" interpretation. In the next section I'll offer a philosophical critique of that interpretation.

The approaches to the two-standpoints interpretation that I shall consider here differ in how they explain the relation between phenomena and noumena. According to one approach, phenomena and noumena are objects, respectively, of the faculties of theoretical and practical reason. That is, when we reason theoretically, we view objects as phenomena; when we reason practically, we view them as noumena. This is the approach to the distinction that has been set out by Korsgaard. But a different approach, championed by Allison, says that phenomena and noumena are objects of different types of "philosophical considerations." This one differs from the first approach in that it does not identify the different ways of considering things philosophically as theoretical and practical reason. That is, it does not say that we think of things as phenomena when and only when we reason theoretically, and we think of things as noumena when and only when we reason practically. This appears to be a distinct advantage if the point is to develop an accurate interpretation of Kant's views. For there seem to be discrepancies between the first approach and Kant's own presentations of the distinction, on the one hand, between phenomena and noumena, and of the distinction, on the other hand, between theoretical and practical reason.

To clarify this last point, consider the way Korsgaard explains her two-standpoints interpretation. She writes, "On what I take to be the correct interpretation, the [transcendental] distinction is not between two kinds of beings, but between things of this world insofar as they are authentically active and the same beings insofar as we are passively receptive to them." [1] She explains further that:

Reason has two employments, theoretical and practical. We view ourselves as phenomena when we take on the theoretical task of describing and explaining our behavior; we view ourselves as noumena when our practical task is one of deciding what to do. The two standpoints cannot be mixed because these two enterprises—explanation and decision—are mutually exclusive.   (204)

In assessing the adequacy of this interpretation it should be observed, in the first place, that Kant was convinced that the ideality of space and time is required for making sense of his transcendental distinction between appearances and things in themselves. But as Korsgaard interprets the transcendental distinction, it seems to reduce to the difference between explaining behavior, and deciding what to do. The ideality of time is not required in order to understand *that* difference, however.[2] So something Kant considered especially important seems to have been left out of Korsgaard's version of the two-standpoints interpretation.

A second point to be observed is that the difference between theoretical and practical reason, as Korsgaard presents them above, should correspond exactly to the distinction between phenomena and noumena. For in her approach the latter distinction depends upon the former. But this is not

---

[1] *Creating the Kingdom of Ends*, 203; cf. also Rawls, *Lectures on the History of Moral Philosophy*, 301.

[2] On views like Korsgaard's, the timelessness of principles of action is often substituted for the Kantian doctrine of the ideality of time. But Kant's epistemological arguments in the Transcendental Aesthetic of the first *Critique* support a much richer theoretical outlook. Kant believed that he needed to establish the ideality of space and time in order to support the transcendental distinction between appearances and things in themselves. The timelessness of practical principles does not seem to play an analogous role in Korsgaard's version of the distinction.

how Kant saw the relation of these two pairs. For him, it was not that the objects of theoretical or speculative reason are exclusively phenomenal, and that we deal with things noumenal only in reason's practical use. Rather, it was that *determinate cognition* of an object—objectively valid, synthetic predication—is possible for theoretical reason only insofar as its object is phenomenal. But it is possible for practical reason even if its object is noumenal (see 4.5). To understand the point here it helps to see that things in themselves are not the inventions and exclusive properties of the standpoint of practical reason. Things in themselves are also acknowledged by theoretical reason; albeit for theoretical reason the thing in itself is a problematic idea. Here is one way Kant explained the point:

> the understanding [theoretical reason], when it calls an object in a relation mere phenomenon, simultaneously makes for itself, beyond this relation, another representation of an *object in itself* and hence also represents itself as being able to make *concepts* of such an object, and since the understanding offers nothing other than the categories through which the object in this latter sense must at least be able to be thought, it is thereby misled into taking the entirely *undetermined* concept of a being of understanding, as a something in general outside our sensibility, for a *determinate* concept of a being that we could cognize through the understanding in some way. (*Pure Reason*, B307; see also A796/B824)

The point here is that Kant assumed things in themselves can be objects of theoretical reason, even if it always subsumes them, illegitimately, under the categories and misleads itself. So things in themselves, noumena, are not dependent upon the standpoint of practical reason, in the way that Korsgaard's approach to the transcendental distinction implies. Their reality is supposed to be independent of whether we consider them from the theoretical or the practical standpoint.

As further evidence that Kant did not treat theoretical and practical reason as standpoints from which objects of this world can be seen respectively as phenomena and noumena, the following passage may be consulted. "[J]ust as the moral principles are necessary in accordance with reason in its *practical* use, it is equally necessary to assume in accordance with reason in its *theoretical* use that everyone has cause to hope for happiness in the same measure as he has made himself worthy of it in his conduct" (ibid., A809/B837). In Korsgaard's approach, the scope of theoretical reason should be limited to the domain of the phenomenal, the domain of natural

CHARACTER FROM TWO STANDPOINTS 135

science. But if this is so, it does not seem *theoretically* reasonable for anyone to hope for happiness in proportion to her worthiness to receive it. *Worthiness to be happy* is not an idea available to us from the theoretical, phenomenal standpoint. So a presupposition of Kant's claim in the sentence just quoted is that the perspectives of theoretical and practical reason can overlap. Each may focus in its different way on some common object. But this is not possible on Korsgaard's approach, where, as she claimed, the theoretical and practical perspectives are supposed to be mutually exclusive. Accordingly, her approach to the relations between theoretical and practical reason on the one hand, and between phenomena and noumena on the other, is not consistent with Kant's.[3]

The second approach to the two–standpoints interpretation seems not to encounter such difficulties. Allison explains the approach he takes as follows: "the transcendental distinction," he writes, "is not *primarily* between two kinds of entity, appearances and things in themselves, but rather between two distinct ways in which the objects of human experience may be 'considered' in philosophical reflection, namely, as they appear and as they are in themselves."[4] On an approach like this it seems easy to preserve the importance of the ideality of time that Kant saw as required

---

[3] Another difficulty with Korsgaard's view is worth mentioning here. It is that her view amounts to what I call "practical solipsism." For her, the standpoint of practical reason is the standpoint of deliberation. But I deliberate for no one but myself. Hence, there should be no object of practical consideration except myself. Korsgaard recognizes this difficulty, as it turns out. But her solution to it seems inadequate. She writes, "you cannot restrict the concepts of freedom and responsibility to yourself in the [practical] context of deliberative choice. If you did, you would think that the only free agent in the world is me-right-now. But the moral law, which according to Kant presents itself to you in exactly these moments, commands that you treat everyone as an end in himself" (*Creating the Kingdom of Ends,* 206). This attempt to eliminate the prospect of practical solipsism by appeal to the content of the moral law's command begs the question. If the perspective of practical reason is deliberative, and if I can deliberate only for myself, then the moral law cannot tell me to treat anyone other than *myself* as an end in itself. I cannot even tell if *there is* anyone other than myself, from just the standpoint of deliberation. That's the solipsistic problem, after all. To step out of the deliberative standpoint and to recognize the existence of something besides myself is to step into the perspective of explanation and description, where there is supposed to be no freedom. Once I do that, I cannot recognize any free choosers or deliberators. In that perspective I cannot even recognize myself as a free chooser and deliberator. It might be offered on Korsgaard's behalf that we do not necessarily deliberate only for ourselves, since we can deliberate collectively. Hence, the practical perspective of deliberation is not solipsistic. But if this suggestion works, then we can prove too much. If we follow this reasoning then we can refute even theoretical solipsism, just by observing that we share experiences with others. Both versions of the argument are, of course, question begging. What is in question for the theoretical solipsist is precisely whether experience can be shared. What is in question for the practical solipsist is precisely whether deliberation can be collective. For Kant's own worries about the problem of "metaphysical egoism" see above, 4.7.
[4] *Kant's Theory of Freedom,* 4.

for his transcendental distinction. It need only be pointed out that in our philosophical considerations of objects as things in themselves it is necessary to regard them as atemporal; while in our philosophical considerations of objects as appearances it is necessary to regard them as temporal.[5] Moreover, the different standpoints as understood in this approach are not identified with the different employments of reason. So here each of theoretical and practical reason could conceivably have as its object either phenomena or noumena.

Allison presents a richer characterization of his approach to the two-standpoints interpretation in the following statements:

Implicit in this [approach] is the necessity of distinguishing between things insofar as they [are] knowable by the human mind and *the same things* as they are "in themselves," that is, as they are independently of the human mind and its cognitive apparatus. The former corresponds to things as they appear, or simply appearances; the latter to things as they are in themselves.... Although things considered in the latter fashion are by definition unknowable by us, we can think of them as possible objects of a divine mind blessed with nonsensible or intellectual intuition. Thus, we can think, although not know, things as they are in themselves. (*Kant's Theory of Freedom,* 4, emphasis added)

From the preceding statements it is possible to see how, on Allison's approach, things in themselves could be objects of theoretical reason, though not of human knowledge. This is not possible on Korsgaard's approach to the two-standpoints interpretation; and that seems to constitute an advantage of Allison's approach.

5.2 Neutral Objects

Two-standpoints interpretations of Kant's transcendental distinction, in general, have been subject to a persistent criticism. It is that they leave us in the dark about *what* is considered from each of the two standpoints.[6]

---

[5] Watkins points out that this approach to preserving the timelessness of noumena may be too easy. It seems to make noumena timeless *by definition,* whereas Kant thought it necessary *to argue* for the timelessness of things in themselves. See Eric Watkins, *Kant and the Metaphysics of Causality* (Cambridge: Cambridge University Press, 2005), 320.

[6] See Robert Greenberg, *Kant's Theory of A Priori Knowledge* (University Park, PA: Pennsylvania State University Press, 2001).

In viewing something from one standpoint we consider it under the conditions of space and time. In viewing it from the other standpoint we are supposed to consider it in abstraction from those conditions. But the problem is how to account for the identity of *it*. What is *it*—let us call it the "neutral object"—that we are presumed capable of considering from either standpoint? And how do we have cognitive access to it?

It is difficult to see how this criticism can be answered in the first approach to the two-standpoints interpretation. Korsgaard characterizes the transcendental distinction in terms of the difference "between things of this world insofar as they are authentically active and *the same beings* insofar as we are passively receptive to them" (emphasis added). This suggests that self-identical things of this world, "the same beings," should be considerable from either standpoint. But it is difficult to understand what these same beings would be. When we consider an object from the point of view of theoretical reason, what we observe is supposed to be importantly different from what we have in view when we consider the same thing from the point of view of practical reason. Take myself as an example. After doing what *I* decided to do, by practical reason, it should be possible for me to explain the action *I* have done, by theoretical reason. And for this it seems that the deciding *I* should be identical with the *I* whose action is explained. But it remains unclear how, on Korsgaard's approach, we can be confident about this identity, or even how we can think it. Neither practical reason nor theoretical reason should enable us to recognize that the *I* considered from either standpoint is identical with the *I* considered from the opposite standpoint. So it seems that this approach to the two standpoints would require some additional, third standpoint on ourselves, our actions, and other things. The things we would consider from the third standpoint would be the neutral objects of this world that can be considered as noumena or phenomena, depending on whether we take the standpoint of practical or theoretical reason. But I am not aware that Korsgaard has identified any additional manner of representing objects, or any third standpoint, that would be adequate for viewing neutral objects. So her account of the two standpoints seems so far incomplete.[7]

This does not seem to be a problem for Allison's approach, however. He sees the two standpoints as "two distinct ways in which the objects

---

[7] See also below, n. 30.

of human experience may be 'considered' in philosophical reflection." So his approach has it that our cognitive access to neutral objects is through ordinary human experience. As transcendental philosophers, presumably, we may view neutral objects of human experience from a standpoint in which we regard them as appearances, conditioned by space, time, and the categories of the understanding. Or, we may view neutral objects of experience from a standpoint in which we regard them as things in themselves, unconditioned by human ways of knowing. This contrasts with Korsgaard's approach, where "philosophical consideration" does not seem required for taking either of the two standpoints on things. She seems to present ordinary people, who are not engaged in philosophical reflection, as capable of explaining things, from the standpoint of theoretical reason, and as capable of deciding what to do, from the standpoint of practical reason. In other words, as Allison sees it, the difference between appearances and things in themselves would be something discoverable only by philosophically sophisticated subjects of experience. But in Korsgaard's view, by contrast, the difference is well understood by ordinary thinkers. Anyone who grasps the difference between explaining and deciding understands it, even if they do not use terms like "phenomena" and "noumena."

Allison's approach to the two-standpoints interpretation seems to improve upon Korsgaard's in its ability to give an account of neutral objects and our cognitive access to them. Yet his approach seems unfaithful to Kant's view, nevertheless. For his approach makes it impossible to employ the transcendental designation "thing in itself" apart from human experience. That is, by Allison's approach, a thing in itself could be nothing more than an aspect of a neutral object; and neutral objects are one and all objects of human experience. Hence, a thing in itself is always identical in some way with an object of experience. Consequently, on Allison's approach it would not be possible to think of God as a thing in itself—unless, of course, we are prepared to think of him also as an object of human experience.[8]

---

[8] Allison has claimed that his own approach to the two-standpoints interpretation has an advantage over others, in that it leaves room for God, and perhaps also for rational souls. "Such objects present no particular difficulty for the ['two-standpoints'] approach," he writes, "because there is nothing in the approach which requires denial of their possibility" (Henry E. Allison, "Transcendental Idealism: The 'Two Aspect' View," in Ouden and Moen, eds., New Essays on Kant, 160). My argument here is that, on the contrary, Allison's approach limits what can be thought of as a thing in itself to just an

In summary then, the philosophical problem facing the two-standpoints interpretations is that they require "neutral objects." In these approaches it is agreed that "noumenality" depends upon one standpoint we can take on something, while "phenomenality" depends upon the other standpoint we can take on *the same thing*. Yet neither standpoint is presumed to have resources available to it for accounting for the self-identity of the thing we may consider as either noumenon or phenomenon. So some third standpoint, or some other mode of cognitive access, will be required if the things considerable either as noumena or phenomena are to be recognizably self-identical. And once it is seen how a thing in itself differs from an appearance, and how these differ from the relevant neutral object, it becomes clear that every thing in itself would be related to an appearance in human experience. It becomes clear, in short, that every noumenon would have to have a phenomenal aspect—including God.[9]

5.3 Justification and Explanation Revisited

In this section and the one that follows I shall point out another serious shortcoming of two-standpoint interpretations. It is that they cannot solve the problem of justification and explanation. Or at least they cannot solve it in a way that saves the relevance of a priori, moral justification. The argument here will be, basically, that on these interpretations, the resources for explaining action are limited to the empirical standpoint. So to the extent that practical reason presents non-empirical justifications for action,

---

aspect of an object of human experience (just an aspect of a neutral object). So it actually precludes our thinking of a God that is not also an object of human experience.

[9] Here it may be proposed that this problem arises only because the expressions "noumenon" and "thing in itself" are treated as equivalent. But it is possible, someone might say, to think of a noumenon as just the intellectual aspect of a so-called "neutral object" that could also be regarded from the phenomenal standpoint, and to think of a thing in itself as just something existing independently of human experience, outside the conditions of space and time. Hence, God could exist as a thing in itself, and it would not be necessary to consider him as a noumenon, or as an aspect of something that could be, in another aspect, an object of human experience. I think this suggestion ultimately fails, however. It implies that when we take the standpoint from which we are supposed to consider something as a noumenon, we must have in this standpoint some tacit accommodation of the other, phenomenal standpoint. For there would be no way to distinguish a noumenon from a thing in itself apart from some consideration of the relation of the noumenon to a phenomenon, or to its phenomenal aspect. And so, in the end, the noumenal and phenomenal standpoints turn out not to be separable, as claimed in setting up the two-standpoints interpretations.

to that extent these interpretations come up short. They cannot show how what would justify action, non-empirically, can also explain it, empirically. Hence, they cannot show how what Kant saw as a priori, moral justification is relevant to human action in the empirical world.

The problem of justification and explanation is, again, that unless we can see how what justifies an action can also explain it, justification is irrelevant (1.11). I have maintained that embracing psychological determinism (3.1) is necessary for solving this problem. For by doing so, we can see how psychological forces incorporated into the maxims of practical reasoning are capable of explaining actions these maxims justify. Recall that a maxim, as a major premise of a practical syllogism (1.3), can justify an action seen as an effective means of producing what it, the maxim, represents as "good."[10] And recall how the force of the psychological incentive incorporated into the maxim (2.2) can cause the agent to act as she recognizes she is justified in acting. This solves the problem, by showing how the maxims of practical reasoning that justify actions can also explain them. But it solves the problem at what many may see as too great a cost. For the assumption of psychological determinism required for this solution requires that free agency be located, conceptually, in another world.

Two-standpoints interpretations might seem capable of solving the problem of justification and explanation much less extravagantly, however. So this may lead some to favor one or another version of the two-standpoints interpretation, despite the problems pointed out just above. For on a two-standpoints interpretation it seems possible to accommodate the psychological determinism needed to solve the problem of justification and explanation, at least in a limited way. Psychological determinism could be relegated to just the empirical standpoint on actions. So viewed from that standpoint, some may say, our actions should be explainable as caused by certain psychological states of agents recognizing rational justifications for action: beliefs and desires, for instance. And from the other standpoint, then, the same actions can be considered free. Hence, the two standpoints on our agency that even Kant himself identified seem to show how it is

---

[10] Actions justified by moral imperatives can be explained by psychological forces (moral incentives) incorporated into maxims, in the same way. These maxims differ from non-moral maxims in the type of "good" they represent (1.5). Actions on moral maxims are not viewed by their agents as means to bring about some good, however (1.7). They are viewed as instances of concepts or conditions represented as good in the maxims: instances of treating humanity as an end, for example; or of avoiding acting on maxims that cannot be willed to become universal law.

possible to embrace both psychological determinism, and freedom. And so it seems unnecessary to invoke the (extravagant) metaphysics of two worlds.

But here I'll argue that accommodating psychological determinism in only this limited way, in just a standpoint from which things are seen as phenomena, makes it impossible to show how a priori, moral justification is relevant to human action.

Take an example of an action that is justified by a categorical imperative of practical reason, as something that ought, morally, to be done. Suppose also that the action is not supported also by any of the agent's natural desires or inclinations, and is perhaps disfavored by all of them.[11] If the empirical standpoint has no resources for explaining how such an action can occur, then from that standpoint the action must be judged impossible. Pure practical reason may of course insist that its justifying, categorical "ought" implies "can." Nevertheless, the standpoint for explaining how an action is possible is the one that views actions and their motivations as phenomena. And from that point of view we cannot explain actions otherwise than in terms of agents' empirical desires or inclinations.[12] Hence, it is impossible to see how some actions justified non-empirically, independently of the desires or inclinations of the agent, can be explained.

It might seem obvious that actions justified non-empirically can always be explained from a non-empirical, intelligible standpoint on rational agency. They may seem explainable from this standpoint through what Kant referred to from time to time as the "causality of freedom," or the "causality of reason." And this need not refer us to any otherworldly mode of causation, some may say. For the causality of reason is, as two-standpoints interpreters usually see it, the causality in this world of a rational agent's *free choice*. The idea would be that from the noumenal or intelligible standpoint, practical reason can be seen as justifying action with its moral principles. And from that very standpoint it can be seen how the rational agent would *freely choose* to act on the basis of those reasons.[13] That is how the

---

[11] Kant evidently saw this as a psychological possibility. See *Groundwork*, 11–12/4:398.

[12] Allison claims: "at the empirical level, at least, Kant is clearly a causal theorist since he holds that 'reasons,' in the sense of beliefs, desires and intentions, are the empirical causes of human action" (*Kant's Theory of Freedom,* 49).

[13] Allison claims:

in those places where Kant speaks of the causality of reason, he is referring to actions supposedly based on principles or imperatives, that is to say, actions performed in virtue of the fact that a rational agent takes them as in some sense reasonable, if not obligatory. But although it is common enough to speak

problem of justification and explanation may seem to be solvable, without invoking any otherworldly, noumenal causality. Allison seems to represent this "free-choice solution" to the problem very well, in elaborating on his Incorporation Thesis:

[I]ncentives (*Triebfedern*) do not motivate by themselves causing action but rather by being taken as reasons and incorporated into maxims. Correlatively, we think of reason as determining the will by legislating to it, that is, by providing the laws or principles ('objective determining grounds') which govern, without causally necessitating, its acts of incorporation or, more simply, its choices. Although reason, according to this picture, is not literally an efficient cause of action, free actions are not regarded as uncaused. It is rather that the act of incorporation is conceived as the genuine causal factor and reason 'has causality' only in the Pickwickian sense that it provides the guiding rule. Moreover, since this act is thought (or presupposed) but not experienced, it is in the specifically Kantian sense an intelligible cause.   (*Kant's Theory of Freedom*, 51–2)

In this passage Allison offers what looks like a solution to the problem of justification and explanation. It would be that when viewed from an intelligible or non-empirical standpoint, a rational agent can be seen as recognizing principles of practical reason that would justify her actions. From this standpoint she can be seen as also having available to her certain incentives. Among them would be the moral incentive of respect for law. Incentives by themselves lack explanatory power, however. This is a key assumption of The Incorporation Thesis. So in order for an incentive to explain an action, as Allison sees it, the agent must choose to incorporate it into her maxim. And by that act of free choice, as an "act of incorporation," the chosen incentive would be able to explain the action that is justified on a priori, rational grounds. The act of incorporation is, according to Allison, "the genuine causal factor" that explains the action.

   But in Chapter 3 I offered several lines of criticism of this type of solution to the problem of justification and explanation. There I criticized The Incorporation Thesis, and offered independent arguments why free choice cannot explain action. So here it will suffice to repeat, only briefly,

metaphorically of the 'power' of ideas or reason, it is clear that principles do not of themselves literally have causal efficacy. Such efficacy pertains rather to the belief in these principles or, better, to the agents who act on the basis of their beliefs. (ibid.)

the reasons why free choice is not explanatory (3.9). A free "executive" choice is a choice to execute an action, for a reason, or on a certain incentive. It does not explain an action because it is part of the very idea of an action that the agent executes it for a reason, or on an incorporated incentive. So since free executive choice is part of what needs to be explained, it is not explanatory. A free "elective" choice, on the other hand, is a choice to execute action on one reason or incentive rather than another. Because different reasons typically support different actions, an elective choice is typically, though not always, a choice to execute one action rather than another.[14] In terms of The Incorporation Thesis, an elective choice is a choice to incorporate one incentive rather than another. But elective free choice is also not explanatory. This is because, in Kant's view, our knowledge of the incentives upon which we choose to act is limited. We can act freely and never know the reason or incentive upon which we act. So we do not control, that is, we do not choose (elect), the incentives upon which we act. Consequently, our actions are not explained by our elective choices.

For these reasons it seems we should be skeptical of the explanatory power of free choice. And so we should be skeptical that the "act of incorporation" emphasized in Allison's elaboration of The Incorporation Thesis above can explain actions justified by a priori rational principles. Hence, interpreting Kant's claims about the "causality of reason" or the "causality of freedom," considered from an intelligible standpoint, does not seem very promising as a solution to the problem of justification and explanation. Actions may still be explained from the empirical standpoint by the agents' beliefs and desires, however. But from this standpoint it is doubtful that actions on practical reason's non-empirical, moral justifications can be explained.

5.4 A Deterministic Account of Moral Motivation

Regarding the previous point about action explanations from the empirical standpoint, it will be worth the effort to review here some comments

---

[14] Sometimes different reasons support executing the same action, so an elective choice can also be a choice to execute the same action on one reason rather than another.

made by Korsgaard. Her assumption is that all human actions, including actions on a priori moral principles, would be fully explainable from the standpoint of theoretical reason. But here I'll argue, against this view, that the explanatory resources available from that standpoint are inadequate to explain action on practical reason's non-empirical, moral justifications. Here are some of Korsgaard's comments on the explanation of morally justified action from a strictly theoretical standpoint:

Insofar as we view our actions as phenomena we must view them as causally determined, but not necessarily as determined by mere desires and inclinations. We can still view them as determined by moral thoughts and moral aspirations; only from this point of view, those must themselves by viewed as determined in us. For instance, I might explain someone's doing the right thing by saying that she did it because she values humanity as an end in itself, and I might in turn explain that fact by showing how she received a moral education.

A deterministic account can be a deterministic account of moral motivation itself—it does not have to bypass morality and pretend we do everything for the sake of happiness. . . . From a merely theoretical and explanatory point of view, moral interest is on a footing with inclination. We may imagine the cynic saying: "it doesn't really matter how she came to treat humanity as an end in itself. It is what she likes to do, so she is still pursuing her own happiness." When moral motivation is viewed theoretically, it can be distinguished from inclination only by its content. Its special *source,* in the agent's autonomy, does not show up. (*Creating the Kingdom of Ends,* 210)

In the statements initiating the above-quoted passage Korsgaard acknowledges that psychological determinism is a presupposition of action explanation. One of her assumptions here seems to be that the presupposition of psychological determinism is consistent with Kantian freedom, nevertheless, so long as it is limited to the empirical standpoint of theoretical reason.[15] But she does not see that standpoint on human actions as limited to

---

[15] In a preceding chapter I presented Korsgaard as an example of someone rejecting psychological determinism as incompatible with Kant's theory of freedom (3.1). As I acknowledged in a note to that discussion, she nevertheless agrees that psychological determinism would be a necessary presupposition of the phenomenal, explanatory perspective on human action. What she denies is that an action considered free, in the noumenal perspective of deliberation, falls under the explanatory presupposition of psychological determinism. The point I made there about Korsgaard's perspectivism can now be presented this way. What Korsgaard must deny, in fact, is that an action on a moral incentive or motive can fall under the presupposition of psychological determinism. If the motive for the action is non-empirical, then it cannot be explained by resources available to the phenomenal, explanatory

explaining them solely in terms of inclination, or the agent's own happiness. She implies that to insist on explaining human action, from the phenomenal point of view, in no other terms but natural, sense-based motivations would be cynical. But it is difficult to see how it could be cynical if the only resources available for explaining action from that standpoint are supposed to be empirical. I do not see how the explainer of action Korsgaard views as cynical would have any other option if he is, as she thinks he must be, explaining from a standpoint that is blind to anything non-empirical. And I think Kant would agree that an explainer of actions like the one Korsgaard imagines would not be cynical. Consider, for example, what Kant wrote in the following passage.

[I]f the conditions for the exercise of our free choice are empirical, then in that case reason can have none but a regulative use, and can only serve to produce the unity of empirical laws, as, e.g., in the doctrine of prudence the unification of all ends that are given to us by our inclinations into the single end of *happiness* and the harmony of the means for attaining that end constitute the entire business of reason, which can therefore provide none but *pragmatic* laws of free conduct for reaching the ends recommended by the senses, and therefore can provide no pure laws that are determined completely *a priori*.   (*Pure Reason*, A800/B828)

This passage shows how Kant assumed reason would justify action if there could be none but empirical explanations of action. Reason's laws could be pragmatic only, in which case it could not be cynical to explain all human actions as motivated ultimately by the prospect of personal happiness.

Korsgaard's view on action explanation seems to me to issue incompatible requirements. She requires that genuine moral thoughts and aspirations be capable of explaining action, and she requires that action explanations originate in the phenomenal standpoint, where psychological determinism is presupposed. But it seems that neither requirement can be satisfied without violating the other. The phenomenal standpoint would present all human actions as explainable by nothing other than prior phenomena of the empirical world. So if these are its only explanatory resources, then no genuinely moral thoughts or aspirations, no recognition of anything

perspective. In that case, it does not fall under the presupposition of psychological determinism. So to the extent that Kantian freedom requires the possibility of action explained by non-empirical incentives, to that extent psychological determinism, as Korsgaard understands it, is incompatible with Kantian freedom.

a priori practical, can explain action. I think we may presume that, for Kant, explanatory thoughts and aspirations simply would not count as genuinely moral unless they can be seen as non-empirical. Another way to put this point would be to say that explanatory desires or motives can be distinguished as genuinely moral only by what Korsgaard refers to as their special source, in the agent's autonomy. But, as she recognizes, this distinguishing mark of moral motivation does not show up in the phenomenal perspective. According to her view, therefore, there should be no reason to think that a deterministic account of Kantian moral motivation can be given.

My contention is that it is possible for genuine moral thoughts and aspirations, which cannot be accounted for wholly in empirical terms, to fall within the scope of deterministic action explanation. But for this we must do what two-standpoint interpreters are unwilling to do. We must acknowledge that we act in two worlds. If we acknowledge this, then we can see our psychologically determined actions in this world as appearances of how we act freely in the other world. We can also see our actions in the empirical world as explainable by psychological forces of "intelligible origin," like the moral incentive of respect for the moral law.[16] This cannot be seen in two-standpoints interpretations, since it would require mixing the empirical and intelligible standpoints.

To understand better how intelligible, "moral motivation" can appear in the deterministic, sensible world, we must now turn to explore Kant's views on the explanatory role of "character."

5.5 Causation and Character

Early in Chapter 1 we saw Kant's definition of "action" as "the determination of the power of a substance as a cause of a certain accident." This definition applies for anything capable of making a difference in the world. The difference a substance makes through action will be either a difference in itself, in one of its own properties, or a difference in the properties

---

[16] This is exactly what Kant was referring to in "Of the Interest Attaching to the Ideas of Morality" (*Groundwork*, 54–8/4:448–53).

of something else. The former type of action is called "inner," while the latter is called "transeunt." The reciprocal influence of substances implied by their membership in a world is transeunt action.[17]

In the sensible world, according to Kant, physical as well as psychological substances, material things as well as thinking subjects, are acting causes. And every cause has a character by which it operates. Its character is constituted by the laws of its causal agency, by the laws that dictate how it acts in response to prior occurrences.

[E]very effective cause must have a *character*, i.e., a law of its causality...through which its actions, as appearances, would stand through and through in connection with other appearances in accordance with constant natural laws...and thus, in combination with these other appearances, they would constitute members of a single series of the natural order.　(*Pure Reason*, A539/B567)

My character is not the cause of my action, however.[18] It is rather that I, as a phenomenal mental substance, am the cause of my actions as effects in the phenomenal world, in accordance with the laws of my character. Just as water performs its freezing action when the temperature drops below $0°C$, so I act in the world, in accordance with my character, and as a consequence of prior events. A causal law forming part of the nature of water, part of what it *is like,* explains water's icing. In the same way, psychological laws of my character explain my actions.[19]

But there is an important difference between actions like water's freezing and my actions. It is that water does not act through representations. It does not see its actions, or their ends, as good. Water, in other words, does not act on desires (1.5). It is not a living being.[20] Neither is it a rational being. Its actions do not follow as conclusions of practical reasoning from maxims,

---

[17] A physical example of transeunt action implied by membership in a world is the action of each material particle in the empirical world upon every other, through attractive force (Newtonian gravity). For Kant's argument that matter must actively affect all other matter, see *Metaphysical Foundations of Natural Science*, in *Theoretical Philosophy after 1781*, 227/4:516–17. The divine act of creation is also a transeunt action; see *Lectures on Metaphysics*, 182/29:823, 329/28:565.

[18] Kant seems once to say otherwise: "His power of choice has an empirical character, which is the (empirical) cause of all his actions" (*Pure Reason*, A552/B580). But he typically identifies character with the concept of "causality," rather than that of "cause."

[19] This is consistent with my actions' being explained by practical reasoning.

[20] Cf. Kant's definition of "life." "*Life* is the faculty of a being to act in accordance with the laws of the faculty of desire" (*Practical Reason*, 8n./5:9n.).

from subjective principles. Kant connected the concept of a maxim with the "empirical character" of a human being when he wrote that,

> every human being has an empirical character of his power of choice, which is nothing other than a certain causality of his reason, insofar as in its effects in appearance this reason exhibits a rule, in accordance with which one could derive the rational grounds of the actions themselves according to their kind and degree, and estimate the *subjective principles of his power of choice.* (*Pure Reason*, A549/B577, emphasis added)

From this statement and the one previously quoted it is evident that Kant thought of our characters as causal laws for our actions. A person's character is a law required in order to fit all of his or her actions as effects in the world into "the single [deterministic] series of the natural order." But the causal law of character, as such, seems also to be a singular summation of a person's various maxims: the "subjective principles of his power of choice [*Willkür*]." Knowing that a causal agent acts according to laws, and observing variabilities of circumstances corresponding with variabilities in its actions, we can formulate (estimate) particular laws for explaining its actions in their circumstances. Where those particular laws are presumed to be self-imposed by the agent, that is, where they are regarded as *subjective* principles of action, they are maxims of the agent's character.

5.6 Empirical and Intelligible Character

Because all of a person's actions would be causally determined through the causal laws of his or her character, by which they fit into the single causal series of nature, Kant concluded that "in regard to this empirical character there is no freedom" (*Pure Reason,* A550/B578). Accordingly, he wrote, "for a subject in the world of sense we would have first an *empirical character,* through which" as in the passage quoted above, "its actions, as appearances, would stand through and through in connection with other appearances in accordance with constant natural laws." "Yet second," Kant continued, "one would also have to allow this subject an *intelligible character,* through which it is indeed the cause of those actions as appearances, but which does not stand under any conditions of sensibility and is not itself appearance" (ibid., A539/B567). This means, as Kant indicated very soon afterward, that the intelligible character "would not stand under any conditions of time." So in contrast to the unfreedom or determinism characterizing empirical character, the intelligible character can be considered free.

The relation between empirical and intelligible character is based on the relation between the person as appearance and as a thing in itself. Kant thought of the empirical character, he said, as "a mere appearance of the intelligible character" (A541/B569). He wrote also that the latter is "the transcendental cause of the former," and is "indicated" through it "as only its sensible sign" (A546/B574). The intelligible character, which cannot be perceived, "would have to be *thought* in conformity with the empirical character, just as in general we must ground appearances in thought through a transcendental object, even though we know nothing about it as it is in itself" (A540/B568).

Worth pointing out here are two importantly different ways commentators have understood Kant's idea of intelligible character. I think both are mistaken, though I think the error of the second way is more serious than that of the first. I'll explain why after outlining and comparing these two different approaches to understanding Kant's conception of intelligible character.

What characterizes the first interpretive approach most clearly, it seems, is the idea that we freely choose our own intelligible characters. Kant defined character as a law of causality, and connected our empirical characters with the determinism of the natural world. This suggests, therefore, that we can have control over our actions in this world only through control over our action-determining empirical characters. Yet we do not control how our empirical characters appear in this world as "signs" of our intelligible characters. So it seems that in order to have control over our actions in this world we must have some kind of control over our intelligible characters. Understandably, then, some have assumed that in Kant's view we freely choose our intelligible characters.[21] Their assumption is that our chosen intelligible characters then appear as our empirical characters, through

---

[21] I think this is Wood's assumption; see Allen W. Wood, "Kant's Compatibilism," in Wood, *Self and Nature in Kant's Philosophy*, 73–101 at 91. See also Bernard Carnois, *The Coherence of Kant's Doctrine of Freedom,* trans. David Booth (Chicago: University of Chicago Press, 1987), 98; and John Rawls, *Lectures,* 299–300. Louden views intelligible (moral) characters as freely chosen; and suggests that empirical moral education can conceivably "shape and influence" intelligible character. See Robert Louden, *Kant's Impure Ethics: From Rational Beings to Human Beings* (Oxford: Oxford University Press, 2000), 59, 136–7.

whose laws our actions are causally determined by prior events. I think this representation of Kant's view of freedom and character is very nearly correct.

But the second interpretive approach to intelligible character views it as consisting in little else besides freedom. According to Allison, for example, "the transcendental idea of freedom . . . provides the content to the otherwise empty thought of an intelligible character." [22] In the first approach we are presumed to choose our intelligible characters by an exercise of freedom. But in this second approach, our intelligible character is virtually identical with our freedom. The second approach is natural for those who interpret Kant's transcendental distinction as a distinction between two standpoints on human actions or agency.[23] They see the empirical character of an agent, or of an action, as referring to our consideration of him, or her, or it, as sensibly determined. And they see the idea of intelligible character as referring to our consideration of an agent or action as noumenal and free. Sometimes in interpretations like this, the aspect of the agent under consideration from the intelligible standpoint is thought of as almost entirely negative. It is thought of as the feature that human sense experience is incapable of grasping. But the intelligible character can be thought to include, positively, whatever must be presupposed in our consideration of the agent as free. This may extend to the agent's rationality, or responsiveness to reasons for action, including also the rational principles of Kantian morality.

---

[22] *Kant's Theory of Freedom*, 45. At one point Allison explains what he calls the otherwise empty thought of intelligible character in terms of "spontaneity," which can be "characterized provisionally as the capacity to determine oneself to act on the basis of objective (intersubjectively valid) rational norms and, in light of these norms, to take (or reject) inclinations or desires as sufficient reasons for action" (5, see also 138, 140). Reath, who takes the same interpretive approach to intelligible character, explains that "The idea of intelligible character is the basis of an incompatibilist model of rational agency. It is a mode of representing agents whose activity is subject to norms, and reflects the point of view that we adopt towards ourselves while we engage in the rational activities of deliberation, choice, judgment, etc." Andrews Reath, "Intelligible Character and the Reciprocity Thesis," *Inquiry* 36 (1993): 419–30 at 421. Piper writes: "our intelligible character consists in the metaphysical predisposition to regard empirical events as instances of abstract universal concepts and principles, and so to transcend, by way of abstract thought, the personalizing and limiting constraints of time and space." See Adrian Piper, "*Kants intelligibler Stanpunkt zum Handeln*" in Hans-Ulrich Baumgarten and Carsten Held, ed., *Systematische Ethik mit Kant* (München/Freiburg: Alber, 2001), 186.

[23] In a way that those who take the first interpretive approach to intelligible character could not easily understand, Allison slips into referring to particular "actions," and to "agency," as having empirical and intelligible characters (see 42, 45). This seems to be a manifestation of his view that the empirical and the intelligible do not characterize separate things, but are different standpoints we can take in considering anything in space and time.

Probably the clearest point of distinction between these two approaches to interpreting Kant's thoughts on intelligible character just outlined is the following. In what I have identified as the first approach, our intelligible characters are all different, or at least they could all be different, and they probably are. But for those taking the second approach, our intelligible characters seem to be all the same. This is not the precise distinction between these two interpretations, it should be emphasized. It is only a clear marker of their difference. On just this point of difference I am in agreement with those who take the first approach. For it seems to me, also, that we would all be different in regard to what Kant called our intelligible characters. I think it is fair to say that in the second approach, what is referred to as intelligible character is actually not character, but something Kant would refer to instead as our intelligible or rational "nature." It is our shared nature as rational agents, which would include our transcendental freedom.

I think Kant's use of words like "character" and its equivalents typically implies differences among us. Rational agents of the same *nature* can be expected to have different intelligible *characters*.[24] Even the same rational agent can be thought of, counterfactually, as having a different intelligible character. And Kant showed that he understood intelligible character in this way, in giving an example of someone blameworthy for telling a malicious lie. He wrote that this liar's having "another intelligible character would have given [him] another empirical one" (A556/B584). The point is that despite his bad upbringing or the influence of bad company reflected in his empirical character determining that he would lie, he is still to blame. His empirical character is after all the appearance of his intelligible character. Since he is free in regard to his intelligible character, he is to that extent free in what he does through his empirical character. Had he a different intelligible character—this is the important point—he would have had a different empirical character, and so he may not have acted as he did.

---

[24] Kant's above-quoted definition of "character" as the law of the causality of every effective cause might not suggest this difference between character and nature. Different effective causes can be supposed to share the same law of their causality, after all. Different physical objects, at least of the same type, operate according to the same causal law(s). Here, however, we would say that such physical objects (of the same type) have the same nature. I think Kant's use of "character" for the law of the causality of every effective cause emphasizes differences in the laws of effective causes. For different human beings, the laws of their causality are subjectively imposed maxims, so "character," not "nature," is the appropriate term for the different laws of their causality. For different physical objects of the same type, "nature," not "character," is appropriate for referring to the same law of their causality.

I think the error of the first approach to interpreting Kant's idea of intelligible character is minor, in comparison with the error of those taking the second approach. Those taking the first approach are misled, I think, into separating the transcendentally free *act*, by which the intelligible character is presumably acquired, from the intelligible character itself. My view is that Kant saw these as identical. That is, it does not seem justifiable to make a noumenal distinction here.[25] The difference, practically speaking, between the noumenal agent's free action and the intelligible character supposed to result from it, or be acquired by it, comes to nothing.

Kant is in a position to say, and in *Religion of within the Boundaries of Mere Reason* he as much as said, that the noumenal basis for an empirical character can be represented as a single, intelligible act (*deed*).[26] So it need not be that in the noumenal world we choose an intelligible character that appears here as our empirical character. It can be instead that the empirical character is grounded in an intelligible character, which is nothing other than a noumenal act. The latter need be nothing other than the action each of us takes as a member of the noumenal world community. It seems to me that Kant refers to the free noumenal act as an intelligible "character" just because of its relation to the empirical character of the free agent. A rational agent's empirical character is therefore best understood, I think, as an ongoing appearance of the difference he or she makes as an active member of the noumenal world (4.3).

5.7 The Allegory of the Play

Imagine now an actors' workshop, with ten or a dozen participants. Each is given the assignment of submitting a short list of psychological traits constituting a dramatic character. And each will later portray the role of the

---

[25] I do not deny that, insofar as the transcendentally free act and the intelligible character are identical, the intelligible character is freely chosen. I cannot deny this, because I think the intelligible act is freely chosen. What I deny is a difference between the freely chosen act and the intelligible character, where the latter is assumed to be acquired by the former.

[26] "Now, the term 'deed' can in general apply just as well to the use of freedom through which the supreme maxim (. . .) is adopted into the [*Willkür*], as to the use by which the actions themselves (. . .) are performed in accordance with that maxim. The propensity to evil is a deed in the first meaning (*peccatum originarium* [an original sin])" (*Religion,* 55/6:31). Here I think the "propensity to evil" that Kant identifies with "a deed" refers to a common feature of everyone's intelligible character. It is justifiably referred to also as our evil "nature," because of its universality in our species (7.1).

character he or she thereby defines. To ensure unity and variety in a plot, the participating actors would meet to coordinate the lists of traits they will jointly submit. Yet they are under a kind of veil of ignorance at this meeting. For they are unaware of their play's plot and setting; they know nothing about their roles apart from the traits they submit. A playwright in residence will later be assigned to write a script featuring the characters determined by the actors' choices. The playwright's assignment, let us imagine, is to author a play lasting fifty to seventy minutes in performance, taking place within the space of the metropolitan area of a major city, with its action spanning a time between two and four days. Every event in the play, actions included, must have a prior natural cause: miracles are excluded. The characters' actions must all be "believable." Any spectator thoroughly knowledgeable of their character traits, and of all other, prior events in the play-world imagined by the playwright, should be capable of predicting every onstage action. Here the explanatory hypothesis of psychological determinism is an undoubted assumption.

In this allegory, the playwright and actors can be seen as enjoying freedom from any determining influences in the dramatic world of the play. The playwright's freedom in creating that world is, in a sense, "cosmological." So also, in a somewhat different sense, is the actors' freedom. Each of the actors occupies two positions in the allegory, which may be understand as related by a kind of identity. Each participates in the workshop community, in a world apart from the space and time of the play. By a communal selection of traits to formulate their onstage characters, each participant affects the selections of every other. And their joint performance of the play can be understood as an effect or appearance onstage of their communal act of authorship, supplemented by the contribution of the playwright. The contents of the dramatic characters, functioning as laws animating the personae onstage, are freely chosen by the actors who play them. And so all their causally determined choices made onstage will depend ultimately upon their preliminary free choices made offstage. The actors are not responsible for the play-world. But they are each responsible for their actions in that world, because their actions onstage are determined, at least in part, by their original choices of character traits.

This allegory illustrates how to conceive of the relation between the same agent's singular, noumenal choice and the plurality of his or her phenomenal actions based on it. The latter take place under conditions quite different from the former, so that the two sets of conditions constitute entirely different worlds. Here the offstage choice of traits of character is merely allegorical. In Kant's view of human freedom, there is no reason to assume that the noumenal agent intentionally chooses traits of character, like the actors in the allegory. The most that can be said is that the noumenal agent's freely chosen action, whatever it may be, appears as the empirical character of the person acting in the world of space and time.[27]

5.8 "Ought" Implies "Can"

Was Kant a fatalist then? His theory of action as interpreted here has it that our empirical characters regulate everything we do in life, under the presupposition of psychological determinism. Yet our empirical characters have been fixed once and for all by a timeless act. So does this mean that everything we do in our lifetimes is for all practical purposes already done? Does it mean that our actions are already written down like so many stage directions in the script of the empirical world? What about " 'ought' implies 'can' "? If our actions are fated through our characters' determining our every move in response to prior events in the world, how can we freely choose to do what we recognize we ought to do? And if we ought to improve our characters, how can we do that?

---

[27] This point is offered to distinguish what I think is Kant's view from the Platonic characterization of it offered by Walker and Allison. "In Kantian terms," writes Walker, "this amounts to the idea that although the whole course of the phenomenal world is fixed, the noumenal self can choose to identify itself with one particular empirical character, which as a result of this identification becomes its 'sensible schema' (*KrV*, A553/B581), and for the conduct of which it thereby incurs moral responsibility"; Ralph C. S. Walker, "Achtung in the *Grundlegung*" in Otfried Höffe, ed., *Grundlegung zur Metaphysik der Sitten: Ein kooperativer Kommentar* (Frankfurt Am Main: Vittorio Klostermann, 1989), 97–116 at 102. Allison describes the mythic situation similarly: "the foundational choice, itself outside of time, supposedly determines the temporally appearing character in its entirety [, and from this] it seems to follow that our freedom is limited to a single 'intelligible act' in which we choose our character. On this reading, then, Kant's position reduces to a variant of the Platonic myth of Er, in which each soul (noumenal self) freely chooses whom to be in a deterministic universe" (*Kant's Theory of Freedom*, 139). In both of these characterizations of the noumenal act its intentional object is a particular empirical character. But I do not see how Kant would be entitled to say that the noumenal choice is a choice of one particular empirical character rather than another. It would be sufficient for Kant's view of the free, noumenal choice that the assignments of empirical characters are merely in some way fitting, or based on the choice. For another analogical application of Kant's idea of noumenal choice see John Rawls, *A Theory of Justice* (Cambridge, MA: Belknap Press, 1971), 255–6.

To address questions like these it will help to begin by interpreting the language of "standpoints" that Kant himself used. Sometimes he distinguished between two standpoints we can take on ourselves (*Groundwork*, 56/4:450), and sometimes between two aspects of sense-objects, including ourselves and our actions (*Pure Reason*, A538/B567). He referred sometimes to "intelligible consciousness" (*Practical Reason*, 83/5:99), evidently in contrast to "sensible consciousness," and to different "modes" of cognition or representation of things: "the mode of thought" and "the mode of sense" (*Denkungsart, Sinnesart; Pure Reason*, A551/B579).

We have seen how Kant's two-standpoints language has been interpreted as grounding his transcendental distinction between appearances and things in themselves. According to this popular line of interpretation, when an object is viewed from the sensible or phenomenal perspective its noumenal aspect is ignored. This is because its noumenal aspect would be unconsiderable from that standpoint. When the same object is viewed from the intelligible perspective, likewise, its phenomenal aspect is supposed to be ignored. Appearances are excluded from consideration in the intelligible standpoint, just as things in themselves are excluded from the sensible standpoint.

Yet Kant's standpoints language suggests a different arrangement. It suggests that he did not see the two standpoints as grounding the transcendental distinction. That distinction, rather, seems to provide the basis for the two standpoints as he conceived them. Kant seems to have seen the two standpoints as taking what I call *perpendicular views* on a common object. While others interpret them as what I call *parallel views,* on a neutral object. The difference is that perpendicular views can intersect; but parallel views cannot. The geometry of standpoints is illustrated in the following table.

Table 5.1.

Perpendicular Standpoints	Parallel Standpoints
Thing in Itself ↓	Appearance Thing in Itself
Appearance → Appearance	| | [neutral object]

Kant, I think, considered the intelligible and sensible standpoints on things as intersecting at *appearances*. The same appearance, that is, can be viewed from either standpoint. So he did not see appearances as excluded from the intelligible standpoint, in the way the two-standpoints interpretation of his transcendental distinction implies. To his mind, the standpoints are different perspectives on the causality of appearances.[28] They contrast in viewing appearances as caused "vertically," let us say, by things in themselves, and as caused "horizontally," by other appearances.[29] In the above diagram, the perpendicular standpoints are represented by vertical and horizontal arrows suggesting these different causal relations. With parallel standpoints, on the other hand, a neutral object is supposed to be the same object considerable from one standpoint as an appearance, and from the other standpoint as a thing in itself. The parallel standpoints on the neutral object are represented in the diagram by vertical lines suggesting parallel points of view.[30] The vertical lines are not arrows, since the two standpoints do not represent causal relations. In parallel-standpoints views, typically, causal relations are considerable only between appearances.

Here is an example of Kant's use of standpoint language related to our present concern about fatalism: "For, the *sensible life* has, with respect to the *intelligible* consciousness of its existence (consciousness of freedom), the absolute unity of a phenomenon. . . ." (*Practical Reason*, 83/5:99). From the

---

[28] The different standpoints on causality are suggested in the following statement:

The human being, who . . . regards himself as an intelligence, thereby puts himself in a different order of things and in a relation to determining grounds of an altogether different kind when he thinks of himself as an intelligence endowed with a will, and consequently with causality, than when he perceives himself as a phenomenon in the world of sense (as he also really is) and subjects his causality to external determination in accordance with laws of nature. (*Groundwork*, 61/4:457, see also *Pure Reason*, A538/B566)

[29] I have addressed the causal "overdetermination" that might be suggested by this arrangement in remarks on Hanna's criticism of the two-worlds interpretation. See p. 118, note 24.

[30] In the diagram I have bracketed the "neutral object" because not all who offer a parallel-standpoints interpretation specify what the neutral object is supposed to be, or even acknowledge its necessity. Above it was explained why Korsgaard's two-standpoints interpretation is incomplete, for not having acknowledged the neutral object (5.2). In view of this apparent incompleteness, however, one might imagine that Korsgaard actually does not see the two standpoints as parallel. It might seem that she has seen no need to acknowledge a neutral object, because, like Kant, she considers the two perspectives to be perpendicular. But I think the reason we cannot read Korsgaard's two standpoints as perpendicular is that she regards phenomena and noumena as standpoint-dependent. Consequently, she cannot regard the object of both her practical and theoretical standpoints as an appearance in space and time. In Kant's perpendicular standpoints, by contrast, the same appearance in space and time is considered in relation to other appearances in the one standpoint, and in relation to a thing in itself in the other standpoint. Parallel-standpoints interpretations see the objects of the two standpoints as different, as phenomena and noumena respectively. Perpendicular-standpoints interpretations see them as the same, as phenomena. This is possible because the latter interpretations do not see phenomena and noumena as standpoint-dependent entities.

intelligible standpoint, in other words, the plurality of a human being's actions can be viewed as a unitary role played out in the theater of the phenomenal world. Notice how, in the statement just quoted, Kant saw freedom and phenomenon as accessible from the same standpoint.[31] Consider also this further example, where Kant compared empirical and intelligible characters.

[F]or a subject in the world of sense we would have first an *empirical character,* through which its actions, as appearances, would stand through and through in connection with other appearances in accordance with constant natural laws. . . . Yet second, one would also have to allow this subject an *intelligible character,* through which it is indeed the cause of those actions as appearances. . . .   (*Pure Reason,* A539/B567)

This passage follows almost immediately after Kant's first suggesting how to think of an object of sense in a "double aspect."[32] Note here how he saw the same objects of sense, in this case, *a subject in the world of sense,* and *actions as appearances,* as common objects of the empirical and the intelligible standpoints on character. This is a hallmark of perpendicular standpoints. From the intelligible standpoint actions as appearances are considered in relation to their free, noumenal cause; from the empirical standpoint the same actions as appearances are considered in relation to their empirical causes.

In the second *Critique* Kant granted that "if it were possible for us to have such deep insight into a human being's cast of mind . . . that we would know every incentive to action . . . as well as the external occasions affecting them . . . we could calculate a [free] human being's conduct for the future with as much certainty as a lunar or solar eclipse. . . ." (83/5:99). In the empirical perspective on human conduct, that is, every action is the necessary effect of prior natural events in accordance with the determining laws of character. Kant's statement here implies that an omniscient observer of the empirical world would be able to judge with certainty that someone recognizing that she *ought* to do something will not do it. That is the same as judging that, considering all relevant empirical data prior to the action,

---

[31] This is not possible in the way Korsgaard interprets the two standpoints we can take on things.

[32] "Of the faculty of such a subject we would accordingly form an empirical and at the same time an intellectual concept of its causality, both of which apply to one and the same effect. Thinking of the faculty of an object of sense in this double aspect does not contradict any of the concepts we have to form of appearances and of possible experience" (*Pure Reason,* A538/B566).

she *cannot* do it.[33] How else could there be predictive certainty in such a case? How else can we predict the occurrence of a solar eclipse tomorrow than by foreseeing that tomorrow the moon *cannot* do otherwise than move between the sun and the earth? In the case of someone's failing to do what she recognizes she ought to do, it could be known in advance, in principle, that her moral incentive will fail "to express its effect in actions only because subjective (pathological) causes hinder it" (*Practical Reason*, 68/5:79). In this empirical perspective on the human being's sensible life, whatever fails to happen when there is an active causal force for its happening fails to happen only because of stronger hindrances to the effectiveness of that force. So here, judging from the empirical standpoint, "ought" would not imply "can."

The empirical standpoint situates every human being's actions within a chain of natural causes over which he has no control (cf., ibid., 82/5:97). But, writes Kant, if "we were capable of another view, namely an intellectual intuition of the same subject . . . then we would become aware that this whole chain of appearances, with respect to all that the moral law is concerned with, depends upon the spontaneity of the subject as a thing in itself" (83/5:99). So there is one view on human actions which sees them all as predictable events that could not have been otherwise, given the character of the human agent and the external occasion of his action. But there is another, intelligible view on the human subject as a thing in itself, a view we can only imagine taking, because we cannot view what underlies its series of appearances. From this standpoint, if we could adopt it, we could see how the unified phenomenon of a sensible life could have been otherwise, and hence how any action-event in its chain of appearances could have been otherwise. "[T]he moral law assures us of this difference between the relation of our actions as appearances to the sensible being of our subject and the relation by which this sensible being is itself referred to the intelligible substratum in us" (ibid.). Because of the moral law, that is, we cannot avoid thinking that whatever we *ought* to do, we *can* do. But in thinking this we adopt a non-empirical, intelligible view of our conduct.

---

[33] Kant said as much in the following comment, which he framed in terms of commission rather than omission: "If I say of a human being who commits a theft that this deed is, in accordance with the natural law of causality, a necessary result of determining grounds in preceding time, then it was impossible that it could have been left undone. . . ." (*Practical Reason*, 80/5:95).

The next sentence Kant wrote was: "From this [intelligible] perspective, which is natural to our reason though inexplicable, appraisals can be justified which, though made in all conscientiousness, yet seem at first glance [i.e., from the empirical perspective] contrary to all equity." He has explained here how justified moral appraisals from the intelligible perspective, which is where "ought" *does* imply "can", may seem "contrary to all equity" from the empirical perspective, where "ought" *does not* imply "can". If we say that the agent who recognized that he ought, morally, to do something could not have done it nevertheless, because his opposing inclinations were too strong, then we are considering the case from the empirical perspective. But this is not how we see things from the intelligible perspective presup posed by the moral law. When we say from this perspective that since he ought to have done it, he could have, we mean that the unitary phenomenon of his character ought to have, and so could have, provided for his doing it.

But if Kant's moral theory tells us that we ought to be better than we have been, doesn't this mean that we ought to, and so that we *can*, alter the moral character of the role we play in the phenomenal world? Wood once responded to such a question in the following way: "Presumably, [Kant's] theory is that for every imaginable course of conduct in the phenomenal world, there is a timeless choice . . . that would yield that course of conduct. Hence there are some such choices whose results in the world of appearance involve changes in empirical character. . . ." ("Kant's Compatibilism," 94). We must be careful here, however, to avoid thinking that moral dissatisfaction with the way things are unfolding in time might lead a noumenal person to alter the phenomenal person's empirical character. Personal moral progress in Kant's theory would imply a change of character from bad to better. But this can be consistent with the idea that empirical character is the temporally developing appearance of a timeless, invariant, noumenal action. We need only stop to consider the perplexities to be encountered in the very idea of character. Consider a physical analogy. A cup of water dropped from a height of one meter will splash. A cup of ice dropped in the same way will bounce. Here, apparently, are two physical objects whose actions differ in the same circumstances just because of their different empirical characters. But the cup of water can undergo a change of physical character at $0°C$ and take on the character of ice; and we know that water's changing to ice at that temperature is, so to speak, "in character." So does the water's change from being something whose character calls for it to splash when dropped, to something whose character calls for it to bounce, constitute a change of character or not? In one sense of character, yes; in another sense, no.

The same equivocation applies in human psychology, though in a way that is more complicated. What must always be factored in here, unlike in the physical world, is that the human being's representation of the laws of her character can subsequently make a difference in her character. Self-consciousness alters the conscious self.[34] So if someone should come to recognize the moral shortcomings of his character, that recognition itself may change his character. And whether it changes his character for the better or the worse must depend, of course, on his character, on the kind of person he is at that time.

But here the charge of fatalism arises most pointedly. From the intelligible perspective on character moral progress is inconceivable, for noumenal becoming is a contradiction. Yet from the empirical perspective, even though change and becoming takes place here, we cannot control it while we are in the stream of becoming. We cannot *make* moral progress here, though it is possible that our empirical characters might *show* moral progress. It may well be that the maxims constituting my empirical character will improve. Or it may be that my recognition of the moral *ought* will generate an increasingly stronger moral incentive compared with inclinations. It may even be that this progress in me can be initiated and sustained only consequent to my recognition that I "ought" morally to initiate and sustain it. Still, whether I will show this kind of progress must depend simply on the chain of causes that drives these evident variations of my empirical character over time. Whether I am to become a better person in the empirical world, as a consequence of recognizing that I ought to, may therefore seem to be left to fate.

This is the charge of fatalism brought against Kant's theory of freedom. In answering it we need only point out that, conceptually, *fatalism* would place the control of my moral development in something outside me: either in natural causes, or in blind chance (cf. *Lectures on Metaphysics,* 411/28:773). So Kant's view is not fatalistic, because it says that the moral development

---

[34] Kant suggested this in part of his famous skeptical argument against a science of empirical psychology: "even observation by itself already changes and displaces the state of the observed object" (*Metaphysical Foundations of Natural Science,* 186/4:471).

of my empirical character is determined by my free, noumenal act. Nature, or part of nature, may contain events prompting alterations in my empirical character. But their efficacy upon my character is nevertheless determined by my own action as a noumenon. It can still be said, therefore, that whether my bad empirical character shows improvement must depend ultimately upon me. Even if bad education, poverty or abuse turn out to be insurmountable obstacles to my moral development, I am the one who made them my obstacles, the one who put them, so to speak, "in my way." [35] Their effect on my becoming better depends not on fate, but ultimately upon me.

5.9 Two Moral Objections

A couple of objections to the idea of timeless free agency in a noumenal world were addressed near the end of the previous chapter. These objections raised metaphysical or epistemological issues. In the final section of this chapter we consider two more objections, both formulated by Ralph Walker, which focus on moral considerations.

The first of Walker's objections to be considered here has been repeated often by others.[36] It is roughly that by supposing that our empirical characters are chosen from a position outside the empirical world we over-expand the scope of moral responsibility. This supposition should make us morally responsible not only for our empirical characters, but also for all of the empirical causes of our characters, even those that precede our births. Walker argues,

in view of the thoroughgoing causal interaction that the Third Analogy [of Kant's *Critique of Pure Reason*] requires, my noumenal self must have freely chosen the entire causal series that makes up the phenomenal world. Perhaps it did so by itself, perhaps in collusion with other noumenal subjects who all happened to agree. Either way, my responsibility extends far beyond my own character: I can be blamed for the First World War, and for the Lisbon earthquake that so appalled Voltaire.[37]

---

[35] This is how Kant puts it in *The Metaphysics of Morals,* speaking of a person's natural inclinations as self-imposed "obstacles" to virtue (197/6:394).

[36] See Bennett, "Kant's Theory of Freedom," 102–4; and Allison, *Kant's Theory of Freedom,* 138–9.

[37] Ralph C. S. Walker, *Kant, the Arguments of the Philosophers* (London: Routledge & Kegan Paul, 1978), 149.

A fair response to this line of objection has been offered by Wood. He reminds us that in his theory of freedom Kant intended to establish nothing more than that we *could be* noumenally free, even while every phenomenal event has a cause. He did not intend to establish that we can know that we are free. Nor did he attempt to say exactly what we do as noumenal free agents that results in our empirical characters, and how it would do so. Consequently, Wood points out, it remains at least possible that owing to our noumenal actions we are each morally responsible for just those empirical deeds we normally impute to ourselves. That is all Kant would have wanted to prove.[38]

It seems that a somewhat better reply to the objection may be available, however. The crucial error made by Walker here, it seems to me, lies in treating empirical characters as events. Kant's Second and Third Analogies in the first *Critique* attempt to demonstrate the thoroughgoing casual connections of all events in the phenomenal world. This makes it certain that every event has prior causes extending back to ancient history. But it is important to recognize that our empirical characters are not events, but *causal laws* of events: specifically, of our actions. Empirical characters are laws by which substances in the phenomenal world operate; and it is absurd to suppose that the laws of empirical causality themselves have prior empirical causes. Kant wrote, as quoted earlier: "But every effective cause must have a *character,* i.e., a law of its causality . . . through which its actions, as appearances, would stand through and through in connection with other appearances in accordance with constant natural laws" (*Pure Reason,* A539/567). So if empirical characters can be correctly understood as laws of causality, then we need not acknowledge any empirical causes of our characters.[39] We therefore can be morally responsible for our empirical characters without being responsible also for any prenatal causes.

---

[38] "Kant's Compatibilism," 92.

[39] Kant may seem at one point to say otherwise: "Because this empirical character itself must be drawn from appearances *as effect,* and from the rule which experience provides. . . ." (*Pure Reason,* A549/B577, emphasis added). It makes no sense, however, that a law of empirical causality, which is how empirical character is defined, should be derived or inferred as an effect of prior appearances. Kant probably referred instead to (knowledge of) empirical character derived from its effects among appearances. In the previous sentence he said as much: A human being's empirical character, he wrote, "is nothing other than a certain causality of his reason, insofar as in its effects in appearance this reason exhibits a rule. . . ." Compare another translation of the "as effect" passage: "this empirical character must itself be discovered from the appearances which are its effect and from the rule to which experience shows them to conform. . . ." Immanuel Kant, *Critique of Pure Reason,* trans. Norman Kemp Smith

But to this reply another objection can be anticipated. Certainly, it will be said, there are character-shaping events in our lives—education, good or bad, adversity, fortune—and the events that cause these events may be caused in turn by prenatal, even ancient causes. So imputing responsibility for our empirical characters should make us responsible for these causes as well. Yet the simple response to this reply is that even if we grant that an event can shape a character, how it can shape a character must depend upon the character. That is, whether a good education will work for me, whether adversity in youth can bring out a later positive outlook, or whether an early string of luck will incline me toward deep resentment as I suffer later setbacks—these outcomes of character-shaping events depend upon the shape of my character when they occur. So the assumption that prior empirical events can affect the development of our characters does not imply that responsibility for our characters would include responsibility for the causes of character-shaping events.

The second line of objection formulated by Walker is that, "From a purely formal point of view, Kant succeeds in showing that the two ideas of [freedom and determinism] are consistent, but at the cost of detaching freedom utterly from the [temporal] context in which it was originally required: that of everyday life and moral appraisal" (148). But this objection misses the mark. It would be on target if Kant thought of the noumenal world as utterly detached from the empirical world. But that is not how he saw their relationship. The timeless noumenal world is what Kant called the "ground" of the appearances making up the phenomenal world. That is, what we do empirically, in everyday life, is dependent somehow upon what we do freely in the noumenal world.

Walker's second line of objection would be on target also if human character were utterly detached from free action; that is, if character's explanatory power were seen as canceled by everyday freedom of choice. In that case, anyone with a bad empirical character would be considered free in his everyday actions to act contrary to the contents of his character, or contrary to his maxims: his own subjective principles. In theory, therefore,

---

(New York: St. Martin's Press, 1965). Compare also, "this empirical character itself must be drawn from appearances, as its effect, and from the rule of these as provided to us by experience . . ." Immanuel Kant, *Critique of Pure Reason,* trans. Werner S. Pluhar (Indianapolis, IN: Hackett Publishing Company, 1996). Kant wrote: *"dieser empirische Charakter selbst aus den Erscheinungen als Wirkung und aus der Regel derselben, welche Erfahrung an die Hand giebt, gezogen werden muß. . . ."*

he could do good every day without the slightest improvement in his character. Or, what seems even more absurd, he could have an exemplary moral character and still exercise his everyday freedom, constantly, to do evil. These contradictions are implied by Walker's assumption, expressed in the second objection, that freedom would be required, originally, for the temporal context of everyday action. But Kant would reject this assumption, and it seems he would be right to do so.

The assumption that we should be considered free to act contrary to the contents of our characters is an assumption that confutes the very idea of a character. Hence, to assume we have character is to assume that freedom is not required for the everyday temporal context of free action. And in that case, to hold someone morally responsible for her everyday actions in their temporal context is to hold her morally responsible for her character. It is to presume, as Kant presumed, that our freedom is originally required not for the everyday temporal context, but for the acquisition of character. Perhaps the reader will tolerate here yet another reference to the problem of justification and explanation. It should be pointed out here that when we require freedom for the temporal context of action in everyday life it becomes impossible to solve that problem. The justifications for our actions that are supplied by practical reasoning are derived from our maxims, the contents of our empirical characters. These maxims include the maxim of morality: our interest, in general, in doing what is right. The explanations for our actions are then supplied by the psychological forces of incentives incorporated into these maxims. If we therefore assume that through everyday freedom of choice we have the power to act independently of our maxims, the laws of our characters, then there can be no explanation for our actions we recognize as justified. It will not do to say that through everyday freedom we can nevertheless choose to act, or not, on the principles by which we recognize actions as justified. This will not do because free choice, as shown near the end of Chapter 3, and as reiterated above, is not explanatory.

The two lines of objection formulated by Walker may seem to present good reasons from moral philosophy to reject the two-worlds, metaphysical interpretation of Kant's theory of action.[40] But these objections turn out to be easy to dismiss. Earlier in this chapter we saw good reasons to reject

---

[40] See also Allison, *Kant's Theory of Freedom*, 138–9.

the more popular alternative to the two-worlds interpretation, which is the "two-standpoints" view. It was shown here that these interpretations seem incapable of providing satisfactory explanations for action justified on purely practical, non-empirical grounds. In the next chapter, on the moral incentive of respect for law, we see how the two-worlds interpretation takes the advantage on this last point, succeeding at a crucial point where its competitor fails.

We began this chapter by outlining a couple of different approaches to the two-standpoints interpretation of Kant's transcendental distinction, between appearances and things in themselves. Then followed a philosophical critique of that interpretation, centering on the "neutral object." This is the self-identical object that presumably can be viewed from either of the two standpoints, respectively, as an appearance or as a thing in itself. The two-standpoints interpretation was further criticized for its inability to solve the problem of justification and explanation. In the middle of the chapter we turned next to Kant's distinction between empirical and intelligible character. In his view, our free actions in the noumenal world result in our having the character we have in the empirical world. That character serves as a "causal law" for our actions, and hence it is central to the explanation of our actions. So since we are free in the noumenal act by which we acquire our empirical characters, our actions in the empirical world are both causally determined and free. This way of making determinism consistent with freedom may suggest empirical fatalism, or it may seem to conflict with Kant's principle that "ought" implies "can." But we saw how these worries can be addressed, in part by clarifying and employing the language of two standpoints in the way that Kant himself used it. We also addressed, in the end, two objections to the idea of noumenal free agency, based on moral considerations. Neither objection represents Kant's views correctly, as we saw. So far, then, the two-worlds interpretation of Kant's theory of action has here proved superior to the problematic, and weaker, two-standpoints interpretation.

6

Moral Motivation

Two-standpoints interpretations of Kant's practical philosophy have difficulty showing how what justifies action, morally, can also explain it (see 5.3). On these interpretations, consequently, it is hard to see how moral justification, expressed in categorical imperatives, can be relevant for human action (see 1.11). But the alternative, two-worlds interpretation defended here has no difficulty on this point, mainly because of the way it accommodates psychological determinism (see 3.1, 5.5).

It will be a principal thesis of the present chapter that Kant viewed respect for the moral law as a psychologically forceful incentive, one that would be capable of explaining actions justified by pure practical reason. The first half of the chapter develops an extended argument showing that respect is the motivating feeling that explains actions appraised in Kant's ethical theory as having "moral worth." It also presents a "phenomenology" of respect, and elucidates some of Kant's comments on how this motivating feeling would be generated. In later sections, beginning with Section 6, the focus shifts to a perennial complaint about Kantian ethics that is related to respect and moral motivation. It is the objection posed by virtue-theorists, and others, who say that Kant's criterion for the moral worth of action is too narrow; because only actions from duty alone, motivated by respect for the moral law, are supposed to have moral worth. Here I'll offer a new response to this complaint. It will be that in Kant's ethical theory, the criterion for an action's having "moral worth" is different from the criterion for an action's being "virtuous." Thus, if an action lacks moral worth, because it is not motivated by respect for the moral law, it could nevertheless be virtuous. The problem-solving distinction to be drawn here, between the moral worth and the virtue of actions, will have some further implications for the moral life as presented by Kantian ethics; and these will be discussed in the final section of this chapter, and in the next, final chapter.

6.1 Moral Incentives

For an action to have what Kant called "moral worth" it must not be motivated, even in part, by any natural desire or inclination. He wrote in a prominent passage in the second *Critique* that "What is essential to any moral worth of actions is that *the moral law determine the will immediately*. If the determination of the will takes place conformably with the law but only by means of a feeling, of whatever kind . . . then the action will contain *legality* indeed, but not *morality*" (62/5:72). This statement has been interpreted as implying that no feelings or psychological forces, of any kind, could explain actions with moral worth. But if that is actually what it implies, then the assumption that human actions are causally determined by psychological forces must not reflect Kant's views. And if it does not, then the two-worlds interpretation of Kant's theory of action may be in trouble. For it, also, will have difficulty showing how actions justified by moral principles can be explained.

The response I'll offer to this apparent difficulty here will be simple. It will be that Kant did not see motivation by the feeling of respect for law as incompatible with the moral law's immediate determination of the will. Hence, he did not deny that action motivated by that feeling would have any "moral worth."

Kant's *Critique of Practical Reason* includes an entire chapter devoted to moral motivation. The first sentences of that chapter are those sentences quoted just above, about immediate determination of the will by the moral law. The chapter's title is "On the Incentives of Pure Practical Reason," in the plural. As I pointed out earlier (2.2), in this chapter Kant identified two different things as the one and only moral incentive. They are the objective moral law, and the subjective feeling of respect for the moral law (see 62/5:72, and 67/5:78). His identifying both the law and the feeling as *the* moral incentive suggests that his concept of "incentive" has both objective and subjective dimensions. It suggests, in other words, that Kant's term "incentive" can refer to an object to be brought about through action, as well as to a subjective, motivational state targeting such an object. For example: an investor's incentive for a new venture is profit, or it is the profit motive. It usually makes no difference whether we explain action in terms of the object the agent is motivated to achieve, or in terms of a subjective state of the agent targeting the object.

A careful reading of the text quoted above shows that there Kant actually did not intend to deny that the feeling of respect can be motivationally effective in morally worthy action, as is sometimes supposed. He wrote that actions lack moral worth "[i]f the determination of the will takes place ... only by means of a feeling, of whatever kind, *that has to be presupposed in order for the law to become a sufficient determining ground of the will. ...*" (emphasis added). But Kant did not think the feeling of respect has to be presupposed for this.[1] He elsewhere described "moral feeling" as a feeling that can arise only as *a consequence* of the thought of the moral law (cf. *Metaphysics of Morals*, 201/6:399), or of its determination of the will. He also classified all other feelings that we could have antecedent to recognizing a command of the moral law as "pathological," not as moral ("practical").[2] In making these comments his assumption was that the thought of an action's being dutiful or right would be the "*sufficient determining ground of the will*"; and this would subsequently give rise to the feeling of respect for the law that makes it dutiful or right. Then the action, following on the strength of that feeling, would be done for the sake of the law (2.6).

Kant's statements on feeling and moral motivation at the beginning of his chapter are meant to exclude the prospect that initially there is something we desire, such as to be happy, or perhaps to receive a heavenly reward, and then we recognize that obeying the law is the way to achieve this, so we comply with the law on the strength of our antecedent desire. He wanted to emphasize that a motivational structure like this would not confer moral worth on actions in compliance with the law. But this would not imply that motivation for actions with moral worth must depend on no feelings whatsoever.

---

[1] Lewis Beck pointed this out several decades ago. See *A Commentary on Kant's Critique of Practical Reason*, 222.

[2] "The feeling that arises from consciousness of this [practical] necessitation [of duty] is not pathological, as would be a feeling produced by the senses, but practical only, that is, possible through a preceding (objective) determination of the will and causality of reason" (*Practical Reason*, 69/5:80, cf. also 65/5:75).

6.2 The Feeling of Respect

Kant referred to the feeling of respect as the "moral incentive," which implies that this feeling would be motivationally effective (2.2). But most commentators have not seen the feeling of respect as an effective motive for moral action.[3] This section outlines three different ways the role of the feeling of respect has been explained, and then presents a critical challenge to all three. In the section to follow we develop an alternative explanation of respect, which presents it as a motivating feeling.

(a) Some see respect for the moral law as a complex mental attitude, having both an intellectual aspect and an affective aspect. The intellectual aspect is seen as the moral agent's consciousness of the law's constraint, while the affective aspect is considered to be a psychological effect of that consciousness. Here recognition of the law's supreme authority is thought to provide a sufficient motive for action, which causes us to feel respect for it. But our feeling is not supposed to play any motivational role. Rather, our recognition of the law's authority is believed to motivate action in obedience to it, and the feeling is something like an emotional side-effect of that motivation.[4]

(b) A slightly different view is that what Kant called the feeling of respect, or of reverence, is nothing other than our recognition of the motivating constraint imposed by the law. It is not a side-effect of that recognition. Here the law's authoritative constraint is supposed to motivate, as in the previous view. But it is said that the only way we can be conscious of this constraint is through feeling respect or reverence for the law.[5] The idea is

[3] See Robert Paul Wolff, *The Autonomy of Reason* (New York: Harper & Row, 1973), 83; A. Murray MacBeath, "Kant on Moral Feeling," *Kant-Studien* 74 (1973): 283–314, 313; Mark Timmons, "Kant on the Possibility of Moral Motivation," *Southern Journal of Philosophy* 23 (1985): 377–98; Onora Nell, *Acting on Principle*, 111; and Ralph Walker, "Achtung in the *Grundlegung*," 98.

[4] Reath, for example, has claimed that "it is the intellectual aspect [of respect] which is active in motivating moral conduct, while the affective side, or feeling of respect, is its effect on certain sensible tendencies" ("Kant's Theory of Moral Sensibility," 287). "[W]hile [a feeling of respect] is produced when the Moral Law determines the will, it is not this affect that motivates" (ibid., 290). See also Allison, *Kant's Theory of Freedom*, 123.

[5] This interpretation is developed in Stratton-Lake, *Kant, Duty and Moral Worth*, 34–9. His argument for it emphasizes something Kant wrote about our knowledge of that feeling: "respect for the law is a feeling that is produced by an intellectual ground, and this is the only feeling that we can cognize completely a priori. . . ." (*Practical Reason*, 62–3/5:73). It is assumed in this argument that if our cognitive consciousness of the moral law's constraint is supposed to *cause* a feeling of respect, then we

that to say we feel respect or reverence for the moral law is merely to offer a different description of what actively motivates us: our consciousness of the law's constraint.

The two preceding views disagree mainly over the etiology of the feeling of respect. They agree in denying that the feeling of respect plays a motivational role in morally worthy action. But they differ on how the feeling would relate to our consciousness of duty, or of the moral law's command. It is caused by that consciousness, according to the former view, and it is identical with that consciousness, according to the latter. Yet this is a very subtle disagreement, which might seem resolvable by the theoretical resources emphasized in a third view. Kant did, after all, recognize a kind of mix of causality and identity in the relation between things in themselves and appearances. The thing in itself is supposed to be a cause of the appearance, and yet the latter is in some way identifiable with the former. Could this have been Kant's view of the feeling of respect: that it is the appearance of a thing in itself? That is the suggestion of the third view.

(c) The third view explains that the feeling of respect could be both *caused by*, and *identical with*, (consciousness of) the moral law's determination of the will. The will can be viewed from two standpoints, it is claimed in this view.[6] From one standpoint we may think of the morally determined will as a thing in itself. From the other standpoint it may be an appearance in our self-consciousness. The former determination of the (noumenal) will by the moral law could therefore *cause* the (phenomenal) feeling of respect, as its appearance in time.[7] But since the feeling would be caused by that of which it is an appearance, this would allow us, perhaps, to see the feeling of respect as both an effect of the moral law's motivating

could not know this a priori; because causal relations are known through experience. Hence, Kant's insistence that the relation between consciousness of the moral law's constraint and the feeling of respect is known a priori implies that they would not be causally related. So since the feeling would not be *caused by* consciousness of the law's constraint, it must be *identical with* that constraint. But this conclusion should be compared with what Kant wrote at *Groundwork*, 64/4:460, where he presented the relation between our consciousness of the moral law's constraint and the feeling of respect as mediated by a "special kind of causality."

[6] See Daniel Guevara, *Kant's Theory of Moral Motivation* (Boulder, CO: Westview Press, 2000).

[7] Guevara writes: "[T]he law's becoming an incentive, or subjective determining ground of our will, is the embodiment of the law: that is, its appearance in an embodied and thus sensible species of rational agents. The law's becoming a subjective determining ground is the law's becoming a motivational feeling, namely the feeling of respect" (106).

determination of the will, and as identical with moral motivation in the empirical world.

In the preceding paragraphs we have the outlines of three ways recent interpreters have attempted to explain the relation Kant saw between moral motivation and the feeling of respect for law. Only in the third interpretation is it allowed that the feeling would somehow play a motivational role in moral action. In the other two interpretations this is explicitly denied. Yet I think each of these interpretations overlooks something crucial: namely, the possibility of moral weakness of will (see 2.3). In an earlier chapter I pointed out a number of places were Kant wrote as if the strength of the moral incentive matters (3.6). I think he believed it matters because he assumed that lack of strength in the moral incentive, which would be moral weakness of will, explains certain kinds of failure to act on moral principles.[8] To explain how moral weakness of will is possible, moral motivation must be seen as depending upon something subjective, and variable from agent to agent. And I think each of the three ways recent interpreters have explained the feeling of respect falters on this point.

The first two ways agree in denying that the subjective feeling of respect plays any motivational role. Each explains moral motivation entirely on the side of the law's authoritative constraint. But we may presume that no one accepting either of these views would agree that the moral law can constrain, and so motivate, *too weakly*. Nor should anyone accepting either view agree that the fault of moral weakness lies in our intellectual consciousness of that constraint.[9] For then failure to act morally, through weakness of will, would evidence either a momentary loss of consciousness of the law's constraint, or a conception of the law's constraint with faint, or diminished understanding. The fault would be wholly on the side of conception or understanding, and we would not then have the classic case of moral weakness *of will*. For a genuine example of weakness

---

[8] It can also explain how a person might sometimes do the right thing but fail to do it for the right reason. If the proper motivation is weak, and if there is another, stronger motive force for doing the same action, then the latter may prevail. Although Kant does not say so, this might be what happens in the example he gives of the shopkeeper who charges a fair price not because it is right to do so, but because it is in his self-interest. It might sometimes be that neither motive is strong enough by itself, but that together they move the agent to act in the right way: a case of "mixed motives."

[9] Both views include, as a necessary component of the consciousness of the moral law's constraint, the idea that the law provides an all-sufficient reason for action. (See Reath, "Kant's Theory of Moral Sensibility," 287, and Stratton-Lake, *Kant, Duty and Moral Worth*, 37–8).

of will is a case of someone caving in to temptation to do what he understands fully well is not right.[10] So there is a problem in each of the first two approaches to understanding the role of the feeling of respect in moral motivation. Neither view can present moral motivation as dependent upon a subjective, psychological force, like the feeling of respect for law. Consequently, neither view can explain how moral motivation can sometimes be too weak for doing what we recognize as right.

The third view of the feeling of respect seems more promising on this point. For it actually identifies respect for the law as a *motivating* feeling. And this should make it possible to see moral motivation as subjectively variable in strength. Yet here there is the following difficulty. In this third view, the feeling of respect is supposed to be the phenomenal counterpart of the noumenal will determined by the law. But how then shall we understand moral weakness, on the phenomenal side, in relation to the noumenally determined will?[11] Perhaps weakness in the motivating feeling is explainable as the phenomenal appearance of some kind of noumenal weakness. Or, something might be lost in the actual "appearing" of the noumenally determined will. It might be assumed that the phenomenally weak will would be only a pale imitation of the noumenal will that would be absolutely, sufficiently, determined by the moral law. Each of these alternatives proves problematic, however.

The latter alternative is somewhat plausible if we think of the feeling of respect as the instantiation in the world of sense of something like a Platonic Idea. The moral law's determination of the will might be absolute or perfect. But its appearance as the phenomenal feeling of respect could be expected to be imperfect, and therefore sometimes too weak. If we

---

[10] It isn't temptation unless one is attracted to something one believes to be wrong, or less good.

[11] Guevara avoids having to deal with this problem. He does not attribute weakness of will to any weakness in what he recognizes as the motivating feeling of respect. He writes: "Weakness of will shows that the causal influence of a moral principle can be overridden. . . . overridden by what? A stronger cause? A stronger force? No. If anything, the answer is simply that we override it, by our own free decision to go against our better judgment or our character or whatnot" (80). It seems to me that Guevara is here expressing something like the free-choice solution to the problem of justification and explanation (3.9). Our action is supposedly explained by our free choice to act contrary to the law we recognize as constraining us, and not by any weakness of a psychological force or feeling. In that case, however, I do not see what Guevara can mean by calling the feeling of respect for law a *motivating* feeling. Evidently the strength or weakness of this feeling does not explain our acting one way rather than another. What explains this, Guevara seems to say, is "our own free decision."

accept this explanation, however, it would be difficult to see why anyone's failure to act morally, through weakness of will, should be imputable to him as *his own* moral failing. On the other hand, the former alternative has the potential to present a similar problem. This interpretation says that weakness in the phenomenal feeling reflects some kind of weakness in the law's determination of the noumenal will. But how could we be morally responsible for weakness attributable to a noumenal activity of the moral law upon our wills?

To account for the imputability of moral weakness it seems we must suppose that the degree or quality of the moral law's determination of each individual's will is in some way up to the individual. It seems to me that this is possible only if we adopt the two-worlds interpretation of Kant's practical philosophy, as defended in the previous chapters. The component of that interpretation that we are specifically concerned with here, and that we shall develop further in Section 5 below, is moral character: intelligible and empirical. But before we can take up this topic it will be best to consider Kant's own explanation of moral motivation a little more closely.

6.3 Motivating Feeling

Kant introduced the feeling of respect for the moral law in an early footnote of his *Groundwork of the Metaphysics of Morals*. He introduced it there as "*self-wrought* by means of a rational concept and therefore specifically different from all feelings [received through the influence of sensible objects], which can be reduced to inclination or fear" (14n./4:402n.). In this section we examine the way Kant understood the motivating role of that feeling.

We may begin by observing that the third view outlined above is not faithful to Kant's conception of feeling in general. That view presents the feeling of respect as the sensible appearance of the morally determined will as a thing in itself. But "feelings" are not what Kant would classify as appearances of things. So it would be a mistake to suppose that the feeling of respect is the sensible appearance of the noumenal will, or of its determination by the moral law. We feel pleasure or displeasure only in the representation of an object, as Kant's view has it. And when we do, the feeling is referred to ourselves and not to the represented object.[12] The pleasure one feels in representing an object doesn't even refer to oneself as an object. That is, my feeling pleasure or displeasure doesn't present me with an idea of myself, or of my will. Feelings may be subjective reactions to sensible appearances, including even bodily or mental activities. They may also be subjective reactions to ideas of things in themselves. But they are not *appearances* of those things. So it is not Kant's view that the feeling of respect is the sensible appearance of the noumenal will. Rather, he claimed that a feeling of respect is a feeling of pleasure or displeasure that arises from the recognition that an action conforms to, or disobeys, the moral law.[13]

In that initial footnote on respect Kant claimed that it is a feeling analogous to both inclination and fear. The analogy is evidently between respect and both painful feelings, of which fear is a species, and pleasant feelings, which are the basis for inclinations. Yet both fear and inclination are motivational states. So, by analogy, it seems that respect for the moral law should also be a motivational state.

Not all feelings of pleasure and displeasure are motivational states, however. Kant explained the pleasures we feel in aesthetic contemplation, the pleasures of the beautiful and of the sublime, as "disinterested" pleasures. As such they are not pleasures "in the existence" of their objects (see *Judgment*, 90−1/5:204−5). By this he meant that these pleasures do not move us to act. In *The Metaphysics of Morals* he contrasted these contemplative pleasures with motivating, "practical" pleasures (41/6:212). He also ranked "moral feeling," or the feeling of respect, among the practical pleasures (see *Practical Reason*, 65/5:75, *Metaphysics of Morals*, 183/6:378). So the feeling of respect for the moral law is not a non-motivating, aesthetic feeling. It is instead a motivating, practical feeling.

It may seem puzzling that Kant would think of a feeling of pleasure as a motivating psychological state. It is easy to understand states of desire or

---

[12] Kant wrote: If a determination of the feeling of pleasure or displeasure is called sensation, then this expression means something entirely different than if I call the representation of a thing (through sense, as a receptivity belonging to the faculty of cognition) sensation. For in the latter case the representation is related to the object, but in the first case it is related solely to the subject, and does not serve for any cognition at all, not even that by which the subject *cognizes* itself. (*Judgment*, 92/5:206)

[13] He often referred to respect simply as "moral feeling" (2.10), and he defined the latter as "the susceptibility to feel pleasure or displeasure merely from being aware that our actions are consistent with or contrary to the law of duty" (*Metaphysics of Morals*, 201/6:399).

inclination as motivating. But pleasures may seem different. It may seem most plausible to think of a feeling of pleasure as motivating just in the sense that it is desired, or in the sense that we are motivated to bring about the condition of our feeling pleasure (see 2.11). So did Kant think that when we act motivated by this feeling we are attempting to satisfy a desire to feel the noble pleasure of respect for the moral law? Or did he perhaps think that we obey the moral law because we are fearful of the moral pain or remorse we would expect to feel if we disobeyed?

This is not how he saw the role of the feeling of respect for law in moral motivation. He made this clear in the following passage from the second *Critique*.

[C]onsciousness of the determination of the faculty of desire is always the ground of a satisfaction in the action produced by it; but this [moral] pleasure, this satisfaction with oneself, is not the determining ground of the action: instead, the determination of the will directly by reason alone is the ground of the feeling of pleasure, and this remains a pure practical, not aesthetic, determination of the faculty of desire. (97–8/5:116)

His view is not that we are motivated to obey the moral law because we anticipate a good feeling, or because we hope to avoid a bad one. It is the other way around. We feel the moral pleasure or displeasure of respect when we are conscious of our contemplated action's relation to the moral law. This moral consciousness, this "determination of the will by the moral law," must *precede* the feeling of respect.

But this last point seems now to raise another difficulty. Why, if the moral law's determining the will is supposed always to precede the feeling of respect, is the latter seen as a practical, motivating feeling? Why isn't the always prior consciousness of our action's relation to the moral law sufficient to motivate?

The answer is that human motivation has two aspects, distinguishable as direction and force. The distinction made earlier between the objective and subjective dimensions of Kant's concept of "incentives" (2.2) is related to these two aspects of motivation. When we are motivated to act we are directed toward some targeted object or end. But we are motivated in that direction either strongly or weakly. For different agents, the objective direction of their motivation may be the same, though its subjective force may differ. The feeling of respect for law, as a practical, motivating feeling, accounts for the subjective force of moral motivation. Here the objective law supplies the direction of motivation, and the subjective feeling of respect supplies its strength. Each can therefore be said to motivate moral action, in its respective aspect of motivation; especially because the latter is supposed to be an effect of the former (2.8). The strength of one's feeling of respect can explain one's acting on a moral principle rather than on an alternative maxim of inclination.

Section 2, above, presented with three competing explanations of the relation Kant saw between the moral law's determination of the will and the feeling of respect. Of these three, it seems that the first and third are correct in presenting the feeling of respect as an *effect* of the moral law's determination of the will. But the first is incorrect in presenting the feeling as a mere side-effect, denying that it plays any motivational role. The third explanation does not deny this, but it is plagued by two related difficulties: first, it incorrectly models the causal relation between the determination of the will and the feeling on the model of the relation between noumena and phenomena; second, the variable motive force of the feeling, in comparison with competing incentives of inclination, is not adequately accounted for in this explanation.

If what has been offered here is a correct interpretation of Kant's view of the feeling of respect for the moral law, then it is a feeling caused by consciousness of an action's relation to the law. When it prevails in motivating action (or omission), it does so through its relative strength as a motive force.

6.4 Phenomenology of Respect

In the second *Critique* Kant wrote that "how a law can be of itself and immediately a determining ground of the will," that is, how a law itself can motivate, without presupposing any feeling for it, or for an object to be achieved by obeying it, "is for human reason an insoluble problem and identical with that of how a free will is possible." So Kant conceded that this aspect of moral motivation simply cannot be explained. But he did not see this as also precluding an explanation of the motivating law's subjective force. "What we shall have to show a priori," he continued, is "not the ground [, which we cannot explain,] from which the moral law in itself supplies an incentive, but rather what it effects (or, to put it better, must effect) in the mind insofar as it is an incentive" (62–3/5:72). This psychological effect is the motivating feeling of respect for the law. It constitutes the subjective, force-aspect of motivation. But this means that it is always comparable to the subjective forces of alternative and competing motivational states. The "strength" of a motive force, in other words, is always gauged in relation to other motive forces coexisting in the agent's psychology (3.7). Consequently, when we refer to respect as a motivating feeling, we refer implicitly also to all other, comparable feelings in the motivational economy of the moral agent. These would be sense-based desires and inclinations.

Any motivational feeling that may be an effect of the objective moral law's determination of the will therefore has necessary implications for all other, comparable feelings of the agent. One way to conceive of these implications would be to suppose that the moral law's determining the will generates a feeling, which then alters the relative motivational forces of other, existing feelings. This would occur in the same way in which the introduction of a new competitor in a game would affect the prospects of the other, existing players. But this is not exactly how Kant presented the etiology and effectiveness of the feeling of respect. His view was that the moral law's determination of the will has (or is) a direct, inhibiting effect on motives and associated feelings of inclination, and the negative effect on them is the same as a positive effect, at least from the perspective of the moral law.[14] "[A]ll inclination rests on feeling," he wrote, so "what infringes upon all the inclinations in self-love has, just by this, a necessary influence on feeling... an effect which on the one side is merely *negative* but on the other side, and indeed with respect to the restricting ground of pure practical reason, is *positive*..." (*Practical Reason*, 64/5:74–5, see also 65/5:75–6, 67–8/5:78–9). So this shows that the analogy of a new player's introduction into a competitive game is not quite accurate.

We can see from his explanation here why Kant would sometimes deny that respect is a feeling of pleasure (see 66/5:77). It does not *feel* like pleasure. There is a sense in which it feels most like displeasure, because it is a feeling

---

[14] On this point see Melissa Zinkin, "Respect for the Law and the Use of Dynamical Terms in Kant's Theory of Moral Motivation," *Archive für Geschichte der Philosophie* 88 (2006): 31–53.

of our being hindered from doing what we please. Yet from the moral law's point of view this is a positive result; and a positive effect on feeling should count as pleasure, again, from the moral law's point of view.[15] So it can be called a moral pleasure, and our feeling it would always presuppose a prior, frustrating and therefore painful effect on inclinations. I think there is more than this in the phenomenology of respect, however. For Kant claimed that the moral law's "negative effect on feeling (disagreeableness) is *pathological*" (ibid., 64/5:75). But he also characterized the feeling of respect as not pathological but "practical only."[16] This suggests that the feeling of respect would be more than just a negative impact on inclinations that is redescribed from a moral point of view.

We have yet to consider an important aspect of the frustrating effect of the moral law on our feelings and inclinations. It is that this constraint is self-imposed. Kant wrote: "since this constraint is exercised only by the lawgiving of [one's] *own* reason, it also contains something *elevating,* and the subjective effect on feeling, in as much as pure practical reason is the sole cause of it, can thus be called *self-approbation* with reference to pure practical reason. . . ." (69/5:81). In moral consciousness we feel a constraint on our doing as we please. It is a constraint that does not yield to considerations of how much or what kind of pleasure may be at stake. So in this experience we are confronted with the limitations of sensibility. Kant described this best, I think, in his explanation of the aesthetic feeling of the sublime. Take the example of what he called the "mathematical" sublime. Confronted with a seemingly infinite magnitude, like the starry night sky, we first feel the unpleasant exhaustion of our sensible capacities. The object of contemplation is simply too vast. But our reason, which outreaches the senses, easily conceives of that which exhausts our sensible capacities. Recognizing the limits of our sensibilities in such a case presupposes that

[15] On the commensurability of pleasure and negative displeasure see *Religion* (48n./6:22n.). See also Immanuel Kant, *Attempt to Introduce the Concept of Negative Magnitudes into Philosophy,* trans. and ed. David Walford and Ralf Meerbote, in *Theoretical Philosophy 1755–1770* (Cambridge: Cambridge University Press, 1992), 219–20/2:181, 233–4/2:196.
[16] Kant wrote: An action that is objectively practical in accordance with this law, with the exclusion of every determining ground of inclination, is called *duty*, which, because of that exclusion, contains in its concept practical *necessitation*, that is, determination to actions however *reluctantly* they may be done. The feeling that arises from consciousness of this necessitation is not pathological, as would be a feeling produced by an object of the senses, but practical only, that is, possible through a preceding (objective) determination of the will and causality of reason. (*Practical Reason*, 69/5:80)

our conceptual capacities are not restricted by the bounds of sense, and so are not of natural origin. *"That is sublime which even to be able to think of demonstrates a faculty of the mind that surpasses every measure of the senses"* (*Judgment*, 134/5:250). The feeling of the sublime is thus an "elevating," positive effect on feeling. But it is a mixed pleasure, since it is dependent upon a prior feeling of displeasure. The same sequence of displeasure giving rise to elevating pleasure or esteem characterizes the "practical" feeling of respect for the moral law.[17]

Not surprisingly, Kant connected the elevating aspect of respect for law with the concept of freedom. He wrote the following about someone motivated by the moral law's determination of his will, independently of any inclination to act accordingly:

> he cognized himself as determined to [do his duty] solely by the law and without any interest, and now becomes conscious of an altogether different interest subjectively produced by the law, which is purely practical and *free;* and his taking this interest in a dutiful action is not advised by any inclination; instead, reason through the practical law absolutely commands it and also actually produces it. . . . (*Practical Reason,* 69/5:81)

Here the agent's consciousness of himself as determined (constrained) by the law is one thing. His consciousness of his having an "interest subjectively produced by the law" is something else. The latter would be an "elevating" effect of the former. It would depend upon some at least vague recognition of freedom from the limitations of sensible inclinations. So it would be a positive feeling of respect that is not merely a frustrating effect on inclinations redescribed from a moral point of view.[18]

---

[17] Here I do not intend to suggest that the elevating feeling of respect for law is the feeling of the sublime. I think Kant distinguished the former as a "practical," "interested" feeling and the latter as a "contemplative," "disinterested" feeling. It seems to me that Walker has conflated this distinction, in his identification of the feeling of respect with the feeling of the sublime (see "Actung in the Grundlegung," 98).

[18] Korsgaard also recognizes the significance of consciousness of freedom for moral motivation. "Kant sees positive freedom as pointing to a higher vocation, the thought of which moves us to moral conduct, and explains how we can take an interest in such conduct" (*Creating the Kingdom of Ends,* 183). But I do not think that in moral motivation we are necessarily moved to act in order to realize a higher vocation, least of all in order to realize our freedom. What Korsgaard says here can be considered correct, but it is not the whole story of moral motivation. We are not moved "to moral conduct," or morally motivated, solely by the thought of a higher vocation. In characterizing the latter she says that "we are members of the intelligible world, and have a higher vocation than the satisfaction of our desires; and (. . .) this provides us with the incentive to be positively free—that is, moral" (175). On the contrary, I think, the incentive for moral conduct is the feeling of respect for the moral law. This

But it should not be thought that this second and elevating feeling of respect would imply subsequent action in obedience to the law. Kant's view was that our feeling respect for the moral law can still fail "to express its effect in actions only because subjective (pathological) causes hinder it" (ibid., 68/5:79). Our inclinations may be initially frustrated as a consequence of the law's determination of our wills. But whether this provides an obstacle psychologically sufficient to overpower those inclinations, so that we actually obey the law, out of respect for it, is another matter. The latter depends upon the strength of the interest (2.7) grounded in the "elevating" feeling of respect. To prevail it must be stronger than competing interests grounded in those constrained though still motivationally forceful inclinations: those "subjective (pathological) causes."[19] We can differ from one another in regard to these subjective conditions, even though we are presumably all the same in regard to the moral law's determination of our wills. The subjective conditions here refer to empirical character (5.6): the laws for our causality as agents in the empirical world.

6.5 Feeling and Character

Kant sometimes used the word "feeling" (*Gefühl*) to refer to particular, datable feelings of pleasure or displeasure. But more often he used it to refer to the capacity or susceptibility for such feelings. In the latter sense the feeling of respect for law would constitute a central component of moral character. The previous chapter made the point that Kant explained empirical character as a causal law of activity in the empirical world (5.5).

---

feeling arises from consciousness of an intellectual (not an inclination-based) constraint on our conduct, and so the feeling of respect motivates moral action as much as our intellectual consciousness of that constraint. Awareness of this constraint is necessarily connected with the idea of freedom, in some sense. And that is how the elevating feeling of respect arises. But it does not produce "the incentive to be positively free—that is, moral." Moral motivation is not a drive or interest in being free(er). It is the incentive merely to obey the law. If the law should command that we act in order to become free(er), by cultivating mastery over inclination, perhaps, then taking on this project, possibly under the name of a "higher vocation," is among the things we may be morally motivated to do. It is not the entire scope of moral motivation, as Korsgaard seems to imply.

[19] Hence Kant's observation in *The Metaphysics of Morals* that it is our obligation, in regard to the elevating feeling of respect, "to *cultivate* it and to strengthen it through wonder at its inscrutable source" (201/6:399).

We saw, further, how specific laws of a human being's character are the subjective principles of his or her will, or maxims. Maxims are supposed to incorporate incentives, as we have seen (2.2). So since the feeling of respect for law has been identified as the moral incentive, this feeling would be "incorporatable" into a maxim of moral character. And maxims serve as major premises of practical syllogisms (1.3), insofar as they represent objects or conditions as "good." Two kinds of goodness Kant identified are "well-being" and "moral good" (1.5). So this distinction suggests that there are therefore two basic kinds of maxims—or two highest maxims: prudential and moral.

The feeling of respect for law would be the subjective incentive incorporated into the moral maxim, into our practical conviction that obeying the moral law is good. The moral law itself, or our obedience, would be the incentive object incorporated into the same maxim. When we recognize an action as falling under our moral maxim, we recognize it as something good to do because it is called for by, or would obey, the moral law of pure practical reason. Kant's view is that we then feel respect in the thought of our doing the action. And the result is that we are motivated to act as we recognize we are commanded to act by the law.[20] But at the same time we may also recognize that what the moral law commands us to do would be contrary to our selfish interests. A maxim of personal happiness or prudence may therefore simultaneously support a hypothetical imperative. It may command that we not do the action that the moral law commands, if so acting interferes with our overall happiness. This prudential maxim will incorporate a feeling-based incentive of inclination as its psychological motive force. So here we have, in these two competing maxims, the classic struggle between reason and desire.

The winner of this psychological contest will be, in every case, the maxim incorporating the motivationally stronger incentive (3.6). The stronger incentive is what explains action on the relevant justificatory principle: on either the hypothetical or categorical imperative. Consequently, we have better moral characters, empirically, to the extent that we are susceptible

[20] Kant assumed that without a feeling of pleasure or displeasure we would be motivationally indifferent to any recognized command of the law. "If we take away the faculty of pleasure and displeasure from all rational beings, and enlarge their faculty of cognition however much, then they would cognize all objects without being moved by them; everything would be the same to them, for they would lack the faculty for being affected by objects" (*Lectures on Metaphysics*, 62/28:246).

to feeling greater moral pleasure and displeasure: to the extent, that is, that our recognition of how our contemplated action conforms to the moral law generates, through feeling, a stronger motive force. This would be greater pleasure and displeasure, and so stronger motive force, relative to the pleasures and displeasures of our sense-based desires and inclinations. Kant confirms this explanation of his view in a definition of "virtue" that is hard to read in any other way: "*Virtue* is the strength of man's maxims in fulfilling his duty. Strength of any kind can be recognized only by the obstacles it can overcome, and in the case of virtue these obstacles are natural inclinations, which can come into conflict with man's moral resolution" (*Metaphysics of Morals,* 197/6:394).

In the next chapter we shall see how Kant explained, as far as he considered it possible to explain, empirical moral character: the so-called "moral disposition" (*moralishe Gesinnung*). There the condition of moral strength and weakness, relative to inclinations, will be seen to depend upon a free, noumenal choice. But for the remainder of the present chapter we turn to what is probably the most controversial doctrine related to Kant's conception of moral motivation.

6.6 Acting From Duty

In order to have "moral worth" an action must be done for the sake of duty alone. This has been one of the more troubling doctrines of Kantian ethics, and there were objections to it almost from the beginning. A verse by Schiller expressed comic ridicule of the doctrine in this way: "Gladly I serve my friends, but alas, I do it with pleasure. Hence I am plagued with doubt that I am not a virtuous person." The mocking reply is: "Sure, your only recourse is to try to despise them entirely. And then with aversion to do what your duty enjoins you."[21] This section further develops the stinging criticism expressed in these lines, and then roughly outlines two ways Kant's recent defenders have responded to it.

Schiller's poetic critique has now been adapted by contemporary critics of Kantian ethics, many of whom advance the cause of virtue ethics.

---

[21] Quoted in Paton, *The Categorical Imperative,* 48. For a contemporary version of roughly the same critique, see Michael Stocker, "The Schizophrenia of Modern Ethical Theories," *The Journal of Philosophy* 73 (1976): 456–66.

With plausible justification, these virtue-theorists have pointed out two related errors in the Kantian theory of moral appraisal. Kantian appraisers mistakenly deny moral worth to actions that actually are virtuous, they say; and Kantians mistakenly attribute moral worth to actions that actually are not virtuous. These critics point out that there are morally good or admirable motives besides respect for moral duty, and they include felt gratitude and kindness, as well as inclinations of parental or familial affection: inclinations that Kant seemed sometimes to deride as "pathological." Other critics have provided examples showing how acting solely from respect for law can sometimes make a person's action morally objectionable, or disappointing. There is something wrong when a husband rescues his wife "from duty alone," or when a father is moved to spend time with his children solely by the thought of its being his duty.

In responding to complaints like these Kant's defenders have taken two general approaches, which I shall here label *the motivational approach* and *the approach of appraisal*. The strategy of those taking the first approach is to clarify, or augment, Kant's theory of human motivation. Often their first step is to show that Kant's theory of motivation and action is, or could be, more sophisticated than critics have recognized. Some say, for example, that it is possible for human motivation to be "overdetermined," in a sense relevant to moral appraisal.[22] An action might be motivated by a virtuous natural inclination such as gratitude, compassion, or parental love. But we could still judge it to have moral worth, provided the motive of respect for law would have sufficed for the action on its own. This "counterfactual sufficiency" of the moral motive might be all that would be needed in order to make an action on inclination morally worthy. That is, it may not be necessary for the motive of duty actually to produce a morally worthy action. Others who take the motivational approach divide human motivation into different levels: most commonly, into primary and secondary motives.[23] An action could be morally worthy even while motivated by a virtuous inclination, it is said. The inclination might serve as the action's primary motive, while the moral motive of duty plays a

---

[22] See Henson, "What Kant Might Have Said: Moral Worth and the Overdetermination of Dutiful Actions."

[23] See Barbara Herman, *The Practice of Moral Judgment* (Cambridge, MA: Harvard University Press, 1993), 1–22.

secondary role, as a kind of limiting condition. In its secondary role the moral motive would ensure that the active, primary motive is kept within moral bounds.

The second general approach is what I call the "approach of appraisal." Those who take this approach respond to virtue-theorists critical of Kantian moral motivation by reinterpreting *moral worth* as a category of moral appraisal.[24] It is clear from the context of *Groundwork* I that Kant introduced "moral worth" in order to clarify the concept of a good will. Some interpreters therefore assume that his ensuing discussion of acting from duty was fundamentally a discussion of good character.[25] The moral worth of character may have been all Kant was interested in illustrating there. He may have thought that the best way to illustrate this special, personal worth is through its motivational sign. Acting from duty alone can be taken as the sign of an underlying moral goodness or worth. So there need be no disagreement between virtue-theorists and Kant, it may be said. It should be possible, even expected, for persons of morally good character to act on any motives that are considered virtuous. Kant's point may have been only that there is a way of acting, namely, *from duty*, that indicates a person's true worth. So he may have been claiming only that in acting on inclinations admired as virtuous a person of good moral character does not manifest his or her personal moral worth. That is done only in acting from duty alone.[26]

---

[24] See, for example, Nelson Potter, "Kant and the Moral Worth of Actions," *The Southern Journal of Philosophy* 34 (1996): 225–41.

[25] See Walter E. Schaller, "Should Kantians Care about Moral Worth?" *Dialogue* 32 (1993), 25–40.

[26] Some commentators take one or the other of the above approaches in defending Kant's views on moral motivation. But it is possible also to combine them. It is possible to say that what Kant was trying to illustrate in discussing "acting from duty" in *Groundwork* I was just good will or personal moral worth (approach of appraisal). And this is only a matter of secondary motivation (motivational approach). A person is morally worthy or good-willed, it has been said, if she "acts from duty" on the secondary level. (See Baron, *Kantian Ethics Almost without Apology*.) This means that on that level of motivation she has a strong commitment to moral ends, or to observing moral constraints. But she can still be morally admired for her actions motivated primarily by virtuous inclinations. According to this mixed approach, the person of good will is someone strongly committed to morality on the secondary level of motivation, but who may allow herself to be moved to action by morally admirable inclinations, when appropriate, on the primary level of motivation. Versions of the mixed approach seem to be taken by Stratton-Lake, *Kant, Duty and Moral Worth*, 60–77, and Guyer, *Kant on Freedom, Law and Happiness*, 287–329. Henson's contribution to the debate can also be seen as mixed in its approach. He offers a motivational model permitting actions' "overdetermination" by moral and non-moral motivation, but he also claims to find two conceptions of "moral worth" in Kant's comments on moral motivation: the "fitness report" and the "battle citation" conceptions.

6.7 Choosing Motives

It will be impossible here to survey and assess the contributions of all who have taken either the motivational approach or the approach of appraisal, or some combination of the two, in responding to virtue-theorists' criticisms of Kantian ethics. But it may suffice here to offer some brief, critical remarks, which can help in laying out a new, and I think more successful line of response to this long-standing difficulty. These remarks will be based on the interpretation of Kant's theory of action developed in previous chapters. In light of this interpretation, which emphasizes psychological determinism and a two-worlds theory of action, I think the approach of appraisal is more sound, psychologically, than the motivational approach.

It is a common conviction among many of Kant's interpreters today that because of our freedom we have the power to choose the motives on which we act. This presumption has been codified in "The Incorporation Thesis" (3.3). It implies that we do not act on one motive rather than another because we are caused to do so by its relative strength. It says that every time we choose to act we select an available incentive to incorporate into our maxim. This "act of incorporation" is then supposed to cause our action, making our chosen incentive the reason or motive upon which we act. Many who take the motivational approach in addressing virtue-theorists' objections presume that we have this kind of control over the motives upon which we act.[27] For they assume that we have the ability to choose whether to let the motive of duty do its work, or to let some other motive move us to action instead. Supposing we elect to do our duty,

---

[27] This presumption may not be required for versions of the motivational approach emphasizing "overdetermination" in the simple sense of having more than enough motivation for a dutiful action. Suppose, for example, that Kant's love of lecturing to students was the inclination that caused him to meet with his classes. According to Henson, this need not imply that his fulfilling his lecturing duties lacked moral worth; for he would also have had a motive of respect for duty that could have caused him to lecture even if he were less inclined to do so, or not inclined at all. Assuming that his motive of duty was strong enough to have caused him to lecture if his inclination had been weaker or absent, then it might be said that his lecturing by inclination still has moral worth. This is a relatively simple version of the motivational approach because it does not involve motives operating on different levels, or as "limiting conditions" on the actions of other motives. But simple motivational approaches like this encounter difficulties in specifying the counterfactual sufficiency or fitness of the motive of duty. It is not easy to state what it means for the motive of duty to be sufficient to cause action in case the inclinations that actually caused the action were weaker, or absent. For development of this point see Noa Latham, "Causally Irrelevant Reasons and Action Solely from the Motive of Duty," *The Journal of Philosophy* 91 (November 1994): 599–618.

we may choose to do it *from duty alone,* or to be moved by an available inclination.[28]

But when we see motives as causes of action, embracing psychological determinism, there is no denying that they do their work through strength or psychological force. One argument for this way of regarding motives focuses on the meaning of "strong" as applied to common-sense motivational concepts like desire and temptation. If the relative strength of a desire, motive, or incentive does not cause us to act on it, there is no plausible explanation of what its strength is the strength *to do.* It is impossible to explain how its strength is supposed to matter (3.7). So this gives us good reason to assume that incentives or motives operate as forceful psychological causes of action. And this implies, in turn, that we are not free to choose which of our available incentives will move us to act.[29] If I therefore have two incentives for the same action, one of which is the motive of duty, and if that one is stronger than the other, it will cause me to act "from duty."[30] It will not be up to me to allow the weaker inclination to cause the action when my motive of duty is stronger, or vice versa. I do not have that kind of control, at least, over my psychological states.[31]

For this reason the motivational approach, taken by many recent interpreters responding to virtue-theorists' criticisms of Kantian ethics, seems misguided. It depends on a common misinterpretation of Kant's theory of action, since it presumes that when we have more than one motive for the same action we can choose between acting on the one rather than the other. Their relative strengths do not matter.[32] The motivational approach,

---

[28] The Incorporation Thesis implies our freedom to choose between doing our duty on the motive of duty and doing it by inclination. Not everyone who accepts The Incorporation Thesis makes this implication explicit, however. Someone who does is Nelson Potter, "Kant and the Moral Worth of Actions," 234. But someone who (I think rightly) rejects our freedom to choose between motives is Walter Schaller, "Should Kantians Care about Moral Worth?", 31–4.

[29] At least we cannot freely choose this in deliberating between courses of action in the empirical world. But that does not mean that we are not free, in a noumenal act, resulting in our having the empirical motives we have, and their relative strengths.

[30] Here, for purposes of simplicity, I ignore the possibility that some third motive for another action might pose an obstacle to my acting on the motive of duty, and might be stronger than my motive of duty, so that my acting dutifully might require the combined strength of both the motive of duty and the second inclination.

[31] Note that if I did have such control, then I could not be always ignorant of the motive on which I act when multiple motives are available for the same action (see 3.9).

[32] I offer this argument against motivational approaches emphasizing multi-leveled motivation with awareness of a certain irony. It is ironic that Herman's leading contributions to the debate over "overdetermination" have been criticized for implicitly assuming that motivating inclinations operate

in other words, is incompatible with psychological determinism. But as we have seen in previous chapters, psychological determinism is required for solving the problem of justification and explanation in Kant's theory of action. So we seem to have good reason to abandon the motivational approach.

6.8 Moral Worth and Virtue

What I have labeled the approach of appraisal is the other strategy for defending Kant's theory of moral motivation against the virtue-theorists' criticisms. It proceeds by clarifying concepts of moral appraisal, without offering any special motivational model. So in taking this approach we may attribute to Kant any plausible model of human motivation, even a model favored by his virtue-theorist critics.[33] Where we disagree with these critics, in taking this approach, will be on the meaning of appraisal terms like "moral worth" and "morally worthy."

This section and the one that follows aim at clarifying Kant's conception of moral worth, especially in relation to his conception of virtue. We may begin here with the suggestion that the adjectives "morally worthy" and "virtuous," as appraisal concepts applicable to actions, have different meanings. Once their difference is clarified, we shall then be able to see how it is consistent for Kantians to deny that an action is morally worthy, *while acknowledging that it is virtuous*. We can therefore respond to Kant's virtue-theorist critics, in general, as follows. We may say that they have assumed,

as psychological causes of action. She has been faulted for overlooking the implications of The Incorporation Thesis, by Allison, *Kant's Theory of Freedom*, 116–17, and by Guyer, *Kant on Freedom, Law and Happiness*, 291–5. What the latter have not recognized, evidently, is that Herman's approach needs The Incorporation Thesis in order to make the distinction between primary and secondary motives. She presumes that we have the freedom to choose whether we shall be caused to do our duty by a primary motive of inclination and not the motive of duty (as primary). But this is impossible if motives are assumed to operate as psychological forces, which is the view of motives attributed to her. Hence, it seems that Herman must actually assume that motives *do not* cause us to act, as psychological forces; and she must suppose, just like her critics who defend The Incorporation Thesis, that we can choose between alternative motives available for the same action.

[33] The critics need only concede, at least as a hypothesis, the possibility of our being moved to action solely by the unique, moral motive of duty. If this point is denied, then the complaint against Kant's theory of moral motivation is quite different. Virtue-theorist critics typically argue, persuasively, that Kantian moral appraisals related to motivation are counter-intuitive. To deny, additionally, the possibility of our being moved to action by a non-empirical motive like respect for the moral law pushes the argument beyond our intuitions related to moral appraisal, into metaphysics.

incorrectly, that "morally worthy" and "virtuous" are equivalent as terms of action-appraisal. That is why they criticize Kant for having denied the moral worth of some actions they consider virtuous, and for having affirmed the moral worth of other actions they see as unvirtuous. But Kantians need not insist that actions lacking moral worth therefore lack virtue. Nor need they assume that actions having moral worth are for that reason virtuous.

Consider Schiller's joking critique once again. The straight-man says, "I am plagued with doubt that I am not a virtuous person." Then follows the punch line: "your only recourse is to try to despise [your friends] entirely. And then with aversion to do [for them] what your duty enjoins you." The Kantian reply, I am suggesting here, can be that acting from duty alone is the criterion for one's action's having moral worth. But it is not the criterion for one's action's being virtuous, or for a person's being a virtuous friend or family member, or whatever. So if you serve your friends gladly, and with pleasure, that is no reason for doubting that you are virtuous. It means only that your actions in service to your friends lack "moral worth." But that, as we shall see momentarily, is nothing to fret.

This answer to the virtue-theorists' criticism proposes that Kant's conception of an action's "moral worth" is different from his conception of an action's "virtue." But is that true? We have a very good reason for thinking it is. The reason is that Kant thought there may never have been an action with genuine moral worth (cf. *Groundwork*, 19–20/4:406–7). But he did not think the same about virtuous actions; at least not about actions on admirable inclinations. "[T]here are many souls so sympathetically attuned that, without any other motive of vanity or self-interest they find an inner satisfaction in spreading joy around them and can take delight in the satisfaction of others so far as it is their own work" (*Groundwork*, 11/4:398). "It is very beautiful," he wrote, "to do good to human beings from love for them and from sympathetic benevolence" (*Practical Reason*, 70/5:82). Actions motivated by inclinations like these can be praiseworthy, in Kant's view: "for example, the inclination to honor, which, if it fortunately lights upon what is in fact in the common interest and in conformity with duty and hence honorable, deserves praise and encouragement. . . ."[34] So Kant evidently saw no ground for doubting that there are actions motivated

---

[34] *Groundwork*, 11/4:398. Kant finished this sentence by denying that actions motivated by praise-worthy inclinations merit "esteem": the type of admiration due actions *from duty*, with true moral worth.

by inclinations of the kind that virtue-theorist critics of his view would call virtuous, and he did not see any reason why acting in these ways should not be encouraged (cf. *Religion*, 67/6:47). But what he doubted, or was at least agnostic about, was whether there may ever have been any actions with moral worth. Pretty clearly, then, his view was that acting in ways that are admirable as virtuous is not the same as acting with moral worth.

Another good reason for thinking Kant saw a difference between moral worth and virtue as concepts of action-appraisal is suggested by the way he developed and published his moral theory. In writing about moral worth in *Groundwork* I, Kant had almost nothing to say about virtue. But twelve years later, in writing about virtue in the second part of *The Metaphysics of Morals,* he likewise had almost nothing to say about moral worth (7.10). We have no indication that Kant changed his mind about moral appraisal of actions and their motives in the years between these two works. He does not seem to have abandoned the appraisal concept of "moral worth" in favor of "virtue." If he had changed his mind about the aptness of these terms he would, presumably, have said so.[35]

Kant's ethical theory provides a well known and at least plausible criterion for appraising actions as morally worthy: they must be done from duty alone. So if there is to be a distinction between moral worth and virtue, then a comparable criterion for applying the latter concept will be required as well. It should also be possible to satisfy the required criterion for acting virtuously, of course. Ideally, it should even be expected. But this last point seems to pose some problems. Here is one: if it is expected in Kantian ethics that we act virtuously, then there should be duties calling for virtuous actions. The concept of "duty" is, after all, the way Kantian ethics deals with moral expectations. Yet this seems to imply a special motive for actions meeting the expectation of virtue: the motive of duty. And that implication would be in tension with the theory's expectation that we act virtuously. So there is one difficulty; here is another: If the criterion for moral worth is supposed to be different from the criterion for acting virtuously, then which way of acting would be better? Given a choice,

---

[35] Kant sometimes corrected himself or revised his terminology in subsequent works, so there is no reason to think that if he had changed his thinking on the appraisal concept of moral worth he would have avoided saying so.

would it be better to act in a way that is morally worthy, or in a way that is virtuous?

Kant's theory of virtue, to which we turn in the next two sections, will provide resources for avoiding theoretical problems like the two just identified.

6.9   Senses of "Virtue"

Above we quoted one of Kant's clearest, most straight-forward definitions of "virtue": "*Virtue* is the strength of man's maxims in fulfilling his duty."[36] This definition makes it difficult to see how Kant could have embraced the problem-solving distinction offered in the previous section. For it seems to imply that only in exercising strong moral resolve, in order to do our duty, can we act virtuously. Hence, the criterion for acting with moral worth seems to be the same, or very near the same, as the criterion for acting virtuously. But in this section we look more closely at different senses of "virtue" found in Kant's ethical writing, in order to see how moral worth and virtue might be more clearly distinguished.

It is important to observe, first of all, that the definition of virtue just quoted defines it as a psychological condition. The definition says that virtue is moral strength of will, or roughly, that moral strength is *a* virtue; perhaps *the only* virtue, or the most important. But in the present context we are interested in virtue not as a psychological condition, but as a concept of moral appraisal. We are interested in Kant's conception of "virtue" in the sense of the term that is comparable to his conception of "moral worth": in the sense of the term that critics have supposed would be equivalent to moral worth in Kantian ethics. So, the definition just quoted is not a definition of "virtue" in the sense in which we are interested. And thus it would not be correct to appeal to that definition in order to show that there would be no difference between virtue and moral worth as appraisal concepts in Kant's moral theory.

We can begin to shed more light on the difference between moral worth and virtue as appraisal concepts by observing yet another appraisal

[36] *Metaphysics of Morals*, 197/6:394. The first definition of "virtue" he published was the cryptic phrase: "moral disposition *in conflict*" (*Practical Reason*, 72/5:84).

concept in Kant's moral theory: the concept of *right*. "Right" is a term of moral appraisal that is in some way comparable to "virtuous." It has been easy to understand "right" as an appraisal concept distinct from "moral worth," because Kant so clearly showed how an action can satisfy the criterion for being right ("according to duty") without being morally worthy. But we should not confuse the distinction between an action's being right and its being morally worthy, with the distinction between an action's being right and its being virtuous. In *The Metaphysics of Morals* Kant distinguished explicitly between duties of right and duties of virtue.[37] A central component of this distinction is that motivation is irrelevant to the criterion for an action's satisfying a duty of right; but it is relevant to the criterion for an action's satisfying a duty of virtue.[38] In other words, an action can be "right" no matter its motive; but an action will not be "virtuous" unless it is motivated in some appropriate way.

The (primary) concepts of appraisal in Kant's moral theory, based on its more complete elaboration in *The Metaphysics of Morals,* are organized in the following table:

Table 6.1.

Action Appraisal (duty):	Motivational Appraisal:
Right (duty of right)	Morally Worthy
Virtuous (duty of virtue)	Virtuous

This table distinguishes virtuous from right as categories of *action appraisal.* It also presents virtuous and morally worthy as distinct categories of *motivational appraisal.* It shows, in other words, that "virtue" is an equivocal term. "Virtue" has at least three senses, two of which are represented on

[37] It was not a new distinction in duties, but had been implicit all along. Even in the *Groundwork* Kant indicated that he hoped someday in a future "Metaphysics of Morals," the groundwork for which he was then establishing, to develop the distinction between "perfect" and "imperfect" duties. This distinction corresponds roughly to what he later distinguished as duties of right and duties of virtue. See *Groundwork,* 31n./4:421n.

[38] Kant usually expresses this point in his claim that duties of right command only actions, whereas duties of virtue command ends of action. What he means by this is that in the latter duties, only, what is commanded is that we have a specific end, like the happiness of others, which motivates us to action. It is possible to satisfy all duties of right through coercion, or motivation by the threat of legal punishment. But this is not possible in duties of virtue; for these specify ends to provide the motivation for action. See *Metaphysics of Morals,* 185–7/6:379–82.

the table. Above we saw how Kant used "virtue" in one sense when he defined it as a psychological condition ("strength of the maxim of duty"). But he used the term in a second sense when he introduced several "duties of virtue." In this second sense "virtue" and "virtuous" are terms of action appraisal, comparable to "right." The action of visiting a friend in the hospital would not be a "right" action, called for by a duty of right. It would be called for by a duty of virtue: "virtue" in the second sense. But "virtue," in its adjectival form, "virtuous," can be used also in a third sense, as referring to a kind of motivational appraisal comparable to morally worthy. Someone who does an action called for by a duty of virtue, with the motivation appropriate for that action, acts virtuously in this third sense. A hospital visit motivated by friendship qualifies as virtuous; it does not meet the criterion for being morally worthy. If it were motivated by duty alone it might have moral worth.[39] But then it would not be, in the third sense, virtuous.

6.10 Ends of Virtue

The difference between right and virtue as types of duty, or as categories of action appraisal, depends ultimately on the fact that human actions are means to ends. We are motivated to act when we have judged acting in a certain way to be a means of bringing about an end we desire, in the broadest sense of "desire" (1.5). The practical syllogism reflects this as a structure of practical reasoning where: 1) a major-premise maxim expresses the goodness of an end; 2) a minor-premise judgment expresses an action's fitness for the end; and 3) the concluding thought of the action as good is motivationally effective (1.3). Acting rationally therefore always involves taking action as a means to an end.[40]

The significance of the ends of actions for Kant's ethical theory may not be obvious, however. To appreciate it fully, imagine that the moral

---

[39] It has been a controversial question whether an action has moral worth when the agent mistakenly believes it is her duty and does it from duty alone. Some assume that moral worth attaches to actions only if they are both right and motivated solely by duty. Others see motivation by duty alone as sufficient for moral worth.

[40] The action and end need not be different, however; actions may be ends in themselves.

law commands only certain kinds of *actions*. Imagine that it never indicates that anything is good to have as an end. Kant argued that if this were so, then there could be no categorical imperative (cf. *Metaphysics of Morals,* 190/6:385). His argument proceeds roughly as follows. First, bear in mind that it is irrational to act for no end. Next, assume as a hypothesis that the moral law commands only that we do or avoid certain actions; assume, in other words, that there are no duties to have any objects as our ends. From these premises it follows that the moral law could never command us to act in ways we do not recognize as means to our already existing ends, the ends of sense-based desire or inclination. Therefore, Kant concluded, if the moral law does not itself supply an end for the actions it commands, it is limited to commanding actions as means to non-moral ends of inclination. It can command only in hypothetical imperatives, and never in categorical imperatives.

So assuming the moral law commands actions by categorical imperatives, we must agree that it also commands that we act on certain ends. A relatively obvious example of an end the moral law commands us to act on is the end of obeying the law. This is not as simpleminded as it may sound, however. It is not that the moral law commands that we obey it. It is rather that it commands that we satisfy our duty for the sake of the moral law. It commands, in other words, that we make our maxim that obeying the moral law is good into a prevailing motive for action.[41]

Here it will suffice to demonstrate just a few other examples of ends Kantian ethics says we ought to have by applying the categorical imperative's formula of universal law. Because there are ends whose abandonment or neglect cannot be willed consistently to become a universal law, it is our duty to have these as our ends, and to cultivate our interest in them. Two familiar examples from Kant's *Groundwork* are the end of helping others in need, and the end of developing our natural talents. The duties to have these ends are there called "imperfect duties." In *The Metaphysics of Morals* they are also called "duties of virtue," and simply, "virtues." In clarifying the distinction between the one end of obedience to the moral law, for the sake of the law, and the several dutiful ends that form the set of virtues,

---

[41] I have put the point this way in order to avoid suggesting that the categorical imperative makes it our duty always to do our duty from duty. That prospect would generate a vicious regress. See W. D. Ross, *The Right and the Good* (Indianapolis, IN: Hackett Publishing, 1988), 5–6.

Kant distinguished between "virtue," in the formal singular, and in the material plural:

Like anything *formal,* virtue as the will's conformity with every duty, based on a firm disposition, is merely one and the same. But with respect to the *end* of actions that is also a duty, that is, what one *ought* to make one's *end* (what is material), there can be several virtues; and since obligation to the maxim of such an end is called a duty of virtue, there are many duties of virtue.   (198/3:395)

"Virtue" is not used here as a concept of motivational appraisal, but in two other ways. It refers to a psychological condition ("conformity with every duty, based on a firm disposition"), and it is used as a concept of action appraisal ("there are many duties of virtue").

To have an object as one's end is to have a maxim indicating that it is good. This is what is meant also by the "incorporation" of an incentive (object) into a maxim (2.2). Incentives can be regarded *objectively*, as objects of desire or as ends, and *subjectively*, as stronger or weaker motivational states. So if there are duties to have certain objects or conditions as our ends, then there are duties to have, and so act on, certain maxims. Maxims are also rules of empirical character, however (5.5). So if there are duties to have certain objects or conditions as our ends, there are duties related to the improvement of characters. We have duties, in other words, to be certain kinds of agents: agents for whom recognition that an action is a means to achieving one of these objects or conditions will generate motivation for that action. Moreover, since these duties are duties of virtue, it is appropriate to appraise a person as virtuous for fulfilling such duties: that is, for having the ends these duties require, as incentives incorporated into maxims, and for acting in order to achieve them. It is appropriate also to appraise such actions as virtuous when their motivation stems from one of these required ends, or stems from the appropriate maxim.

So we can see now how a person can be virtuous for having an end required by a duty of virtue. Someone is virtuous, for example, insofar as she has a maxim of helping others in need—insofar, that is, as she recognizes others' happiness as good. In acting on that maxim she acts virtuously. *But she does not act in a way that is morally worthy.* For in acting to achieve an end like "others' happiness," the virtuous agent acts not in order to do her duty, but directly for the sake of the happiness of others. She has among the principles of her character the virtuous maxim that "helping others is good," and so she is motivated to act when she recognizes actions as helpful to others. She may therefore act this way, virtuously, without recognizing that she has a duty of "helping others." For her acting virtuously it is not necessary that she has acquired her virtuous maxim or end of helping others because she recognized it as a duty of virtue. If she merely happens to like helping others, as did the philanthropist in Kant's example from the *Groundwork,* this implies that she has a virtuous maxim.

In order to do something *right* it is not necessary to recognize what one does as a duty, or to do it because it is required by a duty of right. It is always possible to act *rightly* without one's action's having moral worth. So in Kant's ethical theory it should be possible also to act *virtuously,* or to satisfy a duty of virtue, without acting in a way that is morally worthy. All that would be required for acting *virtuously* in this way is that one act with the motive appropriate to the virtue.

The familiar charges that virtue-theorists have raised against Kantian ethics have presupposed that "moral worth" is the same as what they understand by "virtue," used as an appraisal concept. That is why they have objected, with such plausibility, that Kantian ethics denies the virtue of actions not meeting the "from-duty-alone" criterion. But it has been shown here how in Kant's ethical theory, acting in a way that is morally worthy is not the same as acting in a way that is virtuous. The distinction depends on a difference in the maxims on which a person acts, or, which in this context is the same, on a difference between the ends of the actions.

6.11 The Moral Life

So assuming it is now clear how acting virtuously is different from acting with moral worth, some may ask: Which is better? Should we strive to make ourselves more virtuous, or should we concentrate instead on enhancing our moral worth? Questions like these betray a misunderstanding of what Kant's ethics expects from us, in the broad perspective of living the moral life. First of all, it is not the moral agent's objective to act with moral worth as often as possible, or even to act virtuously. The expectations of Kantian morality are expressed in terms of duties; and these fall into two categories: duties to act in certain ways (duties of right) and duties to have, and cultivate, certain ends (duties of virtue). The latter duties, as we have seen, address the development of character.

Moral worth and virtue, as concepts of motivational appraisal, apply to our actions on account of our maxims, or the ends for which we act. But as agents our focus is always on actions as means to our ends, and not on these appraisal concepts. The distinction between moral worth and virtue rests on the difference between the single end of obedience to the moral law, in the former case, and the several ends that are required by duties of virtue, in the latter. Kant marks this difference in one way, as we saw in a passage quoted above, by observing a distinction between formal "virtue" and material "virtues." We have seen Kant's argument for there being ends we ought to have. The formal end is that of obedience to the moral law. If there is any duty with respect to this end, it is a duty to cultivate or strengthen the subjective incentive of respect for the moral law (*Metaphysics of Morals*, 201/6:399).

At the beginning of the previous section we quoted a definition of virtue as a psychological condition. We can understand that definition better now that we are aware of the difference Kant recognized between formal "virtue" and material "virtues." That definition defines formal virtue, and not any of the material virtues. It presents formal virtue as the strength of a person's maxim of obedience to the moral law; or, as the strength of the moral incentive incorporated into that maxim. This definition connecting virtue with strength is not an isolated comment, but reflects a central theme of Kant's discussion of virtue in *The Metaphysics of Morals*. A rhetorical question he wrote there is, "For what sort of concept can be made of the force and herculean strength needed to subdue the vice-breeding inclinations if virtue is to borrow its weapons from the arsenal of metaphysics, a speculative subject that few know how to handle?" (181–2/6:376). He subsequently referred to virtue as *"fortitude"*: "the capacity and considered resolve to withstand a strong but unjust opponent" (186/6:380). Virtue is next contrasted with *lack of virtue*, which is "moral weakness".[42]

---

[42] 189/6:384, cf. also 194/6:390. Later we read: "It is also correct to say that man is under obligation to [acquire] *virtue* (as moral strength). For while the capacity *(facultas)* to overcome all opposing sensible impulses can and must be simply *presupposed* in man on account of his freedom, yet this capacity as *strength (robor)* is something he must acquire;" (200/6:397). Then, seconding his earlier definition Kant concluded: "Virtue is, therefore, moral strength of a *man's* will in fulfilling his *duty,* [which is] a

In the preceding chapters it has been argued that, in Kant's theory of action, what we choose to do is always a function of the strength of psychological forces of desire, or of incentives. This is another way of saying that what makes the difference in how we choose to act is the relative strengths of our maxims. It is not at all surprising, then, that Kant should think that the strength of the maxim of duty, relative to opposing inclinations, is virtue in the formal sense. In the material sense, the several virtues are attachments or commitments to specific ends, such as the happiness of others and one's own improvement. It is our duty to have these commitments, and commitments to their subsidiary ends. There are even duties to cultivate and strengthen these commitments. Kant provided one example: "It is [an indirect] duty not to avoid the places where the poor who lack the most basic necessities are to be found . . . in order to avoid sharing painful feelings one may not be able to resist. For this is still one of the impulses that nature has planted in us to do what the representation of duty alone would not accomplish" (ibid., 251/6:457).

This has been a difficult comment for many readers to understand. What, after all, *wouldn't* the representation of duty be able to accomplish for the benefit of the poor and the suffering? What, of moral relevance, could our cultivating some *feeling* accomplish that our motive of duty would be incapable of accomplishing? The answer is not that we should cultivate certain natural inclinations in order to make it more attractive for us to choose to do our duty. It is rather that what the poor and suffering sometimes need cannot be given to them through actions motivated by duty alone. Human beings sometimes need others to act on their behalf, out of concern for them, and not solely from duty. For this reason it can be an indirect duty to cultivate and strengthen motivating feelings of sympathy and compassion. Actions taken in regard to this indirect duty—actions intended to strengthen compassion—will have moral worth if they are motivated by the thought of duty. Actions caused through the strength of those feelings can then be appraised as virtuous.

The preceding will serve as an introduction to Kant's reflections on the moral life, and the development of moral character. At the end of the

moral *constraint* through his own lawgiving reason, insofar as this [reason] constitutes itself an authority *executing* the law" (206/6:405). Finally, "the true strength of virtue" is said to consist in "a tranquil mind with a *considered and firm* resolution to put the law of virtue into practice" (209/6:408, emphasis altered).

next chapter we turn to consider his thoughts on the "good will." But before reaching that topic we must say more about Kant's thoughts on the endemic moral weakness of human beings, or "human frailty." This weakness is part of the basis for his assessment of human nature as afflicted by "radical evil." We shall see next how he traces our moral responsibility for this evil to a free, noumenal act—in another world, of course.

The present chapter has focused on motivation for actions appraised as having "moral worth," and for those appraised as "virtuous." In the later sections of the chapter we have concentrated on the difference between these two categories of moral appraisal. We began with the controversial thesis that, in Kant's view, action qualifying as morally worthy can be explained by the feeling of respect for the moral law. The strength of this motivating feeling is the explanatory principle for actions justified by moral principles. Its explanatory power is relatively easy to accommodate on a "two-worlds" interpretation of Kant's practical philosophy. The second half of the chapter focused on a familiar complaint posed by virtue-theorists against the Kantian view of moral motivation. It is that the notorious "from-duty-alone" criterion for moral worth is too restrictive, since many morally admirable actions are not done from duty alone. The response to that complaint offered here was that, as categories of moral appraisal, "morally worthy" and "virtuous" are not the same. So to deny that an action is morally worthy, because it is not done from duty alone, is not to deny that it is virtuous. Kant's ethical theory recognizes certain motives as morally admirable, even if acting on them is not "morally worthy." It also includes duties to cultivate these motives. So it is a mistake to think of the moral life in accordance with Kantian ethics as a single-minded devotion to increasing one's "moral worth." We are not expected to act from duty alone as much as possible, and certainly not as a full-time obsession. We have other ends and incentives to cultivate, and these are bases for an admirable life of virtue.

7

Evil Nature, Good Will

Kant offered a pessimistic view of human nature when he argued that as a species of rational agents we are evil. Yet he did not think that our being evil in this way would preclude our also being in some respect morally good. This chapter is about the puzzling coexistence in human nature of two conditions that Kant called "radical evil" and "good will."

The problem of justification and explanation arises for Kant's theory of action because we are not perfectly rational agents. Just our recognition that we ought to do something does not explain our doing it. To solve that problem it is necessary to show how what justifies action can, nevertheless, explain it, so that justification is not practically irrelevant (1.11). In the preceding chapters I have argued for a controversial solution to the problem. It is that, in Kant's view, the psychological forces of incentives "incorporated" into the maxims that justify our actions can explain our acting on them. The preponderant strength of the incentive incorporated into the maxim upon which we act explains why we act on that maxim rather than another. So this is why, from a moral point of view, it is better to have a stronger moral incentive than a weaker one. And it is also why Kant thought we are morally obligated to cultivate and strengthen our "moral feeling" (*Metaphysics of Morals*, 201/6:399). Why human agency is like this is explained, as far as it is possible to explain, by Kant's doctrine of the "radical evil" of human nature. Our "good will," on the other hand, is the basis for personal moral progress: for struggling with, and hopefully overcoming, our evil nature. At least that is how it will be presented here.

I begin here by examining what Kant meant in calling humanity "evil by nature." I explain what this evil consists in, and how we acquire it, and then I explain three "degrees" of this evil that Kant identified: *frailty*, *impurity*, and *depravity*. Afterwards I turn to his thoughts on the remedy for our radical evil: on how to purify what he called our "evil heart." In the final sections of this chapter, the concepts of "good will" and "virtue" will be compared, in a manner similar to the way "moral worth" and "virtue" were compared in the previous chapter. Here, as there, the aim will be to disentangle some prevailing conceptions of moral worth and virtue, but this time in relation to the concept of a good will. What we shall conclude in the end may be more than a little surprising. For in the end we see why, in Kant's view, everyone would have a good will, and why everyone would also be, to some degree, virtuous.

7.1 Radical Evil

Kant mentioned Jean-Jacques Rousseau near the beginning of his discussion of humanity's evil nature. Rousseau held that human beings are originally good, but become corrupted by society. Kant disagreed, however; for he thought that moral corruption is rooted (i.e., "radical") in our nature. He might have argued against Rousseau in the following way: How could joining with others in society make us evil, if we were not already susceptible to such corruption? If society is what corrupts us, and if we are social by nature, then it must follow that we are corruptible by nature, and so that our nature is evil.[1]

In calling humanity evil by nature Kant meant, first of all, that everyone is evil, "even the best."[2] He meant in addition that we have an innate "propensity" to immorality. He wrote that "By *propensity* (*propensio*) I understand the subjective ground of the possibility of an inclination (. . .), insofar as this possibility is contingent for humanity in general." He noted, for clarification, that "*Propensity* is actually only the *predisposition* to desire an enjoyment which, when the subject has experienced it, arouses *inclination* to it."[3] The "alcoholic gene," would be an example of a propensity rooted

---

[1] I think Grenberg is correct in developing an argument like this against Wood's characterization of radical evil in terms of "unsocial sociability." See Jeanine Grenberg, *Kant and the Ethics of Humility* (Cambridge: Cambridge University Press, 2005), 32–42.

[2] "[W]e my presuppose evil as subjectively necessary in every human being, even the best" (*Religion*, 56/6:32, see also 54/6:30). That some are "best" implies either that there are greater and lesser degrees of evil, or that the scale on which human beings are judged "better" or "best" takes no account of their common evil.

[3] Ibid., 52/6:29; Kant wrote also: "by the concept of a propensity is understood a subjective determining ground of the power of choice *that precedes every deed*, and hence is itself not yet a *deed*" (55/6:31).

in some people. We do not hold them morally responsible for it when we explain it just by heredity; for their being morally responsible for it would imply their having freely chosen it. Yet Kant supposed that we must hold people responsible for a propensity to moral evil. This is because we can think of evil in no other way than as imputable, and therefore as freely chosen.

Two questions can be asked about this evil propensity: In what does it consist? and How is it chosen? We take up the first question in the remainder of this section, and in the one that follows; the second question will be answered subsequently, in Section 3.

The human propensity to evil is not direct. That is, we are not born with a maxim to the effect that "Evil is good," and so we are not predisposed to actions just because we judge them to be evil. Kant would characterize an agent with such a propensity as *diabolical*.[4] The propensity to evil in human beings consists instead in how we are predisposed toward actions we judge to be morally good. As rational agents we are innately predisposed toward obedience to the moral law, since it is presumed that by nature we have a maxim that "Obeying the moral law is good." So our propensity to evil consists precisely in our being predisposed to deviate from that maxim. We can judge that an action is morally justified, or required by duty, and yet not act accordingly, because of contrary maxims of inclination.

There are three fundamental *predispositions* (*Anlagen*) of human nature, in Kant's view (see *Religion,* 50−2/6:26−8). They help explain our innate propensity to evil. Referring to these three in general he wrote that, "By the predispositions of a being we understand the constituent parts required for it as well as the forms of their combination that make for such a being" (52/6:28).

(*a*) The first of the three is a predisposition to *animality*, described in psychological terms as "physical or purely *mechanical* self-love." This includes our basic animal instincts for self-preservation, propagation, and community. Kant explained that "corruption" of these animal instincts leads to what he called "*beastial vices.*"

---

[4] See *Religion,* 60/6:37. We may assume this would mean that, analogous to the case of human beings, such agents might sometimes find it necessary to limit their self-love and inclinations in order to do what is justified by the evil maxim. They could conceivably suffer weakness of will, foregoing an opportunity to do something recognized as evil in order to secure personal happiness.

(*b*) Next follows the predisposition to *humanity,* or the drive to happiness. This too is a kind of self-love, but it is intellectual and not mechanical. It depends on comparisons between human beings, and it generates interests in reputation and equality. From these, he said, may follow jealousy, rivalry and a list of social vices.

(*c*) The third basic predisposition is to *personality.* It is defined as "the susceptibility for respect for the moral law as *of itself a sufficient incentive to the power of choice."* Naturally, there is no potential here for any vice-breeding corruption. As Kant explained, this capacity for the moral feeling of respect for the moral law is "a predisposition onto which nothing evil can be grafted."

These three predispositions may be seen as innate sources of human motivation. Even though some lead to vices, Kant did not regard this as a reason for regarding them as inherently bad or evil: "All these predispositions in the human being are not only (negatively) *good,* (they do not resist the moral law) but they are also predispositions *to the good* (they demand compliance with it)" (52/6:28).

To see how the evil propensity of human nature derives from these elementary predispositions we need only consider a nearly obvious point. As a set of fundamental, practical concerns for human life, the three predispositions generate motivational conflicts in the course of human experience. The same course of action judged good from the point of view of the predisposition to humanity (or on the basis of a maxim of self-love) may be judged bad from the perspective of the moral predisposition to personality. And motivational conflicts that arise from these maxims and judgments must be resolvable in favor of one side or the other, if the human being is to act. Furthermore, episodes of such conflict-resolution may exhibit characteristic patterns in a person's conduct. These regularities would be explainable by some enduring *relation* of the three predispositions that generate these conflicts. The predisposition to humanity may tend to prevail in one person; another may be more strongly predisposed to personality. Such patterns of preference in the psychological determination of action would provide evidence of the underlying, moral quality of a person's empirical character.

7.2 "*Gesinnung*"

A term appearing throughout Kant's writing on moral psychology is "*Gesinnung*." His use of this term in *Religion* is typically translated "disposition," and its significance for explaining the human propensity to evil has been emphasized in recent secondary literature.[5] In writings before *Religion*, however, Kant seems sometimes to have used "*Gesinnung*" as equivalent to "maxim."[6] He also used it frequently in drawing the distinction between dutiful actions prompted by respect for law, and the same actions motivated by alternative, non-moral incentives. In these cases the moral incentive itself is sometimes referred to using "*Gesinnung*," where the presumption is that this incentive explains action.[7] So it appears that in some contexts Kant's use of "*Gesinnung*" can be translated by English "intention" without significant loss of meaning.[8] In contexts like this the phrase "moral disposition," like "moral intention," would have a normative, or an honorific sense. That is, an "evil moral disposition," in this sense of "disposition," would be oxymoronic.

But sometimes, especially in *Religion*, the phrase "moral disposition" is given a less normative, more descriptive sense. In arguing for the doctrine of rigorism, for example, Kant referred to human beings' "disposition as regards the moral law" as never morally indifferent, never neither good nor evil (49/6:24). From claims like this we may infer his belief that the moral

---

[5] See, for example, Allison, *Kant's Theory of Freedom*, 136–45.

[6] See *Practical Reason*, 49/5:56, 71/5:84, 131/5:159, and *Judgment*, 204/5:327.

[7] The following sentences all use "*Gesinnung*," translated "disposition," in referring to the motive for particular dutiful actions. "The disposition incumbent upon [a human being] to have in observing [the moral law] is to do so from duty, not from voluntary liking nor even from an endeavor he undertakes unbidden, gladly and of his own accord" (*Practical Reason*, 72/5:84). "[T]he bounds that practical pure reason sets to humanity [forbid] us to place the subjective determining ground of dutiful actions—that is, their moral motive—anywhere else than in the law itself or to place the disposition which is thereby brought into the maxims anywhere else than in respect for this law...." (73/5:86). "Of every action that conforms to the law but is not done for the sake of the law, one can say that it is morally good only in accordance with the *letter* but not the *spirit* (the disposition)" (62n./5:72). See also 70/5:82. Even in *Religion* Kant used "*Gesinnung*" in referring to the moral incentive: "And so between an evil and a good disposition (the inner principle of maxims) according to which the morality of an action must be judged, there is no intermediate position" (48n./6:23n.).

[8] For further discussion of translations for Kant's various uses of "*Gesinnung*" see G. Felicitas Munzel, *Kant's Conception of Moral Character* (Chicago: University of Chicago Press, 1999), xv–xviii.

disposition of human beings—their disposition (*Gesinnung*) as regards the moral law—must be either good or evil. So here the idea of an "evil moral disposition" seems sensible.

Kant indicated what he meant by "*Gesinnung*" in the context of his discussion of radical evil as follows: "The disposition, i.e., *the first subjective ground of the adoption of the maxims*, can only be a single one, and it applies to the entire use of freedom universally" (50/6:25, emphasis added). It has been said that *Gesinnung* in this sense is the single highest maxim of a human being's character.[9] But this, technically, is not correct. The human being's disposition in regard to the moral law, which accounts for radical evil, is not a maxim. It is instead a ranking of the three predispositions of animality, humanity, and personality as incentives, in which the latter is subordinated to either of the former. In other words, so long as the human being's predisposition to obey the moral law does not predominate the other predispositions, his or her disposition in regard to the law (his or her moral disposition) is evil. Only a perfectly rational being, for whom moral justification would also explain action, would have a moral disposition in which the predisposition to personality predominates. So only a perfectly rational being has a disposition in regard to the moral law that is good. Kant usually referred to this condition as "holiness." Following the doctrine of rigorism, therefore, any disposition in regard to the moral law that falls short of holiness must count as an evil moral disposition: as a natural propensity to evil.

The "highest" or "supreme" maxim of a human being, from which all other maxims are derived by practical reasoning, is in Kant's view a maxim that both *incorporates* and *orders* multiple incentives. The predispositions of animality and humanity can each be regarded as forms of self-love. So we may think of these two as represented by the incentive of personal

---

[9] Allison claims: "Kant states that an agent's *Gesinnung*, or the 'ultimate subjective ground,' of the adoption of maxims is itself a maxim" (*Kant's Theory of Freedom*, 141). But there is no statement to this effect in *Religion*. Allison may have been led to think of the disposition as identical with the highest maxim by Kant's statements here: "This disposition too, however, must be adopted through the free power of choice, for otherwise it could not be imputed. But there cannot be any further cognition of the subjective ground or the cause of this adoption (although we cannot avoid asking about it), for otherwise we would have to adduce still another maxim into which the disposition would have to be incorporated, and this maxim must in turn have its ground" (*Religion*, 50/6:25). It would be natural for Allison to think of the disposition as itself a maxim since, as Kant wrote here, it is something that we *adopt* through an exercise of *free choice*. In light of his Incorporation Thesis, Allison would think of freely choosing as nothing other than adopting a maxim (see above, 3.5).

happiness. We may also see the predisposition to personality as represented by the moral incentive of respect for law. A human being incorporating both of these incentives into his or her highest, unifying maxim can be represented as someone wanting, overall, to be happy and to obey the moral law. Yet in Kant's view happiness and morality would be competing incentives to action. And to adopt a maxim ranking the moral incentive as subordinate to the incentive of happiness (inclination) is to adopt an evil maxim. "[W]hether the human being is good or evil," Kant wrote in *Religion*, "must not lie in the difference between the incentives that he incorporates into his [highest] maxim (not in the material of the maxim) but in their *subordination* (in the form of the maxim): *which of the two he makes the condition of the other*" (59/6:36). In other words, for human beings, the difference between a good nature and an evil nature is not the difference between incorporating the moral law into one's highest maxim, on the one hand, and incorporating happiness into that maxim, on the other. It is rather the difference between ranking the moral incentive above happiness, and ranking happiness above the moral incentive, where both incentives are incorporated into the highest maxim. These different rankings are alternative *forms* of the highest maxim for human beings, as Kant indicated. And he saw human beings as tainted with radical evil because of the evil form of their highest maxim.

So the form of the highest maxim is what Kant referred to as the disposition (*Gesinnung*): "the first subjective ground of the adoption of [subsequent] maxims." It makes sense that the disposition would not be identified as the highest maxim. For if the disposition ranking happiness above the moral law were actually a maxim, then it would be the major premise of the most fundamental practical syllogism of human rational agency. To serve this role the maxim would have to express the thought that "Subordinating the moral incentive to the incentive of happiness is good." It would then be effective in human conduct only with the addition of certain minor premises. These would characterize policies or courses of action as subordinating the moral incentive to the incentive of happiness. So, essentially, this would mean that human beings could not act unless they recognized what they were doing as subordinating morality to their personal happiness. But this hardly makes sense. More sensible is the idea that in their highest maxims, evil human beings regard both happiness and morality as good (see 1.5); yet they do not incorporate the moral law as the stronger incentive, in comparison with the incentive of happiness. The order of their incentives, and hence the way they tend to choose, gives preference to personal happiness.

Kant summarized his conception of human radical evil, accordingly, as follows: "In view of what has been said above, the statement, 'The human being is *evil*,' cannot mean anything else than that he is conscious of the moral law and yet has incorporated into his maxim the (occasional) deviation from it" (55/6:32). This helps answer the first question about radical evil that was asked above (7.1): In what does it consist?

7.3 Explaining Evil

In this section we deal with the second question about radical evil: How is it chosen? That is, how do we, by free choice, incorporate the occasional deviation from the moral law into our highest maxim? The only answer we can give is that this choice of our radical evil is unexplainable.

According to Kant's doctrine of the radical evil of human nature, the moral incentive does not predominate in our highest maxim. This condition is our so-called "disposition" (*Gesinnung*) in regard to the moral law, and it constitutes a propensity to evil actions in our empirical characters. By this propensity we are psychologically predisposed to immoral actions. We tend to prefer actions we recognize as good from the perspective of self-love, over those we recognize as good because they conform to the moral law. I have argued that, according to Kant, this preference is realized in the stronger psychological forces of incentives incorporated into our maxims of self-love.

So I think Kant's view was that we are to blame for every immoral action explained by psychological forces incorporated into our maxims, because we are to blame for the original disposition of those action-explaining forces. These are rooted in our psychology as agents, in the form of our highest maxim of practical reasoning. But how are we to blame for this? How is this evil form of the highest maxim to be explained? If it is evil it must be chosen, according to Kant. But if it is chosen, then wouldn't this imply a still higher structure of incentives, incorporated into a still higher maxim?

Kant's view on our responsibility for our radical evil is sometimes criticized on this point. Brewer, for example, poses the following dilemma. Either the choice of our highest maxim can be assigned to a still higher maxim that governs it, or it cannot be assigned to any maxim at all. But, regarding the first alternative,

To assign a [still higher] maxim to the choice of the highest-level maxim would be self-contradictory, since the maxim governing the choice would then have to be considered our highest-level maxim. Nor [regarding the second alternative] will it help Kant to think of the choice of our highest-level maxim as ungoverned by any maxim, since he would be compelled to understand such a choice as an arbitrary and unreasoned exercise of will.[10]

Kant was aware of the difficulty posed by the first horn of this dilemma. He made this clear in explaining why we cannot attribute the choice of the highest-level maxim to a still higher-level maxim.[11]

But the difficulty expressed in the second horn of the dilemma betrays a misunderstanding of the role of maxims in human agency. For us human beings, who can act only on the basis of maxims, a choice to act independently of our maxims would indeed constitute "an arbitrary and unreasoned exercise of will." But this would not apply for a choice *to be* an agent who can act only on the basis of maxims. Nor would it apply for a choice having this as a consequence. Someone making such a choice need not be understood as acting on a still higher maxim governing or justifying it. And so he or she need not be thought to choose arbitrarily, owing to the lack of a higher maxim. In other words, maxim-less choice and action would be arbitrary and unreasoned for the ordinary human agent acting in the empirical world; but it need not be so for the noumenal agent acting in the intelligible world. Consequently, my act as a noumenal agent may explain my character as an empirical moral agent, or the disposition in regard to the moral law of my highest maxim (4.3, 5.6).[12] And if it does,

---

[10] Talbot Brewer, "The Character of Temptation: Towards a More Plausible Kantian Moral Psychology," *Pacific Philosophical Quarterly* 83 (2002): 103–30 at 125.

[11] "This [evil] disposition too, however, must be adopted through the free power of choice, for otherwise it could not be imputed. But there cannot be any further cognition of the subjective ground or the cause of this adoption (although we cannot avoid asking about it), for otherwise we would have to adduce still another maxim into which the disposition would have to be incorporated, and this maxim must in turn have its ground" (*Religion*, 50/6:25).

[12] Kant wrote: Now, the term "deed" can in general apply just as well to the use of freedom through which the supreme maxim (either in favor of, or against, the law) is adopted in the power of choice, as to the use by which the actions themselves (materially considered, i.e., as regards the objects of the power of choice) are performed in accordance with that maxim. The propensity to evil is a deed in the first meaning (*peccatum originarium*), and at the same time the formal ground of every deed contrary to law according to the second meaning, [i.e., of a deed] that resists the law materially, and is then called vice

then the evil propensity of my empirical character would depend neither on a higher maxim, as the first horn of the dilemma has it, nor need it depend on an arbitrary and unreasoned exercise of will, as proposed by the second horn of the dilemma.

A noumenal choice to be an agent whose choices and actions are explained by maxims and incentives would be unexplainable to human beings; for we can comprehend choices and actions only as justified by practical reasoning with maxims. But what is incomprehensible to us is not necessarily arbitrary. It is incomprehensible to us why we experience the sensible world in three-dimensional space, for example.[13] But this does not justify our calling it "arbitrary," or "unreasoned," that we should experience the world this way. Granted, an atemporal choice of a highest maxim with the moral incentive subordinated to incentives of self-love is *irrational*. This must be so if we place the incentive of the moral law necessarily on the side of reason. But from this it does not follow that such a choice would be an "unreasoned exercise of will." It follows at most only that it is not fully rational, as it should be. And why it is not fully rational is also something we cannot explain. "The rational origin . . . of this disharmony in our power of choice with respect to the way it incorporates lower incentives in its maxim and makes them supreme, i.e., this propensity to evil, remains inexplicable to us. . . . there is no conceivable ground for us, therefore, from which moral evil could first have come in us" (64/6:43, see also *Pure Reason*, A556/B584). So in answer to our second leading question about radical evil, How is it chosen?, the answer has to be that we choose the condition that accounts for our radical evil through our free action in the noumenal world, an action that we of course cannot explain.

7.4 Evil in Three Degrees

Radical evil may come in any of three degrees, as Kant saw it. They are: weakness ("human frailty"), impurity, and depravity ("corruption of

---

(*peccatum derivativum*); and the first indebtedness remains even though the second may be repeatedly avoided (because of incentives that are not part of the law).   (Ibid., 55/6:31)

[13]   The analogy here is suggested by Kant: "we are just as incapable of assigning a further cause for why evil has corrupted the very highest maxim in us, though this is our own deed, as we are for a fundamental property that belongs to our nature" (55/6:32).

the heart"). These conditions have been understood by commentators in different ways, depending often upon their different presuppositions about Kant's theory of action.[14] But some aspects of the degrees of evil are uncontroversial. Weakness, or frailty, is generally acknowledged to be the least evil of the three, while depravity is usually thought to be the worst. Commentators often acknowledge also that it is possible for a person to digress from being less evil to being more evil.[15]

Frailty is described as "the general weakness of the human heart in complying with the adopted maxims." Kant illustrated this condition with the lament of St. Paul: "What I would, that I do not!" (53/6:29, see also above, 2.3). *Impurity* is characterized by "actions conforming to duty [that] are not done purely from duty" (54/6:30). *Depravity*, finally, is "the propensity of the power of choice to maxims that subordinate the incentives of the moral law to others (not moral ones)."

Our original subordination of the moral incentive to the incentives of self-love, in our highest maxim, constitutes our natural propensity to evil. I take this to mean that human beings are, by nature, morally imperfect. Our actions are not explained by the reasons that justify them (see 1.11), but by incentives incorporated into our maxims. And in facing practical conflicts between moral and inclinational maxims, the moral incentive is not forceful enough to prevail in every case. Yet some who recognize this moral shortcoming in their characters may attempt to do something about it. They may resolve to strengthen their moral incentive. Their intention in doing so would be in order not only to resist any future temptation to immoral action, but to bring it about that, for them at least, dutiful actions are done for duty's sake. In Kant's view, perfect achievement of this lofty goal, which would be holiness, is not humanly possible. That is a consequence of the general weakness of human nature: the first degree of radical evil. And this weakness can lead to further evil. In light of

---

[14] See, for example, John R. Silber, "The Ethical Significance of Kant's *Religion*," cxx–cxxiii; Carnois, *The Coherence of Kant's Doctrine of Freedom*, 104–6; Allison, *Kant's Theory of Freedom*, 157–61; and Munzel, *Kant's Conception of Moral Character*, 146.

[15] This is based on Kant's statement about an "evil heart":

Its origin is in the frailty of human nature, in not being strong enough to comply with its adopted principles, coupled with its dishonesty in not screening incentives (even those of well-intentioned actions) in accordance with the moral guide [i.e., "impurity"], and hence at the end, if it comes to this [i.e., "depravity"], in seeing only to the conformity of these incentives to the law, not to whether they have been derived from the latter itself, i.e. from it as the sole incentive. (60/6:37)

212 EVIL NATURE, GOOD WILL

disappointing failures in the resolve to become morally better, that is, stronger, one may sink to the next lower level of evil: impurity.

Impurity is taking no interest in whether one's actions conforming to the law are explained by the moral incentive alone. The impure may well acknowledge holiness as an ideal. But, taking a more realistic attitude, they are satisfied with their compliance with duty even when it may be explained by other motives. Conformity to duty is still considered supremely important. But in the practical thinking of the impure, any number of reasons may account for this conviction: including respect for the law, reputation, honor, satisfaction with oneself, and perhaps even a heavenly reward. The attitude of moral impurity has not "adopted the law *alone* as the *sufficient* incentive but, on the contrary, often (and perhaps always) needs still other incentives besides it in order to determine the power of choice for what duty requires" (53/6:630).

Once conformity to moral duty solely for duty's sake has ceased to engage a person's practical concerns, descent into the lowest level of radical evil is likely to follow. The attitude of the depraved is that the supreme guide in practical life would be a coalition of non-moral interests, under the abstract ideal of happiness. One lives chiefly for enjoyment, reputation, or honor. For the depraved it becomes sufficient merely that moral conduct would serve these interests: that they are not jeopardized by immorality. Kant wrote: "in this case no attention at all is given to the incentives in the maxim but only to compliance with the letter of the law" (60/6:37). In other words, what Kant calls the depraved person would be satisfied with himself if he merely resolved to be an upright person. The fact that his reason or incentive for doing so was just in order to have a good reputation, and to profit thereby, would not trouble him.[16]

---

[16] The relations among the three degrees of evil, and their relations to radical evil itself, have not been well understood. Carnois seems to have considered the third degree, depravity, as equivalent to radical evil itself: "Only the third descriptive level [depravity] enables us to present the very essence of the propensity to evil as it will later be revealed in Kant's a priori analysis in the section devoted to the reality and origin of evil" (*The Coherence of Kant's Doctrine of Freedom*, 105). In Allison's view, on the other hand, the first degree of evil, frailty, is equivalent to the human propensity to evil: "what Kant terms the 'frailty of human nature' or the 'weakness of the human heart' can be seen as compatible with both his conception of freedom and his account of evil if one equates it with the bare propensity to evil itself" (*Kant's Theory of Freedom*, 159). I think we can clear up such confusions in the following ways. First, it is important to take seriously Kant's conception of radical evil as a *propensity* of our nature. As such, it is an innate, original condition that manifests itself once a triggering event is encountered in experience. Its three different degrees are three types of

The human heart can be pure, impure or depraved (corrupted), depending on one's attitude toward the moral imperfection of one's nature.[17] The attitude of purity of heart is characterized by the ongoing struggle to reverse the evil ordering of incentives.[18] The pure in heart remain weak, however; although it is possible that their efforts to strengthen the moral incentive are effective to a degree. The impure, by contrast, do not actively struggle to reverse the order of incentives. They may acknowledge the importance and value of doing the right thing, for the right reason. But they do not work toward the ideal of holiness. In their attitude (*Denkungsart*) toward morality as a guide for human life the impure are worse than the frail, who are pure but morally weak. The depraved, then, are worse than the impure. Their attitude toward morality, and the moral incentive, comes close to indifference.[19] In a sense, the depraved actually resign themselves to the natural, radical evil of humanity. Depravity is the attitude that considers the natural subordination of the moral incentive to self-love to be the norm.

its manifestation. Hence, none of the three degrees of evil is equivalent to the propensity to evil. Its first manifestation in experience is the weakness of the moral incentive, evident in an immoral choice. It stems from the reversal of priorities in the highest maxim, where the moral incentive is subordinated to the incentive of self-love. As a consequence, the explanatory power of the moral incentive turns out sometimes, perhaps often, to be weaker than that of competing incentives of inclination. Frailty is the first and ever-enduring manifestation of the radical evil of human nature. It is therefore easy to see how it might be mistaken, as by Allison, for the propensity to evil itself.

[17] Kant's references to the human "heart," as the locus of moral shortcomings or radical evil, are relatively consistent throughout his writing in practical philosophy, especially in the later texts. Some equate the heart with the faculty of choice (*Willkür*). See, for example, Munzel, *Kant's Conception of Moral Character*, 105. But Kant defined the human heart instead as the "capacity or incapacity" of the *Willkür* "arising from this natural propensity to adopt or not to adopt the moral law in its maxims" (*Religion*, 53/6:29). This statement makes it clear that the heart cannot be the *Willkür;* nor can it be identical with the good or evil propensity, even though a good or evil heart comes along with a good or evil propensity. Kant's saying that the heart *arises* from the propensity suggests that he saw the heart as just the inclinational aspect of the propensity, which develops after the triggering experience: like an addiction developing from a first taste of alcohol. So as an inclination, the heart seems to be a mainly empirical concept. But it should not be seen as an inclination in the sense familiar from Kant's motivational psychology: the habitual desire that develops for an object of sensory pleasure. It is rather an inclination of the faculty of choice, in moral experience, toward either compliance with the moral law, if the heart is good, or deviation from the law, if it is evil.

[18] Heart purity, impurity, and depravity imply an evaluation of the relative importance of the moral law as a reason for action (see 1.10).

[19] Note that one can be indifferent to something, *in attitude*, to which he is not indifferent by nature. The depraved are not morally indifferent, since they still possess a moral maxim incorporating the moral incentive. The point is that they regard the moral maxim and its incorporated incentive with indifference.

7.5 From Bad to Better

Implicit in the preceding section is the prospect of reflection on one's motives and ends, and of adopting policies for guiding one's practical life as a whole. This prospect is not precluded for human beings just because our actions are explained by psychological forces of incentives. For these forces can also explain the adoption of life-altering maxims (1.4, 5.8).

It is a principle of explanation that stronger incentives prevail over weaker ones. But immediate sensory allurements do not always provide incentives stronger than intellectual incentives that can lead to steadfast personal resolutions. The resolution to become a better human being can be powered by the moral incentive, and can receive support from other incentives. Human frailty, the first degree of radical evil, is our susceptibility to defecting from our own adopted policies, in moments of weakness. So self-awareness of this susceptibility may prompt some to attempt to strengthen their moral resolve. Others, Kant suggests, are led into compromising strategies, and hence into deteriorating degrees of evil. He described a natural digression from relatively innocent frailty, through impurity, to depravity (60/6:37). Yet the possibility of such digress suggests the possibility, on the other hand, of progress, from bad to better. No matter how evil we are, Kant thought, it must be possible to make ourselves better. This is just because we ought to: "the command that we *ought* to become better human beings still resounds unabated in our souls; consequently, we must also be capable of it" (66/6:45).

But are we not also expected to recover from our radical evil? Why does the command that we ought to become better human beings not also imply that we ought to convert from radical evil to radical goodness? There are deep mysteries here, and possible grounds for far-reaching criticisms of Kant's view. The problem is that radical evil is something we are presumed to bring upon ourselves, through a timeless, intelligible "deed" (55/6:31). How, then, could this original turn to evil be reversed?

It must be said, first of all, that Kant remained convinced that the stain of radical evil *ought* to be removed. This would imply, therefore, that it *can* be removed, though perhaps not through human efforts alone. Supernatural cooperation would be required here, Kant thought; and for this a human being must "make himself antecedently worthy of receiving it" (65/6:44).

Does this tell us that Kant could not after all have endorsed a noumenalist theory of freedom, according to which a change of timeless, intelligible character from evil to good would be metaphysically inconceivable? It does not seem necessary to draw this conclusion.

Kant seems to have been well aware of the paradox implied by noumenal conversion, whether it be a conversion from evil to good or the opposite:

> How it is possible that a naturally evil human being should make himself into a good human being surpasses every concept of ours. For how can an evil tree bear good fruit? But, since by our previous admission a tree which was (in its predisposition) originally good did bring forth bad fruits, and since the fall from good into evil (if we seriously consider that evil originates from freedom) is no more comprehensible than the ascent from evil back to the good, then the possibility of this last cannot be disputed.   (66/6:45)

Recall that the doctrine of rigorism excludes not only a mixture of good and evil, but also a position of indifference (49/6:24–5, see above 3.4). Recall in addition that we can be radically *evil* only if we have brought this condition upon ourselves, freely. For these reasons, it seems, we can be evil only if we have arrived at this condition from being good (66/6:45). Hence, the very idea of radical evil already implies a noumenal conversion, which Kant himself recognized as implying an incomprehensible change.

His view was that in the highest maxim of each human being the moral incentive is subordinated to self-love. This results in our being to some degree evil: either merely frail, or else impure or depraved. We ought to correct this situation, however; because we ought to be good rather than evil. Yet we must become good through our own effort. And this seems to require nothing less than our changing a timeless condition, by the only means available to us: temporal action. This prospect seems hopeless. But in *Religion* Kant claimed, nevertheless, that through satisfactory moral progress over time one can hope to become *a good human being*. The hope is not to undo what is logically impossible to undo, but rather to do what can and ought to be done, and what in the eyes of God must be equivalent to becoming a good human being.

This requires first a temporal conversion in moral attitude or "cast of mind" (*Denkungsart*), resulting in purity of heart. Kant's assumption seems to be that near the beginning of moral experience every morally frail human being can be expected to degenerate to the second degree of radical evil, which is impurity. The impure do not see moral justifications as by themselves providing sufficient reasons for action. So the reversal of this conviction would be a return to moral purity. Yet this is not the same as having a moral incentive *always strong enough* to prevail over any other, competing incentive. That is why the person converted to a pure heart will remain frail, still mired at least to some degree in radical evil. So beyond the conversion to purity of heart there is also required what Kant saw as an endless progress in strengthening the moral incentive, through ever diminishing degrees of frailty.

If by a single and unalterable decision a human being reverses the supreme ground of his maxims by which he was an evil human being (. . .), he is to this extent, by principle and attitude of mind [*Denkungsart*] a subject receptive to the good; but he is a good human being only in incessant laboring and becoming; i.e., he can hope—in view of the purity of the principle which he has adopted as the supreme maxim of his power of choice, and in view of the stability of this principle—to find himself upon the good (though narrow) path of constant *progress* from bad to better. For him who penetrates to the intelligible ground of the heart (. . .), for him to whom this endless progress is a unity, i.e., for God, this is the same as actually being a good human being (pleasing to him); and to this extent the change can be considered a revolution.   (68/6:48, see also *Practical Reason,* 103/5:123)

The propensity to evil endures throughout human experience, as is to be expected from its origin in a noumenal deed. So what ought to be done about it in human experience is all that can be done: nothing short of coming to recognize the moral law as providing an all-sufficient justification for action, i.e., purity of heart, and then making progress, endlessly, in strengthening the moral incentive. Only such moral progress, if it is unending, would suffice to make the radically evil human being good.

Kant was convinced that becoming good requires supernatural cooperation. "[T]he human being must . . . make himself worthy of receiving it; and he must accept this help (which is no small matter), i.e. he must incorporate this positive increase of force into his maxim: in this way alone is it possible that the good be imputed to him, and that he be acknowledged a good human being" (65–6/6:44). The first step, as explained above, is the sincere conversion to purity of heart. But after that the requirement for *being acknowledged as good* is not any change of a timelessly adopted disposition. The only possible remedy for our timeless evil deed is unceasing, temporal progress from bad to better. This amounts to ever strengthening the action-explaining moral incentive within us, in order to be recognized in the eyes of God as a good human being.

7.6 Three Views on the Good Will

Considering what Kant wrote at the beginning of the *Groundwork of the Metaphysics of Morals*, it seems that to be a good human being, or to be a good person, is to have a good will. Most interpretive work on this concept of good will has focused, understandably, on the early sections of *Groundwork* I. This is where Kant introduced the concept, and attempted to clarify it through the related concept of moral worth. But more than a few commentators have recognized that although these two concepts are closely related, having a good will and acting with moral worth are not the same. "Moral worth is the mark of good willing in the sphere of action," writes Herman; she adds, "It is not the only expression of a good will."[20] According to Allison, "the central concept of a good will, which the introduction of the notion of moral worth was intended to clarify, refers precisely to the underlying character or disposition of the agent."[21] Like Allison, most commentators seem to think that Kant in some way equated having a good will with having a good moral disposition (*Gesinnung*), or being a good or virtuous person.[22] In the recent literature on Kant's moral theory, the prevailing view of the good will suggests that there are undoubtedly some human beings who have one, and who

---

[20] *The Practice of Moral Judgment*, 34–5.   [21] *Kant's Theory of Freedom*, 136.

[22] "[T]he concept of a good will or character is the concept of virtue," wrote Warren G. Harbison, "The Good Will," *Kant-Studien* 71 (1980): 47–59 at 56. "Only a good will makes a person morally good," according to Thomas E. Hill, Jr., *Dignity and Practical Reason* (Ithaca: Cornell University Press, 1992), 69. See also Roger J. Sullivan, *Introduction to Kant's Ethics* (Cambridge: Cambridge University Press, 1994), 74; and Roger J. Sullivan, *Immanuel Kant's Moral Theory* (Cambridge: Cambridge University Press, 1989), 140. According to Rawls, "The primary virtues . . . are those the secure possession of which constitutes a good will. . . ." (*Lectures on the History of Moral Philosophy*, 154, cf. also 178). Alasdair Macintyre compares Kant's conception of good will to Aristotle's notion of excellence of character in *After Virtue*, 2nd edn. (Notre Dame, IN: University of Notre Dame Press, 1984), 154. Cf. also Karl Ameriks, "Kant on the Good Will," in Otfried Höffe, ed., *Gurndlegung zur Metaphysik der Sitten: ein kooperativer Kommentar* (Frankfurt am Main: Vittorio Klostermann, 1989), 45–65, esp. 59; and Brewer, "The Character of Temptation," 110. See also Patrick R. Frierson, *Freedom and Anthropology in Kant's Moral Philosophy* (Cambridge: Cambridge University Press, 2003), 122ff.

therefore act relatively often with "moral worth," but most do not have a good will.[23]

Yet in the opinion of a minority of interpreters, it seems that none of us would have a good will. For they see Kant's conception of having a good will as a humanly unattainable ideal. So they think that not even the best or most virtuous among us would have a good will. We may call this view "good-will perfectionism." Louden expresses a perfectionist view of the good will, which he distinguishes from "virtue," when he writes that "Virtue is only an approximation of the good will, because of the basic conflict or tension in human wills. Kant's virtuous agent is [only] a human approximation of a good will. . . ."[24] For roughly the same reason, Korsgaard has claimed that the good will is to be understood as only an ideal will, or as a "perfectly rational will."[25]

But in contrast to these perfectionists stands a third group of interpreters, whose view can be labeled "good-will universalism." They represent the opposite extreme from good-will perfectionists, because they think that every rational being must have a good will. Universalists see having a good will as a condition of the possibility of being virtuous or vicious, and even for having duties. In the words of Höffe, for example, "One can speak of duty only when, in addition to rational desires, there are competing inclinations, that is, when there is a bad will in addition to the good will."[26] Paton expressed a similar view: "This good or rational will Kant takes to be present in every rational agent, and so in every man, however much it may be overlaid by irrationality."[27]

[23] In a challenge to the majority view's identification of good will and virtue, Dean argues that probably most human beings have a good will, since most are influenced in some way by moral beliefs. See Richard Dean, *The Value of Humanity in Kant's Moral Theory* (Oxford: Clarendon Press, 2006), 97.

[24] Robert Louden, "Kant's Virtue Ethics," *Philosophy* 61 (1986): 473–89 at 478.

[25] *Creating the Kingdom of Ends*, 123–4, 240. Others, who may not explicitly endorse this perfectionist view of the good will, seem also to conceive of the requirement for having a good will as so demanding that it appears that only a perfect will could qualify. "[A] good will is a will which could under *no* circumstances form intentions that violated the principle of autonomy," according to Tom Sorell, "Kant's Good Will and Our Good Nature," *Kant-Studien* 78 (1987): 87–101 at 93. Warner Wick writes similarly, "to have a good will is simply to have a character whose aims and choices are in complete [!] accord with the moral law"; Immanuel Kant, *The Metaphysical Principles of Virtue*, trans., J. Ellington (Indianapolis, IN: Bobbs-Merrill, 1964), lii.

[26] Otfried Höffe, *Immanuel Kant*, trans. M. Farrier (Albany, NY: SUNY Press, 1994), 142.

[27] H. J. Paton, *The Categorical Imperative*, 169. A passage from Kant's *Groundwork* seems to confirm this idea, when it is translated to imply that even a scoundrel must have a good will, because he would be, from the standpoint of freedom, "*conscious of possessing a good will* which, on his own admission, constitutes the law for the bad will belonging to him as a member of the sensible world"; Immanuel

Kant's emphasis on the radical evil of human nature in *Religion* may suggest that the perfectionists have the correct interpretation of his view. A good will, as perfectionists see it, would belong to all and only those who are what Kant would have called good by nature. In contrast to radically evil human beings, those with a good will must have a natural propensity to good. They would be those who, in a free, noumenal act, incorporate the moral law as the preponderant incentive into the highest maxim of their characters. As a consequence, they would always comply fully with the moral law. So since experience shows that no human beings are like this, it should be clear that none of us has such a good will, just as the perfectionists suppose. Still, considering other views Kant expressed in *Religion,* there may be something to be said in favor of the majority view, that having a good will is being a good or virtuous person. Even if we are all evil by nature, we are evidently still capable of converting to purity of heart, and of embarking on the path of endless progress. Having a good will, and so being virtuous, may well be equivalent to having, subsequent to a moral conversion, a pure but still humanly frail heart. Kant did write at least once in *Religion*, contrary to the perfectionist view, that "An evil heart can coexist with a will that is in the abstract [*im allgemeinen*] good."[28]

Yet contrary to both perfectionism and the majority view, Kant wrote also in *Religion* that "for the human being, who despite a corrupted [or depraved] heart *yet always possesses a good will,* there still remains hope of a return to the good from which he has strayed" (65/6:44, emphasis added). Here, even those who are evil to the worst degree possible for human beings are said to possess a good will. Everyone must have a good will if we follow this statement, which supports the universalist interpretation.

Kant, *Groundwork of the Metaphysics of Morals,* trans. H. J. Paton (New York: Harper, 1964), 123/4:455, emphasis added. (But Kant's German sentence here lacks any verb of possession in the emphasized clause, so it does not actually say that the scoundrel is conscious of "possessing" a good will.) Wood's interpretation of Kant's view of the good will is not very far from Paton's. He writes: "Kant's view is that most of us display a rich mixture of good will and evil will, often in ways that entangle evil maxims with good ones and make it difficult for us even to tell the one from the other." Allen Wood, "The Good Will," *Philosophical Topics* 31 (Spring and Fall 2003): 457–84 at 471. Wood's interpretation accommodates good-will universalism, though he does not present any reason to think that no one could lack a good will. His interpretation seems in tension with Kant's "rigorism," however (see 3.4).

[28] 60/6:37 (cf. also 108/6:97). Elsewhere in *Religion* the translators use "in general" and "universally" for "*im allgemeinen.*"

7.7 Good Will in *Groundwork* I

We would very likely go awry in understanding Kant's conception of a good will if we relied only on his comments on good will found in *Religion*. His explicit analysis of the concept, from *Groundwork* I, should not be overlooked. But in that place we find a number of comments counting decisively against good-will perfectionism. Kant opens with the famous claim that "It is impossible to think of anything at all in the world, or indeed even beyond it, that could be considered good without limitation except a *good will*" (7/4:393). If he held a perfectionist view of good will it is not likely that he would lead off his analysis of the concept by locating a good will even *possibly* in this world. In those introductory comments a good will is said also to (help) correct the influence on the mind of recognizably human goods like power, riches, and honor.[29] But this is hard to explain if Kant sided with the perfectionists in thinking that human beings can at best only approximate a good will. Furthermore, admirable human qualities like moderation, self-control, and reflection are called "conducive to this good will itself" and admired because "they can make its work much easier." But this makes no sense if a good will is only a perfectionist ideal for us. Self-control does not seem in any way conducive or useful for the work of a good will if we see it as an unattainable, perfectly rational will.

Good-will perfectionism seems to be ruled out by comments appearing at the beginning of *Groundwork* I. But another plausible interpretation of good will, based on Kant's *Groundwork*, can be ruled out by what appears in *Religion*. This is a conception of good will that treats it as a wholly episodic concept, and denies it any dispositional relevance. What makes this a plausible understanding of Kant's conception of good will as analyzed in *Groundwork* I is that he discussed the concept there almost completely in terms of episodes of acting with moral worth, or of acting from duty. According to this conception of the good will, therefore, one has a good will, or not, only in relation to particular actions. A good will of this sort is not a quality of character that endures over many episodes of action, or

---

[29] "Power, riches and honor, even health and that complete well-being and satisfaction with one's condition called *happiness*, produce boldness and often arrogance as well unless a good will is present which corrects the influence of these on the mind. . . ." (*Groundwork*, 7/4:393).

in conduct over the course of time. The episodic conception of good will seems equivalent just to acting with a (morally) good intention, and not with having any enduring, dispositional readiness to act that way. In the episodic sense, one might have a good will in one action, and then lack good will entirely in the very next action, twenty seconds later.

Most recent interpreters have denied that Kant's conception of the good will should be understood as merely episodic. But few of the arguments for this denial are textually based.[30] Concentrating on just the thoroughly episodic analysis of good will Kant provided in *Groundwork* I, merely in terms of acting from duty, it seems impossible to justify the assumption that good will is supposed to be a dispositional concept. The two claims from *Religion* quoted just above, however, show conclusively that Kant could not, at least at the time he wrote that text, have thought of good will only episodically. In one comment, as we have seen, he referred to the good will "in general" (*im allgemeinen*); in another comment, he referred to always possessing a good will despite a corrupt, evil heart. The second of these seems to provide the strongest evidence against the episodic conception of good will. So like the conception of the good will offered by the perfectionists, it seems that any conception of the good will as purely episodic must be rejected as well.

We must not overlook the scoundrel or cool villain of the *Groundwork*, however. In arguing for a good will's unlimited goodness, prior to his analysis of the concept in terms of episodes of acting from duty, Kant seems to have given an example of someone lacking a disposition of good will. "[W]ithout the basic principles of a good will," he wrote, "the coolness of a scoundrel makes him not only far more dangerous but also immediately more abominable in our eyes than we would have taken him to be without it" (8/4:394). Interpreters favoring good-will universalism would not expect Kant ever to offer such an example. At least this seems to be the only place where his texts prompt us even to imagine someone lacking a good will.[31]

---

[30] Paul Guyer, who acknowledges that in *Groundwork* Kant did not use the dispositional term "virtue" as a synonym for "good will," has at least offered some sketchy textual evidence suggesting that he elsewhere applied the term "virtue" to what he (Guyer) supposes is equivalent to a disposition of good will. See *Kant on Freedom, Law and Happiness,* 305.

[31] He does, of course, provide clear examples of people not acting from duty alone, and so lacking moral worth in their actions. To someone embracing the episodic reading of good will these must also count as examples of people lacking good will. They count as examples of lack of good will also for those who adopt dispositional conceptions of good will so rigorous as to imply that having a good will

And in support of their view it seems open to universalists to discount some of what we find in Kant's early reflections on the concept of good will. The first three or four paragraphs of the *Groundwork* might be read as expressing only pretheoretical intuitions that he assumed were common to ordinary moral consciousness, or "folk morality."[32] He need not be read in these early passages as giving us a clear example of someone who would lack a good will. Kant proves his point there well enough, it might also be said, even if his example is only *per impossible*: if we imagine someone calculating and cool but without a good will (although this is impossible in a rational human being, according to the good-will universalists), how dangerous and abominable he would seem for that coolness! So considering both the singularity and vagueness of the *Groundwork*'s scoundrel example, it is hard to count it as weighty evidence against good-will universalism.

7.8 Moral Strength

But shouldn't a good will have to be *earned*? Isn't it supposed to be an achievement won through moral struggle? According to Rawls, "a good will is not a gift. It is something to be achieved; and results from an act of establishing a character, sometimes by a kind of conversion that endures when strengthened by the cultivation of the virtues and of the ways of thought and feeling that support them" (*Lectures*, 155). If this is correct, then the universalist interpreters are misguided.

Kant does explain, as we saw above, that personal moral progress requires a conversion to purity of heart: "If by a single and unalterable decision a human being reverses the supreme ground of his maxims by which he was an evil human being (. . .), he is to this extent, . . . a subject

requires always doing one's duty *from duty alone*. It is hard to find textual evidence for this brand of rigorism, however; and Kant's claim from *Religion* that even the morally corrupt always have a good will counts against his being this kind of rigorist.

[32] Nelson Potter makes this point also, although not in support of a universalist interpretation of good will. See Nelson Potter, "Kant and the Moral Worth of Actions," 228. It must be acknowledged that this point is in tension, also, with the previous argument against good-will perfectionism. If we cannot take everything Kant wrote about good will in *Groundwork* I as adequately reflecting his view of the concept, then several claims he made there cannot count, decisively anyway, against perfectionism. Still, the number of comments about the good will that tend to discredit perfectionism is considerably higher than the one example that tends to discredit universalism. And the text supporting universalism later, in *Religion*, counts strongly against perfectionism.

receptive to the good" (*Religion* 68/6:48). But to be receptive to the good is not the same as being good; for as Kant adds in the next clause describing the convert receptive to the good, "he is a good human being only in incessant laboring and becoming." The goodness that can be *earned* here, and for which conversion to a pure heart is the necessary first step, is achievable only through unceasing progress. There is accordingly no point before the end of one's life at which goodness can be achieved. But it seems doubtful from his statement above that Rawls thought of a good will as something to be achieved only by life-long moral progress.

Perhaps having a good will should require having a pure heart, plus the additional moral achievement of a will "strengthened by cultivation," as Rawls put it. Ameriks has expressed a view like this, making moral strength criterial for having a good will. We have a good will in this sense when we are strong enough ordinarily to do our duty, from duty—though we might sometimes cave in to temptation in extraordinary circumstances. "Even when a person with such a good will fails to act from duty in a trying circumstance," writes Ameriks, "his goodness is there in the fact that it took such a circumstance to bring him down."[33] Goodness of will might therefore consist in not just a pure heart, but also in a *strong* moral commitment, with a "high *degree* of resistance to temptation" (62). We do admire such strength, of course. But here the question should be whether Kant could reasonably have considered a *strong* volitional commitment to morality to be essential for having a good will. Although he never called a morally strong will a good will, he did seem to say, often, that moral strength is "virtue."[34] His published works in ethics include explicit discussions of good will, in the *Groundwork*, and of virtue, in *The Metaphysics of Morals*. But nowhere in these texts are good will and virtue equated. These terms seem therefore to refer to different concepts. And moral strength of will seems always to go, conceptually, with virtue; never with good will.

Besides this textual argument against equating the achievement of moral strength with having a good will there is another, conceptual difficulty with that equation. The problem arises from the fact that strength is a relative concept. Something's strength is always relative to any counterforce it can

---

[33] "Kant on the Good Will," 58.

[34] "*Virtue* is the strength of man's maxim in fulfilling his duty" (*Metaphysics of Morals*, 197/6:394).

endure or overcome in its causality.[35] But something is "strong" only in relation to a reference class. "Strong" is like "tall" and "rich." Being strong requires others who are weaker, just as being tall requires others who are shorter. So if a person of good will is someone who has achieved a *morally strong* will, then she owes the goodness of her will partly to the moral weakness of others.[36] And if everyone's moral strength were equal, then no one would have a good will.[37] For this reason, also, a maxim of striving to achieve a good will could not qualify as a universal law of nature. So attempting to *earn* a good will, as a morally strong will, could not be our duty. It would be morally wrong![38]

We have no evidence for Kant's having recognized this logical point about a morally strong will. But we should presume that he did recognize it. So we should presume that he did not think that having a good will requires achieving some degree of moral strength, or of resistance to temptation, compared with most others. We seem to have good reasons for assuming Kant thought it at least possible for human beings to have a good will. Yet if we think of a good will as something to be achieved, then the problem becomes how to specify the criterion for that achievement. The criterion cannot be that one achieves a good will when one achieves a will that is *morally strong*. Nor can it be that one achieves a good will when one's moral resolve becomes adequate to defeat contrary inclinations over 50 percent of the time. This would be arbitrary. Why should "over 50 percent" be good? Why not "over 70 percent"?

[35] About the strength that is virtue Kant writes, accordingly, that "Strength of any kind can be recognized only by the obstacles it can overcome, and in the case of virtue these obstacles are natural inclinations" (ibid.).

[36] In that case, too, one person's progress in achieving a good will is at the same time someone else's moral digress.

[37] Everyone can be exactly seven feet high, and everyone can have exactly a million dollars. But the point is that then no one would be tall, and no one would be rich. If it seems that everyone could have a will with strength sufficient for almost always choosing to do their duty in the face of tempting inclinations (96 percent of the time?), the point is that under these circumstances no one would have a "strong" will, just as no one is tall when everyone is exactly seven feet high. If the strength of everyone's will to duty were the same, why should "almost always" choosing duty over tempting inclinations be the criterion for strength of will? Why couldn't everyone be said to have a strong will when duty would win out over inclination merely 51 percent of the time? Why, even, should 51 percent be the threshold? Choosing 51 or 96 percent as the criterion for being "strong" is as arbitrary as choosing seven feet in height as the criterion for everyone's being "tall," and a million dollars as the criterion for everyone's being "rich."

[38] It would not be wrong to act on a maxim of "strengthening" one's will to duty, however. Everyone can will to act on this maxim because having a "stronger" will can imply only a comparison with one's earlier self, and not with anyone else.

It might appear that a satisfactory requirement for achieving a good will would be making the conversion from impurity to a morally pure heart. But even the relevance of this conversion to goodness of will is questionable. In his analysis of good will in *Groundwork* I, Kant analyzed that concept in terms of episodes of acting solely from duty. But he later gave indications in *Religion* that he understood good will as a dispositional concept. Dispositions are to be understood in terms of their episodic manifestations, of course. So it seems that "acting from duty" must inform our understanding of the dispositional good will. But the moral achievement of a "pure heart" does not seem to be required for episodes of acting from duty, in the way that a good will is presumably required. We can infer this from the fact that the degree of radical evil Kant called impurity does not preclude acting from duty. Someone without a pure heart does not consider the morality of an action to be always by itself a sufficient justification for doing it. But this is compatible with being moved to action solely from duty, or solely in view of the rightness or morality of an action. Kant wrote in his definition of "impurity" that the impure heart "*often* (and perhaps always) still needs other incentives besides [the moral law] in order to determine the power of choice for what duty requires" (53/6:29, emphasis added). He therefore does not seem to have thought that those lacking purity of heart *never* act from duty. So he seems not to have reserved application of the concept of good will only for those who have achieved moral purity. For this reason, the dispositional condition of purity of heart that we are expected to achieve as a station in our life-long progress from bad to better does not seem to be what Kant had in mind in writing about the good will.[39]

7.9 Personality

Universalist interpreters maintain that every human being must have a good will, as a basic condition even for having duties. So they do not think

[39] The same considerations expressed here regarding "purity of heart" apply to the conception of the good will that sees a person with a good will as nothing other than someone self-determined to rebel against radical evil, through a moral conversion. As Frierson sees it, "Kant articulates [his] conception of a good will as a 'new man,' a will that engages in a 'revolution' against its radical evil" (*Freedom and Anthropology*, 122). If this were the criterion for having a good will, then Kant would not have explicated the concept of good will correctly in *Groundwork* I, when he offered merely examples of morally worthy actions, from duty alone.

of a good will as something to be achieved. Kant himself also indicated in *Religion* that even the most evil human beings, those with depraved or corrupt hearts, always possess a good will (65/6:44).

But how, then, should we understand good-will universalism in relation to Kant's initial analysis of good will in terms of morally worthy action from duty? The answer, it seems, is that in discussing motivation from duty alone Kant was pointing to a uniquely moral incentive for action: respect for the moral law. The universality of the good will seems accordingly to derive from the universality of that incentive in human nature. As we have also seen above, that incentive can be traced to a fundamental predisposition to personality. The difference it may actually make in practical life can be expected to vary in individual moral agents, of course. But it is present in everyone as an innate predisposition to fulfill the commands of morality. The good will, so conceived, would therefore be possessed even by those Kant described as morally corrupt.

Seeing the good will as a dispositional source of the incentive for actions exhibiting "moral worth," as discussed in *Groundwork* I, also helps illuminate Kant's thoughts on human dignity. About this unique worth he wrote: "that which constitutes the condition under which alone something can be an end in itself has not merely a relative worth, that is, a price, but an inner worth, that is *dignity*." He then concluded, "Hence morality, and humanity insofar as it is capable of morality, is that which alone has dignity" (*Groundwork,* 42/4:34–5). The inner dignity or moral worth of all human beings stems from their innate capacity for being moved to action by the moral incentive of respect for law. This is their predisposition to personality, which would be the dispositional condition manifested in episodic actions *from duty alone*, or in actions with moral worth. A careful comparison of two passages found in Kant's *Groundwork* indicates, similarly, that the absolute, incomparable worth of the good will is something possessed by *every* human being. In the early paragraphs of the *Groundwork* he wrote about the good will that "it is good in itself, and regarded for itself is to be valued incomparably higher than all that could merely be brought about by it in favor of some inclination and indeed, if you will, of the sum of all inclinations" (8/4:394). Later, he wrote: "But suppose there were something the *existence of which in itself* has an absolute worth. . . . Now I say that the human being and in general every rational being *exists* as an end in itself. . . . (36–7/4:428). The context of the latter claim makes it clear that the objects of inclination are only conditionally valuable. They depend, for any value they may have, on the absolute, unconditional worth possessed by every rational being. It is very hard to see how the incomparable worth of every human being, which Kant discussed in the middle section of *Groundwork*, could be different from the unlimited, absolute worth that only the good will is said to possess, at the beginning of that text.[40]

Kant explained the good will initially in terms of actions from duty, prompted solely by the moral incentive. Considered dispositionally, this explanation points us ultimately to the human predisposition to personality as the final term in the analysis of good will. So considered, therefore, it is also an endorsement of the universalist interpretation. We have thus reached the conclusion that, as he conceived the idea, every human being has a good will, of incomparable worth; and that actions motivated purely by respect for the moral law, if there are any, would manifest this moral worth. This is true despite the radical evil afflicting each one of us as a member of the human race. Our good will, therefore, which is our original predisposition toward obedience to the moral law, would be the basis for universal human dignity.

7.10 Good Will and Virtue

In the previous chapter it was pointed out that "virtue" can refer to a psychological condition. The same can be said, of course, about Kant's conception of "good will." In our earlier focus on virtue as a concept of moral appraisal we showed why it would be a mistake to suppose that, in Kantian ethics, appraising an action as "morally worthy" is equivalent to appraising it as "virtuous." Here, in this final section, we shall consider some reasons for thinking that it would also be a mistake to equate "good

---

[40] Dean seems to agree, in observing that "Kant claims that a good will has an incomparable value in every imaginable circumstance, and humanity has a value that is incomparable and independent of inclination. And, given the Kantian framework in which they are embedded, these claims amount to the same thing" (*The Value of Humanity in Kant's Moral Theory*, 42). Somewhat surprisingly, however, Dean is no universalist about the good will. He writes: "A good will is the will of a being who is committed to acting morally, who gives priority to moral principles rather than to acting simply to satisfy her own desires, inclinations, impulses, or sentiments" (24). He argues, further, that even though some may not have a good will, Kant's moral theory requires that they be treated with the respect due those who have good wills (see 94–5).

will" and "virtue," as psychological conditions. Despite this, however, one of our conclusions here will be that just as we all possess a good will, so there is a sense in which we are all to some degree virtuous. This will follow from the way Kant sometimes defined the psychological condition of virtue.

Interpreters taking what was above called the perfectionist view of the good will usually distinguish good will from virtue. For if a good will is an unattainable ideal for us, as they say, then attaining the condition of virtue would hopefully be within our reach. Universalist interpreters may wish to distinguish good will from virtue, also. For if everyone is supposed to have a good will, just as we all possess incomparable human dignity, then virtue may be thought to distinguish the best of us, who would have it, from the rest of us, who do not. But there is also this option for universalists: that we are all virtuous, just as we all have a good will, but the morally best among us are the most virtuous.

Kant's theory of virtue provides for a clear separation between a good will and virtue, in at least one meaning of the latter term. For, as seen in the previous chapter, he distinguished between virtue in the *formal* sense and in the *material* sense (6.9). In the material sense there would be many virtues, like benevolence, gratitude, loyalty, and so on. So virtue in this sense is pretty clearly different from the singular good will. But virtue in the formal sense is also singular. And a passage quoted earlier from *The Metaphysics of Morals* defines virtue in this sense as "the will's conformity with every duty, based on a firm disposition." Another passage claims, similarly, that "*Virtue* is the strength of a man's maxims in fulfilling his duty."[41] These

---

[41] 197/6:394. This definition of virtue in terms of strength is not an isolated comment. It reflects a central theme of Kant's discussion of virtue in *The Metaphysics of Morals*. He writes there also, "For what sort of concept can be made of the force and herculean strength needed to subdue the vice-breeding inclinations if virtue is to borrow its weapons from the arsenal of metaphysics, a speculative subject that few know how to handle?" (181–2/6:376). He subsequently refers to virtue as "*fortitude*": "the capacity and considered resolve to withstand a strong but unjust opponent" (186/6:380). Virtue is next contrasted with *lack of virtue*, which is "moral weakness" (189/6:384, cf. also 194/6:390). Later we read: "It is also correct to say that man is under obligation to [acquire] *virtue* (as moral strength). For while the capacity *(facultas)* to overcome all opposing sensible impulses can and must be simply *presupposed* in man on account of his freedom, yet this capacity as *strength (robur)* is something he must acquire" (200/6:397). Then, seconding his earlier definition Kant concludes: "Virtue is, therefore, moral strength of a *man's* will in fulfilling his *duty*, [which is] a moral *constraint* though his own lawgiving reason, insofar as this [reason] constitutes itself an authority *executing* the law" (206/6:405). Finally, "the true strength of virtue" is said to consist in "a tranquil mind with a *considered and firm* resolution to put the law of virtue into practice" (209/5:408, emphasis altered).

claims at least suggest that virtue in the formal sense would be equivalent to the good will, especially considering the way Kant attempted to explicate the latter concept in *Groundwork* I, in terms of acting from duty. But above we rejected the suggestion that a good will would be a morally strong will, since no adequate sense of "strong" is available for this.

So we can see from the preceding definitions why virtue in the formal sense would not be equivalent to good will. Yet it is a good question now whether these definitions of virtue are also susceptible to the same difficulties that arise when the criterion for a good will is thought to be its strength. For, again, the common meaning of "strong" would make the criterion for virtue relative. Those who would qualify as virtuous because they are strong would owe their virtue to the weakness of others. Or a virtuous person would be considered to be someone doing her duty, from duty, perhaps over 50 percent of the time, or over 70 percent, or whatever. The precise degree of strength that would distinguish the virtuous from the unvirtuous would have to be arbitrary, in other words.

Still, Kant did not define virtue in the formal sense as any *particular degree* of strength of the maxim of duty. His definitions do not imply any criterion that could be used to distinguish those who have virtue from those who do not. That is, he did not write that a person is virtuous if her disposition or maxim of duty is *strong*. He wrote instead that virtue is *strength*. And this is actually consistent with everyone's possessing virtue, to some degree; especially if we suppose that what makes a person virtuous is an incentive to action that is psychologically forceful. For every incentive, as a psychological force, would have some degree of strength. And because this is so, the strength of the moral incentive, incorporated into the maxim of duty, could sensibly be labeled "virtue," in the formal sense.[42] The idea would be that a person's formal virtue is just the strength of her moral incentive, and the variability of this strength, from person to person, accounts for personal differences in this conception of virtue. So there would not be anyone who lacks virtue in this sense, if no one can lack the psychologically forceful feeling of respect for the moral law.

As we saw above, however, everyone also suffers from the "frailty" of human nature. This means that in the nature of human beings the moral

---

[42] On virtue as strength see also Stephen Engstrom, "The Inner Freedom of Virtue," in Mark Timmons, ed., *Kant's Metaphysics of Morals, Interpretive Essays* (Oxford: Oxford University Press, 2002), 289–315 at 304.

incentive, or "virtue" as we are now calling it, is subordinated to the forces of inclinational incentives; in some cases more so than in others. Not surprisingly therefore, Kant first characterized virtue in the following way: "[our] proper moral condition, in which [we] can always be, is *virtue*, that is, moral disposition *in conflict* (*Practical Reason,* 72/5:85).

So the Kantian moral psychology with which we are left, whether right or wrong, presents respect for law and inclinations as constantly antagonistic motive forces, and presents virtue as pitted perpetually against vice, as its antagonist. It presents the moral life as an incessant struggle against the "evil" predominance of inclination and self-love over respect for the moral law. And if we add to this picture Kant's theory of action in the noumenal world, then we are all in this struggle together, and by our own free choice. Next, in the concluding section of the book, we briefly consider some of his thoughts on what we may hope to get out of this lifelong moral struggle.

This chapter has laid out the basic elements of Kant's views on the evil nature of humanity, and of our good will. Overall the aim has been to show how having an evil nature can be compatible with having a good will. To have a good will, it has been argued, is just to be incitable to action by the thought of conformity to the law, as we all are to some degree. And that incentive, whenever it explains an action, accounts for its "moral worth." Yet we ourselves enjoy a comparable moral worth or dignity, just insofar as we can be incited to action by this psychological force. To say that the human moral "disposition" is naturally evil is only to say that, by nature, the action-explaining forces of inclination and self-love are predominant in us. In Kant's view there is no path to overcoming our evil nature apart from striving continuously to make moral progress in strengthening respect for the moral law—that is, apart from attempting to become ever more virtuous, in the formal sense. If the fault in our human natures lies in our own timeless, noumenal deed, its remedy can be nothing other than our own endless, empirical progress.

Conclusion: Grounds for Hope

The seven preceding chapters have laid out the main theses of the theory of human action that is presupposed by Kant's moral theory. Among them are: that we always act on maxims, as principles of practical reasoning; that our maxims provide the basis for imperatival justifications of our actions; and that they also provide the basis for motivational explanations of actions, through the psychological forces of the incentives they incorporate. The latter point implies that Kant would have accepted psychological determinism. And this is controversial; since many see psychological determinism as undermining human freedom. But here it has been explained how Kant held that our freedom of choice belongs to a noumenal world, apart from space and time; and how through a noumenal act we each freely determine the contents of our characters in this empirical world; and that as different as we are in regard to moral character, we are all basically evil ("even the best"). Our evil nature consists in our not being completely good (holy): in our not being predisposed, necessarily, to do whatever we recognize we are morally justified in doing.

This brief, concluding section sketches some of Kant's thoughts on what can be called the human predicament, and, in view of it, on what we may justifiably hope. To be human is to act always, and only, on maxims: in ways we think of as good. Yet "good" here is ambiguous. So there is a sense in which each of us is, within him- or herself, fundamentally divided on what to do. We want to do what secures our own well-being, and we want to do what we see as good overall, or as morally good. But we do not seem to make any progress in achieving the one as we work toward the other. On the one hand, considering what it means to be morally good, we cannot achieve this while we work toward our own personal well-being or happiness. On the other hand, it is not impossible that we should secure our happiness by becoming morally better. But nothing in the natural, sensible world guarantees our achievement of happiness as a consequence of our moral improvement. In fact, any number of empirical conditions or events provide evidence that moral choices preclude, or at least restrict, personal happiness. What is worse, we naturally favor personal well-being. Good intentions, conscientiously moral resolutions, have comparatively little staying power. And we can eliminate neither inclination nor conscience; neither the basis for our happiness nor our respect for the moral law.[1]

One presupposition of recognizing our condition as a predicament is that it shouldn't be this way. This is a central presumption of Kant's doctrine of humanity's "radical evil." A second presupposition is that there should be a way out of the predicament. This is an idea behind Kant's doctrine of the "highest good."

The ambiguity in practical reason's guiding concept of "good," between personal well-being and moral good, is the basis for our predicament. Yet this duality in our basic goods should be representable, through practical reason, as a normative totality. That is, there should be some rational conception of the complete good, which somehow encompasses both of our principal guiding interests. But for this a harmonious *compromise* of morality and happiness is out of the question. The rational conception of overall good cannot be the condition of morality and happiness each obtaining a fair share. Since morality's demands are absolute, its interest will not be served at all by making any concession, as a bargaining price, to effect some ideal coalition of moral and inclinational satisfactions. So the attainment of complete goodness is possible only in one way, according to Kant: practical reason must present morality as the condition of happiness. That is, it must be rational for us to see compliance with morality's absolute demands as making us worthy of happiness. That way, if we make ourselves morally good, or at least morally better, it should be rational for us to expect a corresponding increase in happiness. The realization of happiness proportioned to virtue, for all, is Kant's conception of the "highest good."

---

[1] I have called this the human predicament. But it is more aptly named the *normative predicament.* There could be other, non-human rational agents similarly dedicated to both morality and the realization of other goods.

Yet events in the sensible world, upon which the satisfaction of our inclinations depends, do not operate according to the principle that virtue deserves happiness. We may be rationally justified in expecting to be happy if we comply with morality's demands. But we can have no guarantee that conditions in the sensible world will satisfy that expectation. For this reason, Kant claimed, it is rational to *hope* for happiness we deserve, in a world beyond the sensible world. He also saw this hope as giving us rational grounds for postulating our immortality, and God's existence. Our souls must survive the deaths of our sensible bodies in the natural world if they are to enjoy happiness corresponding to our virtue, he thought. And an omniscient judge, who is also an omnipotent benefactor, is required in order to distribute happiness in exact proportion to virtue.[2]

A world apart from the sensible world is already implied by Kant's theory of human freedom. So also is the existence of God, as creator of that world, and facilitator of the community of its noumenal substances (see 4.5). Kant's doctrine of the highest good, and our rational hope for its realization, adds omniscience, omnipotence, justice, and beneficence to God's attributes.[3] But what remains puzzling in this doctrine is our condition in the afterlife, apart from the sensible world.

Some of Kant's comments locate the afterlife in the intelligible, noumenal world.[4] In fact, in lectures he made the point that each of us is already in either noumenal heaven or hell.[5] Our transition to the afterlife, he said, will be merely a change from sensory to intelligible intuition of the world.[6]

---

[2] See *Pure Reason*, A804–19/B832–47, and *Practical Reason*, 102–10/5:122–32.

[3] See *Practical Reason*, 115–16/5:139.

[4] "Thus only in the ideal of the highest *original* good [i.e., God] can pure reason find the ground of the practically necessary connection of both elements of the highest derived good, namely of an intelligible, i.e., *moral* world. . . . we must necessarily represent ourselves through reason as belonging to such a world, although the senses do not present us with anything except a world of appearances. . . . " (*Pure Reason*, A810–11/B838–9).

[5] "Now if a human being, whose will is well-meaning which devotes itself to exercising the rule of morality, was righteous in the world, he is already in this world in community with all righteous and well-meaning souls, be they in India or in Arabia, only he does not yet see himself in this community until he is liberated from sensible intuition. Likewise an evil being is also already here in the community of all knaves who abhor one another, only he does not yet see himself in it" (*Lectures on Metaphysics*, 105/28:299; see also 103–4/28:297, 283/29:219, 292/28:445).

[6] "But when the soul separates itself from the body, then it will not have the same sensible intuition of this world; it will not intuit the world as it appears, but rather as it is" (ibid., 104/28:297). "We are now already conscious through reason of finding ourselves in an intelligible realm; after death we will intuit and cognize it and then we are in an entirely different world that, however, is altered only in form, namely, where we cognize things as they are in themselves" (283/29:920). See also 353/28:593.

We do not "go" anywhere after we die, since heaven and hell are not spatial. Rather, through death we shift from empirical awareness of the world to finding ourselves in a noumenal community befitting our degree of virtue.

In the previous chapter we saw how, since it must be possible to become good human beings, our unceasing moral progress must be possible. But this suggests that our immortal souls would remain at least temporal beings after their connections with our bodies are broken. For how could our moral progress be unending if it would end with the deaths of our sensible bodies? Kant was relatively clear, in a number of places, that he viewed bodily death as the point of transition to another world. Yet he did not accept any exotic hypothesis of continuous reincarnation.[7] Sometimes he seems to present the afterlife as the perpetual existence of the soul in a world that is at least temporal.[8] And the moral condition in that world, especially the distribution of happiness, is presumably a causal consequence of actions in this world.[9] Yet seeing things this way would make the world of the afterlife identical with this sensible world. For as we saw earlier, continuity of the time series across cause–effect relations suffices for the continuity of the world in which cause and effect occur (4.1).

So Kant gives us reasons for thinking that the afterlife is noumenal, and so atemporal. But he also gives us reasons for thinking that it would be, somehow, a temporal extension of the sensible world. One line of response to this confusion would be to say that Kant's comments on the afterlife refer vaguely to our existence in a timeless, noumenal world, which we cannot comprehend or describe except in illusory temporal terms. But to offer this as a solution to the problem seems to undermine the rationality of our hope for the highest good: for happiness in proportion to our moral worthiness to receive it. For that hope must be illusory also, if the time between now and our hope's future fulfillment turns out to be illusory. And

---

[7] See ibid., 282–3/29:919, 390/28:689, 408–9/28:769.

[8] "[H]appiness consists in progress. In the future world we will thus be in progress either toward happiness or toward misery, but whether this will continue to eternity we cannot at all know" (ibid., 353/28:593, see also 409/28:770, and *Practical Reason*, 102–3/5:122–3). It should be observed here, however, that Kant's arguments against idealism and "metaphysical egoism" attempt to demonstrate that self-consciousness requires the existence of external objects, in space (see 4.6). So by these arguments our self-consciousness in a merely temporal but not spatial world, and presumably then our happiness, may not be possible.

[9] "[W]e must assume the moral world to be a consequence of our conduct in the sensible world" (*Pure Reason*, A811/B839).

without rational grounds for that hope now, Kant claimed, morality seems pointless.[10] So also must the created world: for "reason says to [human beings] that the duration of the world has worth only insofar as the rational beings in it conform to the final end of their existence; if, however, this is not supposed to be achieved, then creation itself appears purposeless to them, like a play having no resolution, and affording no cognition of any rational aim."[11]

Here we cannot make any further progress in resolving these interpretive puzzles related to the afterlife, and the overall point or purpose of morality. One theme of the preceding chapters has been that moral justification would be pointless unless what justifies our actions can also be shown to have explanatory power. Another has been that though such power would imply psychological determinism, it need not compromise human freedom. For we can be assumed to act freely in another world, with the result that all of our actions in this world are deterministic consequences of prior events. We can be supposed, through a free, noumenal choice, to have determined the characters we portray on this cosmic stage. But why this supposition would be so, we cannot know. We can only assume that there would be a reason for all this. And that reason would make the hope for our future happiness proportioned to virtue a rational hope; as rational as the assumption that our empirical play would have its purpose and plot.

---

[10] "If, therefore, the highest good is impossible in accordance with practical rules, then the moral law, which commands us to promote it, must be fantastic and directed to empty imaginary ends and must therefore in itself be false" (*Practical Reason*, 95/5:114; see also *Pure Reason*, A811/B839, and *Lectures on Metaphysics*, 97/28:288).

[11] "The End of All Things," in *Religion*, 198/8:331.

Bibliography

Albrecht, Michael, "*Kants Maximenethik und ihre Begründung*," *Kant-Studien* 85 (1994): 129–46.

Allais, Lucy, "Kant's One World: Interpreting 'Transcendental Idealism,'" *British Journal for the History of Philosophy* 12 (2004), 655–84.

Allison, Henry E., *Idealism and Freedom* (Cambridge: Cambridge University Press, 1996).

——*Kant's Theory of Freedom* (Cambridge: Cambridge University Press, 1990).

——"Transcendental Idealism: The 'Two Aspect' View," in Bernard den Ouden and Marcia Moen (eds.), *New Essays on Kant* (New York: Peter Lang, 1987).

Ameriks, Karl, "Kant on the Good Will," in Otfried Höffe (ed.), *Gurndlegung zur Metaphysik der Sitten: ein kooperativer Kommentar* (Frankfurt am Main: Vittorio Klostermann, 1989).

——"Recent Work on Kant's Theoretical Philosophy," *American Philosophical Quarterly* 19 (1982), 1–23.

Atwell, John E., *Ends and Principles in Kant's Moral Thought* (Dordrecht: Martinus Nihoff, 1986).

Baron, Marcia, *Kantian Ethics Almost Without Apology* (Ithaca, NY: Cornell University Press, 1995).

Baumgarten, Alexander Gottlieb, *Ethica Philosophica* (1751), repr. in Immanuel Kant, *Kant's gesammelte Schriften,* vol. 27 pt. 2. no. 1 (Berlin: Walter de Gruyter, 1923).

——*Metaphysica*, Halle: Carol Herman Hemmerde (1757), repr. in Immanuel Kant, *Kant's gesammelte Schriften* vol. 15 (Berlin: Walter de Gruyter, 1923).

Baumgarten, Hans-Ulrich and Held, Carsten, *Systematische Ethik mit Kant* (München/Freiburg: Alber, 2001).

Beck, Lewis White, *A Commentary on Kant's Critique of Practical Reason* (Chicago: University of Chicago Press, 1960).

——*Early German Philosophy; Kant and his Predecessors* (Cambridge, MA: Belknap Press, 1969).

——"Kant's Two Conceptions of the Will in their Political Context," in Ronald Beiner and William James Booth (eds.), *Kant and Political Philosophy* (New Haven, CT: Yale University Press, 1993).

Beiner, Ronald and Booth, William James, eds., *Kant and Political Philosophy* (New Haven, CT: Yale University Press, 1993).

Bennett, Jonathan, "Kant's Theory of Freedom," in Allen W. Wood (ed.), *Self and Nature in Kant's Philosophy* (Ithaca, NY: Cornell University Press, 1984).

Bittner, Rüdiger, *Doing Things for Reasons* (Oxford: Oxford University Press, 2001).

Blackwell, Richard J., "Christian Wolff's Doctrine of the Soul," *Journal of the History of Ideas* (1961), 339–54.

Brewer, Talbot, "The Character of Temptation: Towards a More Plausible Kantian Moral Psychology," *Pacific Philosophical Quarterly* 83 (2002), 103–30.

Broad, C. D., *Kant: an Introduction* (Cambridge: Cambridge University Press, 1978).

Bubner, Rüdiger, "Another Look at Maxims," in Predrag Cicovacki (ed.), *Kant's Legacy: Essays in Honor of Lewis White Beck* (Rochester, NY: University of Rochester Press, 2001).

Carnois, Bernard, *The Coherence of Kant's Doctrine of Freedom*, trans. David Booth (Chicago: University of Chicago Press, 1987).

Cicvacki, Predrag, ed., *Kant's Legacy: Essays in Honor of Lewis White Beck* (Rochester, NY: University of Rochester Press, 2001).

Clarke, Samuel, *The Works of Samuel Clarke*, vol. II (London: J. and P. Knapton, 1738), repr. (New York: Garland Publishing Company, 1978).

Collins, Arthur W., *Possible Experience* (Berkeley, CA: University of California Press, 1999).

Corr, Charles A., "Christian Wolff's Distinction between Empirical and Rational Psychology," *Studia Leibnitiana Supplmenta* (1975), 195–215.

Cox, J. Gray, "The Single Power Thesis in Kant's Theory of the Faculties," *Man and World* 16 (1983), 315–33.

Dean, Richard, *The Value of Humanity in Kant's Moral Theory* (Oxford: Clarendon Press, 2006).

Deleuze, Gilles, *Kant's Critical Philosophy: The Doctrine of the Faculties*, trans. Hough Tomlinson and Barbara Habberjam (Minneapolis, MN: University of Minnesota Press, 1984).

den Ouden, Bernard and Moen, Marcia, eds., *New Essays on Kant* (New York: Peter Lang, 1987).

Engstrom, Stephen, "The Inner Freedom of Virtue," in Mark Timmons (ed.), *Kant's Metaphysics of Morals, Interpretive Essays* (Oxford: Oxford University Press, 2002).

Falkenstein, Lorne, "Hume's Answer to Kant," *Noûs* 32 (1998), 331–60.

Findlay, J. N., *Kant and the Transcendental Object* (Oxford: Clarendon Press, 1981).

Fodor, Jerry A., *The Modularity of Mind: An Essay in Faculty Psychology* (Cambridge, MA: MIT Press, 1983).

Foot, Philippa, *Virtues and Vices* (Berkeley, CA: University of California Press, 1978).

Frierson, Patrick R., *Freedom and Anthropology in Kant's Moral Philosophy* (Cambridge: Cambridge University Press, 2003).

——"Kant's Empirical Account of Human Action," *Philosophers' Imprint* 5 (December 2005), 1–34.

Funke, G. and Kopper, J., *Akten des 4. Internationalen Kant-Kongress* (Berlin: Walter de Grutyer, 1974).

Gerhardt, Volker, Horstmann, Rolf-Peter, and Schumacher, Ralph, eds., *Kant und die Berliner Aufklärung, Akten des IX. Internationalen Kant-Kongress*, Bd. III (Berlin: Walter de Gruyter, 2001).

Gram, Moltke S., ed., *Interpreting Kant* (Iowa City, IA: University of Iowa Press, 1982).

Greenberg, Robert, *Kant's Theory of A Priori Knowledge* (University Park, PA: Pennsylvania State University Press, 2001).

Grenberg, Jeanine M., "Feeling, Desire and Interest in Kant's Theory of Action," *Kant-Studien* 92 (2001), 153–79.

——*Kant and the Ethics of Humility* (Cambridge: Cambridge University Press, 2005).

Guevara, Daniel, *Kant's Theory of Moral Motivation* (Boulder, CO: Westview Press, 2000).

Guyer, Paul, *Kant on Freedom, Law and Happiness* (Cambridge: Cambridge University Press, 2000).

——ed., *The Cambridge Companion to Kant* (Cambridge: Cambridge University Press, 1992).

Hanna, Robert, *Kant, Science and Human Nature* (Oxford: Oxford University Press, 2006).

Harbison, Warren G., "The Good Will," *Kant-Studien* 71 (1980), 47–59.

Harper, William L. and Merboote, Ralf, eds., *Kant on Causality, Freedom, and Objectivity* (Minneapolis: University of Minnesota Press, 1984).

Hatfield, Gary, "Empirical, Rational and Transcendental Psychology: Psychology as Science and as Philosophy," in Paul Guyer (ed.), *The Cambridge Companion to Kant* (Cambridge: Cambridge University Press, 1992).

Henson, Richard G., "What Kant Might Have Said: Moral Worth and the Overdetermination of Dutiful Action," *Philosophical Review* 88 (1979), 39–54.

Herman, Barbara. *Moral Literacy* (Cambridge, MA: Harvard University Press, 2007).

——*Morality as Rationality* (Cambridge, MA: Garland Press, 1990).

——*The Practice of Moral Judgment* (Cambridge, MA: Harvard University Press, 1993).

Hill, Thomas E. Jr., *Dignity and Practical Reason in Kant's Moral Theory* (Ithaca, NY: Cornell University Press, 1992).

Höffe, Otfried, *Immanuel Kant,* trans. M. Farrier (Albany, NY: SUNY Press, 1994).
—— ed., *Gurndlegung zur Metaphysik der Sitten: ein kooperativer Kommentar* (Frankfurt am Main: Vittorio Klostermann, 1989).
Hudson, Hud, *Kant's Compatibilism* (Ithaca, NY: Cornell University Press, 1994).
—— "*Wille, Willkür,* and the Imputability of Immoral Actions," *Kant-Studien* 82 (1991), 179–96.
Hume, David, *A Treatise of Human Nature,* ed. David Fate Norton and Mary J. Norton (New York: Oxford University Press, 2000).
Irwin, Terrence, "Morality and Personality: Kant and Greene," in Allen W. Wood (ed.), *Self and Nature in Kant's Philosophy* (Ithaca, NY: Cornell University Press, 1984).
Johnson, Robert N., "Weakness Incorporated," *History of Philosophy Quarterly* 15 (1998), 349–67.
Kant, Immanel, *Anthropology from a Pragmatic Point of View,* trans. Victor Lyle Dowdell (Carbondale, IL: Southern Illinois University Press, 1978).
—— *Attempt to Introduce the Concept of Negative Magnitudes into Philosophy,* trans. and ed. David Walford and Ralf Meerbote, in *Theoretical Philosophy 1755–1770* (Cambridge: Cambridge University Press, 1992).
—— *Correspondence,* trans. and ed. Arnulf Zweig (Cambridge: Cambridge University Press, 1999).
—— *Critique of Practical Reason,* trans. and ed. Mary Gregor (Cambridge: Cambridge University Press, 1997).
—— *Critique of Pure Reason,* trans. Norman Kemp Smith (New York: St. Martin's Press, 1965).
—— *Critique of Pure Reason,* trans. Werner S. Pluhar (Indianapolis, IN: Hackett Publishing Company, 1996).
—— *Critique of Pure Reason,* trans. and ed. Paul Guyer and Allen W. Wood (Cambridge: Cambridge University Press, 1998).
—— *Critique of the Power of Judgment,* ed. Paul Guyer, trans. Paul Guyer and Eric Matthews (Cambridge: Cambridge University Press, 2000).
—— "The End of All Things," in *Religion within the Boundaries of Mere Reason and Other Writings,* trans. and ed. Allen W. Wood and George di Giovanni (Cambridge: Cambridge University Press, 1998).
—— *Groundwork of the Metaphysics of Morals,* trans. H. J. Paton (New York: Harper, 1964).
—— *Groundwork of the Metaphysics of Morals,* trans. and ed. Mary Gregor (Cambridge: Cambridge University Press, 1997).
—— *Kant's gesammelte Schriften,* vol. 15; vol. 27 pt. 2. no. 1 (Berlin: Walter de Gruyter, 1923).

—— *Lectures on Ethics,* ed. Peter Heath and J. B. Schneewind, trans. Peter Heath (Cambridge: Cambridge University Press, 1997).

—— *Lectures on Metaphysics,* trans. and ed. Karl Ameriks and Steve Naragon (Cambridge: Cambridge University Press, 1997).

—— *Metaphysical Foundations of Natural Science,* trans. Michael Friedman, in *Theoretical Philosophy after 1781,* ed. Henry Allison and Peter Heath (Cambridge: Cambridge University Press, 2002).

—— *The Metaphysical Principles of Virtue,* trans., J. Ellington (Indianapolis, IN: Bobbs-Merrill, 1964).

—— *The Metaphysics of Morals,* trans. Mary Gregor (Cambridge: Cambridge University Press, 1991).

—— *On the Form and Principles of the Sensible and Intelligible World* [*Inaugural Dissertation*], in *Theoretical Philosophy, 1755–1770,* trans. and ed. David Walford and Ralf Meerbote (Cambridge: Cambridge University Press, 1992).

—— *Prolegomena to Any Future Metaphysics that will be Able to Come Forward as Science,* trans. Gary Hatfield, in *Theoretical Philosophy after 1781,* ed. Henry Allison and Peter Heath (Cambridge: Cambridge University Press, 2002).

—— *Religion within the Boundaries of Mere Reason and Other Writings,* trans. and ed. Allen W. Wood and George di Giovanni (Cambridge: Cambridge University Press, 1998).

—— *Religion within the Limits of Reason Alone,* trans. Theodore M. Greene and Hoyt H. Hudson (New York: Harper & Row, 1960).

Kerstein, Samuel J., "Kant's (Not So Radical?) Hedonism," in Volker Gerhardt, Rolf-Peter Horstmann and Ralph Schumacher (eds.), *Kant und die Berliner Aufklärung, Akten des IX. Internationalen Kant-Kongress,* Bd. III (Berlin: Walter de Gruyter, 2001).

Kemp Smith, Norman *A Commentary to 'Kant's Critique of Pure Reason'* (New York: Humanities Press, 1962).

Kitcher, Patricia, "Kant's Argument for the Categorical Imperative," *Noûs* 38 (2004), 555–84.

—— "What is a Maxim?" *Philosophical Topics* 31 (Spring and Fall 2003), 215–43.

Korsgaard, Christine M., *Creating the Kingdom of Ends* (Cambridge: Cambridge University Press, 1996).

—— *The Sources of Normativity,* ed. Onora O'Neill (Cambridge: Cambridge University Press, 1996).

Latham, Noa, "Causally Irrelevant Reasons and Action Solely form the Motive of Duty," *The Journal of Philosophy* 91 (November 1994), 599–618.

Locke, John, *An Essay Concerning Human Understanding,* ed. Peter H. Nidditch (Oxford: Clarendon Press, 1975).

Louden, Robert, *Kant's Impure Ethics: From Rational Beings to Human Beings* (Oxford: Oxford University Press, 2000).

—— "Kant's Virtue Ethics," *Philosophy* 61 (1986), 473–89.

MacBeath, A. Murray, "Kant on Moral Feeling," *Kant-Studien* 74 (1973), 283–314.

McCarty, Richard, "The Maxims Problem," *The Journal of Philosophy* 99 (January 2002), 29–44.

—— "Moral Weakness as Self-Deception," in Hoke Robinson (ed.), *Proceedings of the Eighth International Kant Congress* (Milwaukee, WI: Marquette University Press, 1995).

Macintyre, Alasdair, *After Virtue*, 2nd edn. (Notre Dame, IN: University of Notre Dame Press, 1984).

Mackie, J. L., *The Cement of the Universe* (Oxford: Clarendon Press, 1974).

Meerbote, Ralf, "Kant on the Nondeterminate Character of Human Actions," in William L. Harper and Ralf Merboote (eds.), *Kant on Causality, Freedom, and Objectivity* (Minneapolis: University of Minnesota Press, 1984).

—— "Which Freedom?" in Predrag Cicvacki (ed.), *Kant's Legacy: Essays in Honor of Lewis White Beck* (Rochester, NY: University of Rochester Press, 2001).

—— "*Wille* and *Willkür* in Kant's Theory of Action," in Moltke S. Gram (ed.), *Interpreting Kant* (Iowa City, IA: University of Iowa Press, 1982).

Mendelssohn, Moses, *Philosophical Writings,* trans. and ed. Daniel O. Dalstrom (Cambridge: Cambridge University Press, 1997).

Michalson, Gordon E. Jr., *Fallen Freedom: Kant on Radical Evil and Moral Regeneration* (Cambridge: Cambridge University Press, 1990).

Munzel, G. Felicitas, *Kant's Conception of Moral Character* (Chicago: University of Chicago Press, 1999).

Nell, Onora, *Acting on Principle* (New York: Columbia University Press, 1975).

O'Neill, Onora, "Agency and Anthropology in Kant's *Groundwork*," in Yirmiyahu Yovel (ed.), *Kant's Practical Philosophy Reconsidered* (Dordrecht: Kluwer Academic Publishers, 1989).

—— "Autonomy: The Emperor's New Clothes," *Proceedings of the Aristotelian Society* (suppl.) 77 (2003), 1–21.

—— *Constructions of Reason, Explorations in Kant's Practical Philosophy* (Cambridge: Cambridge University Press, 1989).

Paton, H. J., *The Categorical Imperative, A Study of Kant's Moral Philosophy* (Chicago: University of Chicago Press, 1948).

Peters, Curtis H., *Kant's Philosophy of Hope* (New York: Peter Lang, 1993).

Piper, Adrian, "*Kants intelligibler Stanpunkt zum Handeln*," in Hans-Ulrich Baumgarten and Carsten Held (ed.), *Systematische Ethik mit Kant* (München/Freiburg: Alber, 2001).

Potter, Nelson, "Does Kant have Two Concepts of Freedom?" in G. Funke and J. Kopper (eds.), *Akten des 4. Internationalen Kant-Kongress* (Berlin: Walter de Grutyer, 1974).

—— "Kant and the Moral Worth of Actions," *The Southern Journal of Philosophy* 34 (1996), 225–41.

—— "Maxims in Kant's Moral Philosophy," *Philosophia* 23 (July 1994), 59–90.

Prauss, Gerold, *Kant über Freiheit als Autonomie* (Frankfurt am Main: Vittorio Kolstermann, 1983).

Rawls, John, *Lectures in the History of Moral Philosophy*, ed. Barbara Herman (Cambridge, MA: Harvard University Press, 2000).

—— *A Theory of Justice* (Cambridge, MA: Belknap Press, 1971).

Reath, Andrews, "Hedonism, Heteronomy and Kant's Principle of Happiness," *Pacific Philosophical Quarterly* 70 (1989), 42–72.

—— "Intelligible Character and the Reciprocity Thesis," *Inquiry* 36 (1993), 419–30.

—— "Kant's Theory of Moral Sensibility: Respect for the Moral Law and the Influence of Inclination," *Kant-Studien* 80 (1989), 284–302.

Robinson, Hoke, ed., *Proceedings of the Eighth International Kant Congress* (Milwaukee, WI: Marquette University Press, 1995).

Ross, W. D., *The Right and the Good* (Indianaplis, IN: Hackett Publishing, 1988).

Schönfeld, Martin, *The Philosophy of the Young Kant* (Oxford: Oxford University Press, 2000).

Schaller, Walter E., "Should Kantians Care about Moral Worth?" *Dialogue* 32 (1993), 25–40.

Schopenhauer, Arthur, *The World as Will and Representation*, vol. II, trans. E. F. J. Payne (New York: Dover, 1958).

Searle, John R., *Rationality in Action* (Cambridge, MA: MIT Press, 2001).

Seigfried, Charlene, "The Radical Evil in Human Nature," in G. Funke and J. Kopper (eds.), *Akten des 4. Internationalen Kant-Kongress* vol. II., 2nd edn. (Berlin: Walter de Gruyter, 1974).

Silber, John R., "The Ethical Significance of Kant's Religion," in Immanuel Kant, *Religion within the Limits of Reason Alone,* trans. Theodore M. Greene and Hoyt H. Hudson (New York: Harper & Row, 1960).

—— "The Importance of the Highest Good in Kant's Ethics," *Ethics* 73 (1963).

Sorell, Tom, "Kant's Good Will and Our Good Nature," *Kant-Studien* 78 (1987), 87–101.

Stocker, Michael, "The Schizophrenia of Modern Ethical Theories," *The Journal of Philosophy* 73 (1976), 456–66.

Stratton-Lake, Philip, *Kant, Duty and Moral Worth* (London: Routledge, 2000).

Sullivan, Roger J., *Immanuel Kant's Moral Theory* (Cambridge: Cambridge University Press, 1989).

—— *Introduction to Kant's Ethics* (Cambridge: Cambridge University Press, 1994).

Timmons, Mark, "Kant on the Possibility of Moral Motivation," *Southern Journal of Philosophy* 23 (1985), 377–98.

—— ed., *Kant's Metaphysics of Morals, Interpretive Essays* (Oxford: Oxford University Press, 2002).

Walker, Ralph C. S., "Achtung in the *Grundlegung*" in Otfried Höffe (ed.), *Grundlegung zur Metaphysik der Sitten: Ein kooperativer Kommentar* (Frankfurt Am Main: Vittorio Klostermann, 1989).

—— *Kant, the Arguments of the Philosophers* (London: Routledge & Kegan Paul, 1978).

Wallace, R. Jay, *Normativity and the Will: Selected Papers on Moral Psychology and Practical Reason* (Oxford: Oxford University Press, 2006).

Watkins, Eric, *Kant and the Metaphysics of Causality* (Cambridge: Cambridge University Press, 2005).

Westphal, Kenneth, *Kant's Transcendental Proof of Realism* (Cambridge: Cambridge University Press, 2004).

—— "Noumenal Causality Reconsidered: Affection, Agency and Meaning in Kant," *Canadian Journal of Philosophy* 27 (June 1997), 209–45.

Wick, Warner, "Introduction" to Immanuel Kant, *The Metaphysical Principles of Virtue*, trans., J. Ellington (Indianapolis, IN: Bobbs-Merrill, 1964).

Williams, Bernard, *Ethics and the Limits of Philosophy* (Cambridge, MA: Harvard University Press, 1985).

Wolff, Christian, *Preliminary Discourse on Philosophy in General*, trans. R. J. Blackwell (Indianapolis, IN: Bobbs-Merrill, 1963).

—— *Vernünfftige Gedancken von der Menschen Thun und Lassen, zu Beförderung Ihrer Glückseeligkeit* [*Deutsche Ethik*] (Frankfurt, 1733); facs. (Hildesheim: Georg Olms, 1976).

—— *Vernünfftige Gedancken von Gott, der Welt und der Seele des Menschen, Auch Allen Dingen Überhaupt* [*Deutsche Metaphysik*] (Halle, 1751); facs. (Hildesheim: Georg Olms, 1983).

—— *Vernünfftige Gedancken von Gott, der Welt und der Seele des Menschen, Auch Allen Dingen Überhaupt, Anderer Theil* (Frankfurt, 1740); facs. (Hildesheim: Georg Olms, 1983).

Wolff, Robert Paul, *The Autonomy of Reason* (New York: Harper & Row, 1973).

—— "Remarks on the Relation of the Critique of Pure Reason to Kant's Ethical Theory," in Bernard den Ouden and Marcia Moen (eds.), *New Essays on Kant* (New York: Peter Lang, 1987).

Wood, Allen, "The Good Will," *Philosophical Topics* 31 (Spring and Fall 2003), 457–84.

—— "Kant's Compatibilism," in Allen W. Wood (ed.), *Self and Nature in Kant's Philosophy* (Ithaca, NY: Cornell University Press, 1984).

—— *Kant's Ethical Thought* (Cambridge: Cambridge University Press, 1999).

—— ed., *Self and Nature in Kant's Philosophy* (Ithaca, NY: Cornell University Press, 1984).

Yovel, Yirmiyahu, *Kant and the Philosophy of History* (Princeton, NJ: Princeton University Press, 1969).

—— "Kant's Practical Reason as Will: Interest, Recognition, Judgment and Choice," *The Review of Metaphysics* 52 (December 1998), 267–94.

—— ed., *Kant's Practical Philosophy Reconsidered* (Dordrecht: Kluwer Academic Publishers, 1989).

Zammito, John, *The Genesis of Kant's Critique of Judgment* (Chicago: University of Chicago Press, 1992).

Zeller, Eduard, *Geschichte der Deutschen Philosophie seit Leibniz* (Munich: R. Oldenbourg, 1873); facs. (New York: Johnson Repr., 1965).

Zinkin, Melissa, "Respect for the Law and the Use of Dynamical Terms in Kant's Theory of Moral Motivation," *Archive für Geschichte der Philosophie* 88 (2006), 31–53.

.

Index